Business Communications 199'

The Marketing Series is one of the most comprehensive
and sales available from the UK today.

Published by Butterworth-Heinemann on behalf of The Chartered Institute of Marketing,
the series is divided into three distinct groups: *Student* (fulfilling the needs of those taking
the Institute's certificate and diploma qualifications); *Professional Development* (for those on
formal or self-study vocational training programmes); and *Practitioner* (presented in a more
informal, motivating and highly practical manner for the busy marketer).

Formed in 1911, The Chartered Institute of Marketing is now the largest professional
marketing management body in Europe with over 60,000 members located worldwide. Its
primary objectives are focused on the development of awareness and understanding of
marketing throughout UK industry and commerce and in the raising of standards of
professionalism in the education, training and practice of this key business discipline.

The CIM Student Workbook Series: Marketing

Certificate

Business Communications 1997–98
Misiura

Marketing Fundamentals 1997–98
Lancaster & Withey

Sales and Marketing Environment 1997–98
Oldroyd

Understanding Customers 1997–98
Phipps & Simmons

Advanced Certificate

Effective Management for Marketing 1997–98
Hatton & Worsam

Management Information for Marketing and Sales 1997–98
Hines

Marketing Operations 1997–98
Worsam

Promotional Practice 1997–98
Ace

Diploma

International Marketing Strategy 1997–98
Fifield & Lewis

Marketing Communications Strategy 1997–98
Yeshin

Strategic Marketing Management 1997–98
Fifield & Gilligan

The Case Study Workbook 1997–98
Fifield

Business Communications 1997–98

Shashi Misiura

Published on behalf of
The Chartered Institute of Marketing

Butterworth-Heinemann
Linacre House, Jordan Hill, Oxford OX2 8DP
A division of Reed Educational and Professional Publishing Ltd

ℛ A member of the Reed Elsevier plc group

OXFORD   BOSTON   JOHANNESBURG
MELBOURNE   NEW DELHI   SINGAPORE

First published 1997

British Library Cataloguing in Publication Data
A catalogue record for this book is available from the British Library

ISBN 0 7506 3576 2

Set by Graphicraft Typesetters Ltd., Hong Kong
Printed and bound in Great Britain by the Bath Press, Bath

Contents

A quick word from the Chief Examiner

I am delighted to recommend to you the new series of CIM workbooks. All of these have been written by either the Senior Examiner or Examiners responsible for marking and setting the papers.

Preparing for the CIM Exams is hard work. These workbooks are designed to make that work as interesting and illuminating as possible, as well as providing you with the knowledge you need to pass. I wish you success.

Trevor Watkins
CIM Chief Examiner,
Deputy Vice Chancellor,
South Bank University

Preface

Welcome to the third edition of the CIM/Butterworth-Heinemann workbook for students of Business Communications.

In this edition I have updated some of the text and theory presented in past CIM examination papers (at the back of the book) in their entirety, together with a complete set of model answers and an examiner's report. A number of past examination questions together with their full model answers also appear in each chapter. I have also added a few new sections and extended some others. In particular, there is now a full introduction to Written Communication 2, emphasizing the planning of *persuasive* messages and some new activities appear in the first chapter. In the chapter on Information technology, a new section on 'Video Technology and its application to business communications' should make interesting reading.

I hope that you enjoy working from this highly successful book and that it prepares you thoroughly in the subject of Business Communications and the CIM examination. I wish you every success.

Finally, I would like to dedicate this edition to my best friend and 'spiritual sister', Ansuya Sodha (ben) and her dear family, Vinod, Sandip and Nina.

Shashi Misiura

Acknowledgement

My grateful thanks to Richard Taylor, Commissioning Editor at Butterworth-Heinemann for all his advice and guidance.

How to use your CIM workbook

The authors have been careful to structure your book with the exams in mind. Each unit, therefore, covers an essential part of the syllabus. You need to work through the complete workbook systematically to ensure that you have covered everything you need to know.

This workbook is divided into ten units. Each unit contains the following standard elements:

Objectives   tell you what part of the syllabus you will be covering and what you will be expected to know having read the unit.

Study guides   tell you how long the unit is and how long its activities take to do.

Questions   are designed to give you practice – they will be similar to those you get in the exam.

Answers   give you a suggested format for answering exam questions. *Remember* there is no such thing as a model answer – you should use these examples only as guidelines.

Activities   give you the chance to put what you have learnt into practice.

Exam hints   are tips from the senior examiner or examiner which are designed to help you avoid common mistakes made by previous candidates.

Definitions   are used for words you must know to pass the exam.

Extending activity sections   are designed to help you use your time most effectively. It is not possible for the workbook to cover *everything* you need to know to pass. What you read here needs to be supplemented by your classes, practical experience at work and day-to-day reading.

Summaries   cover what you should have picked up from reading the unit.

A glossary is provided at the back of the book to help define and underpin understanding of the key terms used in each unit.

Understanding business communication

In this introductory unit you will:

- Understand why communication is a fundamental activity in which we are all continuously engaged.
- Examine the five stages in the communication process.
- Identify the barriers to successful communication both generally within the organization and specifically in dealing with other international cultures.
- Define business communication.
- Consider the formal and informal communication routes within organizations.
- Recognize the different channels used to communicate internally and with the external business environment.
- Study the various types of communication network that can be established within the organization.

By the end of this unit you will:

- Understand the whole communication process and identify your communication needs.
- Be aware of the main barriers to communication and how to eliminate them.
- Appreciate the nature of organization structures, lines of authority and links in the chain of command.
- Be able to identify the type of communication network within which you operate, its advantages and limitations.

This unit covers the introductory part of The Chartered Institute of Marketing (CIM) syllabus for business communication and will be your first opportunity to become familiar with the layout and teaching style of the workbook.

The content is designed for you to develop personal skills in a range of business communications which are covered under the broad headings of written, verbal and visual communication and to use these effectively in the marketing and sales functions in order to communicate both with external markets – customers, suppliers and other groups – and also the internal market – colleagues, superiors, subordinates and shareholders.

In this unit you will be presented with a number of topics that look at the communication process and its importance in business, especially to the function of marketing. This is the foundation for your understanding and appreciation of what it takes to be an effective communicator both professionally and personally. The specific skills you need to acquire and the equipment and tools that facilitate the business communication process are briefly addressed, but discussed in more detail in subsequent units.

The process of communication is not necessarily a smooth one, with frequently encountered barriers that can constrain this important activity of sending information from one party to another, through a selected medium or channel, often with a requirement for feedback. You must therefore be prepared to tackle all the questions and activities that guide you through the important issues of business communication and prepare you for more detailed analysis of specific activities in later units.

Be prepared to ask questions of people around you who may have more knowledge or experience of business communication and therefore know the dos and don'ts of effective communication. This is always a constructive learning exercise.

The study time for completion of this unit will be approximately 8 hours, with another 6 required for the questions, tasks and to analyse the past examination questions and model answers.

There are a number of recommendations I would like to suggest which apply not only to this introductory chapter, but also to the others that follow.

Firstly, the key to success in any examination has to begin with a *complete study* of the subject. You must therefore not 'skip' any of the units or topics presented in the units, but aim at finishing each one within a certain period of time, well before the examination is to take place, so that revision time is available.

Your first task should therefore be to look quickly through the book, both to familiarize yourself with the nature of this subject and the topics to be covered, and also to add up the study time required, so that a personal study plan can be devised. For example, you may wish to dedicate one hour three times per week. If this is sufficient time to complete the units, cover the tasks and revise for the examination, then as long as you stick to it there should be no problem. However, you need to continuously assess the speed with which you are able to digest the material and carry out the tasks set, because although there are guidelines given, everyone has their own study pace.

Secondly, you need not only *breadth* of knowledge but *depth* of knowledge. The former is achieved through completion of the course of study (this will include time spent with a lecturer or tutor at a college, or your own study of the material presented in this book, possibly both), but you will need to spend a considerable amount of time going through the tasks and questions and model answers in this book, together with a close analysis of the past examination paper (June 1995, at the back of the book). A full set of model answers is given. The majority of questions at the end of the units are also past examination questions with a full model answer.

What about a study plan?

I have already suggested that you should have a *set period* each week for the study of one or more units. The ideal period for you may be one block of time or perhaps a smaller amount each, or every other, evening from the beginning of the course of study until the examination. Each student will have a unique set of circumstances that determines the study time that can be allocated and might even change from week to week. However, as far as possible do try and stick to the same *routine*, as this will then become absorbed into a normal weekly pattern of events.

When you have decided how to structure your week incorporating the study of material from this book, work out *how much can be achieved* and try to complete this amount. Do not try and push yourself beyond the study time, as you will dilute the effect of the study already undertaken and possibly not take in any more either.

Where do I start?

I suggested above that your first step should be to 'flick through' the book in order to become familiar with the unit headings and therefore the scope of the subject of business communication as required by the CIM for the Certificate in Marketing and Selling.

At this stage, you might also like to do a calculation of the total study time required and then plan 'backwards' from one or two weeks before the examination, so that you also have enough time for revision and last-minute preparation. Remember, you need to be able to work at *your own pace* with this material, so be generous rather than tight with the amount of time that you may require. (You won't necessarily know this until one or two units have been completed.)

You are now ready to begin study of the first unit.

What do I do now?
Firstly, read through the entire unit, quickly but making sure that you are getting a good 'feel' for the information which is presented.

Next, read through the unit again, but this time pausing at the questions, activities and other tasks.

The choice is now yours. You can either attempt these as you study the unit for the second time, or go back to them after the unit has been completed.

I would suggest that you do the latter, because your level of knowledge after having studied the unit for a second time will be greater and you will therefore be in a stronger position to attempt the tasks.

Finally, before moving on to the next unit, make sure that you have a good 'working knowledge' of the material in the text, have learned all definitions and would be able to attempt a similar examination question with the appropriate level of answer as that given in the unit.

One way of cross-referencing that you have learned enough material in the unit is by looking back at the *objectives* given at the start of the unit and simply answering 'yes' or 'no' to the points! The *revision tips* at the end of the unit are designed to achieve the same principle.

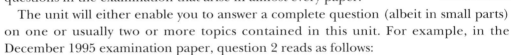

The introductory chapter to this book serves two purposes. The first is to give you a foundation of knowledge and understanding on the subject of business communication. The second purpose is to prepare you for questions in the examination that arise in almost every paper.

The unit will either enable you to answer a complete question (albeit in small parts) on one or usually two or more topics contained in this unit. For example, in the December 1995 examination paper, question 2 reads as follows:

Question 2
In a recent marketing article by Alan Mitchel he quotes from a recent Smythe Dorward Lambert report on internal communication that says that information and ideas can flow more quickly . . . *direct communication can improve morale . . . reduce costs and empower employees.* But at the same time, the new communication channels create a dilemma of directness *where there is greater accessibility to top managers via E-mail, there can be less face to face interaction and where there is communication overload.*

(a)   Illustrate in a diagram the process of internal communication which occurs in an organization, explain possible barriers to effective communication.

(12 marks)

(b)   Give examples of situations in organizations which accurately describe the underlined points mentioned above.   (8 marks)

A full model answer to this question is given at the end of the unit.

The other points that you need to know are as follows:

1   The first question in the examination will always be *compulsory* (see Section A in the June 1995 paper at the back of the book and accompanying guidelines) and worth 40% of the total marks.

The question will be made up of two or more parts and each part will be given a mark allocation. The mark allocation reflects the *relative importance* of this part of the question and therefore *how much time you should spend on it*, compared to the other parts; this is the case for all two or more parts to a question, both in Section A and Section B.

The compulsory question is likely to draw upon several *different parts of the syllabus* and therefore many of the units in this book. You must be prepared for this. The full examination paper with accompanying model answers to the June 1995 paper at the back of this book is designed to help you.

2   Section B comprises of a further nine questions, each of which has a maximum 20 marks allocation. You must answer only *three* of these questions.

Some will be allocated 20 marks for the whole question, whilst others will be in two or more parts, as explained above.

Once again, the questions are likely to draw upon several topics in a unit or from two or more units in this book. *You therefore need a complete knowledge of the subject in order to succeed in the Business Communication examination.*

3   One further point which is crucially important is that the paper (and this book) will invariably use examples from the world of marketing. The reason for this is that whilst the principles of business communication apply to all organizations, both private and public sector, large and small, local, national and international, you are working towards a *Certificate in Marketing or Selling* and are therefore expected to be able to discern and appreciate these principles in the context of a marketing or selling environment and related academic knowledge.

You must therefore *simultaneously revise* the other subjects in the Certificate in Marketing or Selling that you are studying or be expected to draw upon *practical experience* in your responses, from time to time.

In question 2 from the December 1995 paper quoted above, the example used is not specifically from a marketing or selling document, but this will not always be the case.

I will address the issues of interpreting the examination questions, presenting your responses and so on later in the unit and also in the guidelines at the back of the book.

The purpose of communication

Why communicate?

Communication is a process that enables us to learn about other people through sharing experiences and passing information, which is important in establishing and building relationships, whether they are domestic, social or business and professional. Effective communication skills are required throughout our lifetime in order to achieve the following:

- Make our needs clearly understood and to understand those of others.
- To give and receive instruction.
- To initiate action.
- To carry out negotiations successfully.
- To interest, stimulate and persuade individuals or groups to be motivated either in their work (e.g. colleagues) or to trigger consumption behaviour.

QUESTION 1.1

Why is communication important to business organizations?

Business organizations can make powerful statements about themselves through a range of communication initiatives which are expressed through their written, verbal and visual business communications, such as letter presentations, use of symbols, logos, styles of lettering and colour, and in their effectiveness in face-to-face interactions such as meetings, interviews or personal selling. Organizations can also communicate through their general business environments, i.e.

their location, the type and size of building or offices occupied and the interior and exterior design and layout – all factors which communicate either cost-effective business decisions or status and level of sophistication.

Businesses also make statements about their quality, image and market positioning through the products and services they design, develop, produce and market, together with the type of packaging used and other 'added-value' benefits offered, such as after-sales service.

In total, these factors give an overall impression of the business organization that creates its corporate identity, i.e. its individual house style which is used to communicate with internal and external markets and to make it distinct from the competition, usually designed to gain advantage in the marketplace. Research has shown that all types of business messages, verbal, written and visual, gain a higher profile and better perception of the organization if they are presented in a consistent manner, i.e. at every opportunity on all material.

The *internal market* is a term used to describe those who are involved with the internal processes of a business organization such as employees, shareholders and the board. The internal market has a collective responsibility for maintaining the house style through all their communication initiatives, whether this means writing a letter or designing a promotional campaign. However, they also have communications needs, such as the desire for information on corporate activities, budget allocations or company involvement in projects, which may enhance their loyalty and commitment to the firm. An example may be the sponsorship of an environmental campaign or local charity.

The *external market* is the total of the individuals and groups who have an indirect relationship with the business organization. One example is the mass market who are communicated through a poster campaign to stimulate their awareness of a product, service or issue. On the other end of the relationship between customer and organization is the supplier, who also has distinct communication needs, for example if he or she must increase stock to tie in with an anticipated surge in production which will meet the increased demand stemming from a new advertising campaign.

ACTIVITY 1.1

Write below a checklist of all the reasons that you can think of for communication to take place, using real examples from your own personal experiences.

1

2

3

4

5

6

7

8

9

10

QUESTION 1.2

What is business communication?

The main reasons for people to communicate in business organizations, internally and externally, are as follows:

- To *build relationships* internally and externally with individuals and groups.
- To give *specific instructions* to others on a range of business matters, both procedural and strategic.
- To *disseminate information* on a range of corporate matters such as the mission statement, policy issues or, in the case of the external market, on price changes or new promotional initiatives.
- To *share ideas and values* on general organizational issues, possibly to maintain or subtly change the corporate culture.
- To share ideas and values on work-specific issues or procedural tasks.
- To *negotiate* matters of policy such as a joint venture or merger.
- To *discuss* or negotiate on personal or professional matters such as remuneration and other higher- and lower-level hygiene factors.
- To *motivate, interest and stimulate* employees for commitment and loyalty to the firm.
- To create an awareness of the organization, its products or services and *persuade* the external market, for example to make a purchase decision or to request further information.
- To receive feedback in order to monitor whether the communication was understood and the reaction of the recipient to the message.

DEFINITION 1.3

certain. defin
lefinition *n.* s
precise mean
distinct, clea
lefinitive *a.* fi
something; r

Business communication is the process by which information is transferred and received from one individual or group to another both within and outside the organization. The communication can take place verbally or non-verbally and uses a number of different *channels* to transmit the message: written communication, verbal and non-verbal communication such as speeches and body language and visual communications such as charts and posters. All these channels have their distinct advantages and disadvantages and must be used selectively. This will be discussed in more detail later in the workbook.

Business communication is a critical success factor for any organization as it is the sole activity that helps to unite people in working towards goals and establishes and builds important relationships with both the internal and external markets.

The functions of marketing and sales interface with the external market both directly and indirectly more than any other in the business organization. In particular, marketing will be involved with the design and production of a range of communication initiatives such as brochures and leaflets for the external market, letterheads and logos which are used for internal and external communication on letters and memos and many face-to-face communications, where effective use of verbal and non-verbal skills will be required.

If you are engaged in business activity, try this activity to facilitate your learning and understanding of business communication.

What are your professional communication needs?

Internal communication

1 Make a list of the people with whom you communicate at work, for example your line manager, other colleagues and juniors. Briefly state the type of information you *receive* from them, whether these are instructions, information, advice, etc. Use the space below.

Name   *Position*   *Type of information received*

(a)

(b)

(c)

2 Make a list of the people with whom you communicate at work and briefly state the type of information you *send* to them, examples include feedback, informal or formal, reports, advice or other information. Use the space below.

Name   *Position*   *Type of information sent*

3 Which channels are used in your organization to *send* and to *receive* information? Explain briefly why they are chosen *relative* to other methods.

Channel	Send information	Receive information	Reason
Telephone			
Memo			
Letter			
Report			
Brief			
Fax message			
Telex message			
Computer-based system (be specific) e.g. E-mail, CD Rom			

You should have appreciated from this activity that the channels above serve specific functions, which stem from distinct communication needs. For example, memos are usually used for (brief) internal communications and letters are used for sending information or answering a request from an external source, such as would be the case in addressing a customer complaint. The *content* and *approach* are critical to your effectiveness and efficiency as a communicator and also in the type of feedback you will receive. In terms of the communication process, this is one aspect (the elements and style of message) that you can *control*.

These days many organizations are conscious of the *cost* of sending written documents and are increasingly using electronic techniques such as E-mail. Electronic technologies also have the advantage that they are fast, although the *fastest* method for receiving feedback is to use the telephone (assuming that the recipient is available), though this has the disadvantage that it is not possible to have a *formal record* of the conversation.

In terms of both internal and external communication, it should be clear that the channel used should be a *planned activity* and one that is *convenient* to both sender and receiver. The *needs* of the recipient in terms of the *level* and *type* of communication is a starting point in planning the business communication *message*. We shall return to this shortly.

QUESTION 1.3

What would you consider to be the most important skills needed to communicate *effectively* in a business context?

Where will you begin in answering this question – analysing your own practice or that of others around you?

If you are studying this subject at college or in another group situation, use the technique of brainstorming to begin answering this question and then analyse briefly each response given.

ACTIVITY 1.3

These days a vast amount of communication, particularly in the business context takes place through electronic systems and machines. Can you think of some examples of these systems and machines and the way in which they allow communication to take place? Make a list below.

System/machine	Purpose
1	
2	
3	
4	
5	

ACTIVITY 1.4

Based on your professional (work) and personal (domestic or social) experience, choose two people who have the ability and skill to communicate effectively. Rate their skills on the chart below.

Skills	Scale (√ the boxes 5 = high (i.e. a very good) rating and 1 = low (poor communication skill rating)	Name 1					Name 2					Yourself				
		1	2	3	4	5	1	2	3	4	5	1	2	3	4	5
A. *Verbal*																
(i) on the telephone																
(ii) in meetings																
(a) large (10+ people)																
(b) small (1–9 people)																
(iii) in interviews e.g. appraisals																
(iv) in demonstrating something, for example the use of a business machine																
(v) face-to-face communication generally																
(a) professionally																
(b) socially																

The Rating Scale (1–5) is based on giving 5 if you/the person has a **high** level of skill and a 1 if you/the person has a *low* level of skill in their various spheres of communication.

Skills		Name 1					Name 2					Yourself				
B. *Non-verbal* (Body language)																
(i) facial gestures, e.g. smiles																
(ii) eye movements, e.g. widening and narrowing in different situations																
(iii) arm gestures, e.g. folding, embracing																
(iv) hand gestures																
(v) posture, e.g. the way he/she stands or sits																
(vi) body movements, including head movements																
C. *Written*																
(i) in letters																
(a) internal																
(b) external																
(ii) in memos																
(iii) in reports																
(iv) in briefs																
(v) in advertising copy																
(vi) in press releases																
(vii) in job descriptions																
(viii) in job specifications																

Skills	Scale (√ the boxes 5 = high (i.e. a very good) rating and 1 = low (poor communication skill rating)	Name 1					Name 2					Yourself				
		1	2	3	4	5	1	2	3	4	5	1	2	3	4	5
D. Visual																
(i) in presenting charts																
(ii) in presenting graphing																
(iii) in presenting tables																
(iv) in presenting pictures/ pictograms																
(v) in presenting maps/cartograms																
E. Electronic Equipment																
(i) in sending telex messages (if applicable)																
(ii) in sending fax messages																
(iii) in sending E-mail messages																
(iv) other (please specify)																

In your observations you should have concluded that successful communicators use a range of written, verbal (and non-verbal), electronic and visual skills to get their message across, but will select a particular one to suit a situation. Some people have a 'natural' ability to communicate through a particular medium, e.g. the telephone because they speak clearly, or letters because they have a good command of the written language. The key to successful business communication is the ability to *express* yourself clearly and concisely, allowing the recipient to provide feedback, if appropriate.

For face-to-face interactions, it is important not just to demonstrate clear, concise and articulate *speech* characteristics but to use a range of non-verbal cues, such as gestures and eye movements that enhance the communication process and make the message easier to understand.

In written communication it is vital that the message has been carefully composed to reflect the *needs* of the recipient and that the style of presentation and method of communication are suitable for the audience, whether it is through a memo, report or sharp sales letter in a direct-mail initiative.

Visual communications are achieved through graphics, colours, and lettering styles which help to make a message clear and distinct. These are particularly effective when used in combination with other written communications such as reports as they 'cut down' written text and are generally easier to follow.*

In conclusion to this lengthy but hopefully interesting and revealing activity, you will have understood that successful business communicators (or those wishing to improve their business communication skills) have (or should have) five main attributes:

* Visuals enhance the *appeal* of a message and are therefore generally better in competing for the attention of a recipient. However, the way in which the message is *perceived* is open to individual interpretation and on the whole is beyond the control of the sender.

- *Credibility*, i.e. they are highly believable and trustworthy in terms of the content of their communication/message with which you, as a recipient, feel completely comfortable. Indeed, this is vital for successful managers and those involved in the leadership of others.
- *Precision*, this is linked to the first point and relates not just to the ability to articulate words, sentences and phrases into a meaningful communication but also helps to create a communication experience whereby the recipient(s) share the same 'mental picture' as that of the sender.
- *Perception* – a successful communicator will be able to anticipate and predict how his/her message will be received and therefore shape it accordingly. The response of the recipient(s) (which may be presented in written format, verbally or non-verbally) will then be assessed by the sender and if necessary further communication will take place to adjust for misunderstandings.
- *Control* – linked to the point above about perception is the feeling that you should now be getting, which is that successful communicators are able to control their message to a great extent and also to generate (mostly) the required response, if appropriate.
- Finally, one of the most important (natural) skills possessed by successful communicators is that of congeniality, in other words the ability to be pleasant and friendly, either in written, verbal or non-verbal communication, even if the message is serious and possibly very bad news.

The communication chain

Communication is a *chain* of events which has *five* distinct dimensions (Fig. 1.1):

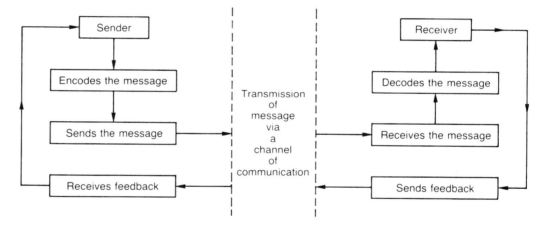

Figure 1.1   The process of communication.

1   The sender has the need to communicate.
2   The need is translated into a message (encoding).
3   The message is transmitted.
4   The receiver gets the message (decoding).
5   The receiver interprets the message and provides feedback.

1   The need to communicate is *intrinsic*, but the *perception* of a message will be unique, therefore in the process of *conceiving* an idea, you will inevitably make assumptions and leave out details that seem unimportant. However, others will not perceive in the same way, therefore you must appreciate the *needs* of your recipient, their possible interpretation(s) and *plan* your message accordingly.
2   Messages may be *expressed* in a number of different ways depending on the purpose of the communication, subject or topic to be related, the needs of the recipient and your own personal skills in communication. In the process of *encoding* you will select bits of information and organize them for transmission. The first step is to decide what and how much to say; if a message contains too much information it is difficult to absorb, but if you do not include enough, it will not meet with the expectation of the recipient and may leave room for misinterpretation.

3 The *medium* you choose for transmission will depend on the message to be conveyed, location of the recipient, speed, convenience and degree of formality required. The usual internal methods are memo, report, telephone and face-to-face interaction.

   Technological advances in electronic office equipment such as computer-based systems for sending electronic mail copies of documentation have made it possible to send communications from one location to another quickly and effectively. This is discussed more fully in the last unit.

4 *Decoding* is in the interpretation of the message that has been received and will have been successful if the recipient has absorbed the message and assigned to it the meaning which the sender intended.

5 *Feedback* (or lack of) is the response that the recipient sends back to the sender and is a key element in the communication process because it enables the sender to *evaluate* the effectiveness of the message. Feedback may take the form of verbal (telephone call, face-to-face interaction etc.), non-verbal communication or action (body language, etc.) or written messages.

Feedback is the key element that creates a *cycle* in the communication chain, enabling the information that is sent to be *reviewed* when it is received back and on this basis further communication initiatives or corrective action can be taken as necessary.

There are two types of feedback, negative and positive.

Positive feedback consists of the following:

- General agreement on the content of the message, expressed either verbally, for example by saying 'yes', or through non-verbal communication, such as a nod of the head.
- Written communication through an internal memo or letter from a client confirming that the message has been received and understood, evident by the type and tone of the message.
- Specific action that is taken, of which the sender subsequently becomes aware, for example an increase in orders through a direct-mail initiative with a new customer, or an increase in purchases following an advertising campaign.

Negative feedback would consist of the following:

- Disagreement with the communication message that is expressed verbally, for example, by the recipient saying 'no' or a shake of the head that is indicated non-verbally.
- Written communication expressing disagreement or disappointment with respect to the message that had been received.
- Clear misunderstanding of the communication, which may be expressed verbally, non-verbally or in written format.
- Silence or no communication received back.

DEFINITION 1.4

certain. defi
definition *n.* s
precise mean
distinct, clea
definitive *a.* fi
something; i

The communication process consists of:

- *Encoding* – putting thought into symbolic or word form, ready for transmission.
- *Transmission* – the process of sending the message, via a selected channel or medium, for example, telephone call or advertisement.
- *Decoding* – the message is received and meaning assigned by the recipient.
- *Feedback* – the message is communicated back to the sender.

The barriers to communication

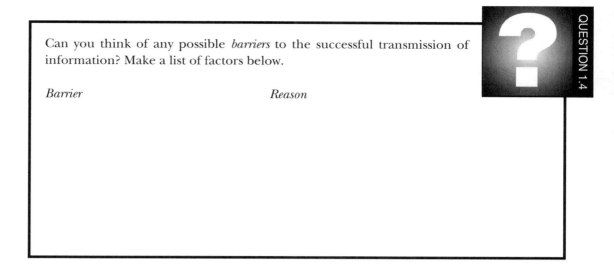

Can you think of any possible *barriers* to the successful transmission of information? Make a list of factors below.

Barrier   *Reason*

Barriers to communication may arise from the sender, receiver or due to other factors in the environment during transmission of the message (Fig. 1.2).

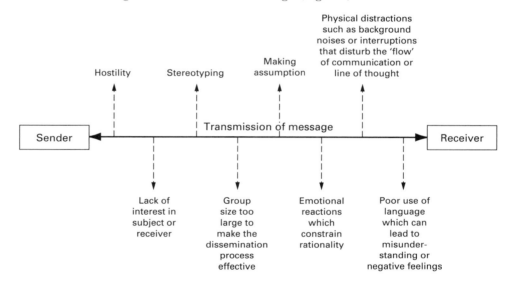

Figure 1.2   Barriers to communication.

Barriers to communication in business can arise from any of the factors above, which leads to an unclear message and a greater chance of misunderstanding or misinterpretation on behalf of the recipient.

The whole process of communication needs to be handled with even greater care when dealing with 'unfamiliar' business people, in terms of language, culture (including protocol), dress and behavioural codes, etc. Good practitioners of business communication will realize that most of these barriers are controllable and steps must be taken to avoid them.

Practical initiatives include reading or learning about the person or group with whom you are to interact, making contact with them prior to a face-to-face meeting to get a feel for their level of sophistication in business, language ability and other behavioural factors as mentioned above. Michael Johnson and Robert J. Morain, in their book *Cultural Guide to doing Business in Europe* (Butterworth-Heinemann, 1992), discuss a range of countries and the difficulties in conducting oneself in an unfamiliar business environment due to language, culture and non-verbal communication differences.

Broadly speaking, they argue that in the international business environment, following protocol, trying not to make assumptions, avoiding stereotyping and having both a positive and non-competitive attitude can go a long way to removing these potential barriers to communication, especially if one is not fluent in the relevant language or conversant with general norms and values of the society and culture.

Internal communications

In dealing with the internal market, it is equally important to reflect the needs of the recipient. For example, verbal, non-verbal and written communication will usually be different when addressed to the chief executive compared to that communicated to a colleague in the department. Internal barriers to communication can arise from the complexity of the structure of the organization, i.e. the levels through which a communication must travel to reach its destination – the more there are, the greater the chance of the message being lost or distorted.

Many organizations have responded positively to this real or potential problem by initiating worker participation schemes at different levels, through consultative committees which influence tactical decisions and worker representatives, who can affect policy-making at board level.

In Germany, the Government has legislated for compulsory works councils in organizations that have more than 2000 employees, where 50% of the representation comes from the staff below management level. The works council acts as a powerful communication channel to management and helps to shape both strategy and planning. The 'tangible' benefits have been increases in productivity, motivation, loyalty and commitment.

A number of businesses have changed their organizational structures to make the internal communication process more effective, or have invested in electronic information technology systems to make the process of communication much faster and more efficient.

In May 1994 in *Personnel Today*, an Industrial Society report into employee communications based on a survey of 1000 organizations, found employers spending around £300 per employee per annum on communication activity and suggested that this would pay dividends in terms of a knowledgeable and motivated workforce which would help in achieving greater competitive advantage in the marketplace.

The most popular channel for communicating between employees was found to be through team briefings, the most important aspect of which was *listening* to the staff and finding out what they think and feel about their working environment and role.

Figure 1.3 illustrates the results of the findings into effective communication methods within the business organizations in the Industrial Society survey.

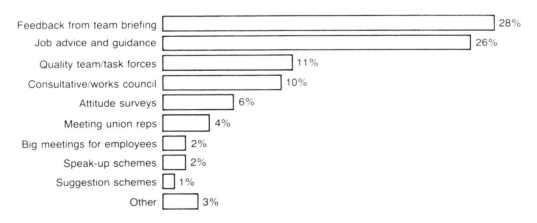

Figure 1.3 Effective communication methods. (Source: Industrial Society.)

ACTIVITY 1.4

Consider the most likely barriers to communication in your role, both within the organization and in contact with the outside business environment. Write a checklist and suggest ways in which they can be eliminated.

Typical barriers e.g. noise, lack of understanding in subject/topic)	Internal (State how and why the barrier arises)	External (State how and why the barrier arises)
1.		
2.		
3.		
4.		
5.		
6.		

In summary, during the process of planning a message and its transmission, it is important to keep distracting background noise (such as telephone calls or chattering) to a minimum as this can distort a message or cause you to lose concentration in sending the message and receiving feedback, especially in verbal communication.

The key to successful communication lies in understanding your customer (both internal and external) and in responding to their needs with the appropriate level and style of written and spoken language which is clearly expressed. Suitable body language in verbal face-to-face communication is also important.

The sales force

The sales force, for the large part, represent an 'absent workforce' and advances in electronic techniques have made the whole system of business communication more efficient in keeping them in touch.

Salespeople need a regular supply of information from the sales department or organization about a complete range of issues – those that may affect them as a result of the external business environment such as competitor activity, or as a result of activities from the sales and/or marketing functions, such as changes in price or promotional activity which has raised the awareness of a particular product, brand or service or changed the level of demand.

Salespeople must also provide information back to the office on customers' orders, reactions to new proposals and projects or products/services, etc. Indeed, many sales and marketing initiatives are designed to respond to this feedback from 'grass roots' and therefore provide a higher level of service to customers. These activities can lead to a differentiation in the consumer's perception, which can only be positive. They also need reactions to their communications, for example, to identify whether a salesperson can offer a particular price to secure a contract or order.

Clearly, different channels will fulfil the variety of communication needs of salespeople. Regular internal correspondence such as memos and reports can be copied to them, or for faster communication, this can be transmitted through electronic techniques such as E-mail or fax machines, if facilities are available. The majority of salespeople have access to a telephone and, increasingly, cellular 'mobile' phones, and this provides a vital communication link for regular and fast flow of information and feedback.

Formal communication routes through organizations

There are four *levels* of communication within organizations:

1 Intrapersonal (communicating with yourself through notes and memos).
2 Interpersonal (communicating with an internal colleague for an appraisal interview or with an external client to assess his or her needs for a particular product or service).
3 Individual to group (e.g. giving a speech at a briefing or conducting a meeting).
4 Group to individual (e.g. team presentation to the chief executive on the spending needs of the marketing department in the forthcoming year).

These levels of communication are all *personal* methods of communication and are achieved either formally, for example in selection interviews, or informally, for example a dialogue or discussion amongst colleagues at a sales conference.

However, whether communication takes place formally or informally, it takes place within the context of the organizational structure which demonstrates the lines of authority and links in the chain of command as shown in Figure 1.4.

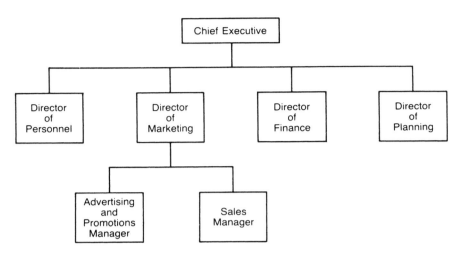

Figure 1.4 Organizational chart of a firm with a typical hierarchical structure where, in this case, the function of marketing encompasses the sales activity.

In most organizations, information will flow upwards, downwards, horizontally and diagonally. These are discussed below.

Upwards, vertical information takes place to superiors such as executives and managers who depend on lower-level employees for grassroots information on the achievement towards targets, individual and team performance levels, general grievances and opportunities. The methods used include group meetings, employee surveys and written communication in the form of reports, memos and suggestion systems.

Downwards, vertical information takes place to subordinates, mainly to make them more effective in their jobs and to provide updates on company policy and strategies. The methods used include interviews between line manager and employee, meetings, workshops and seminars or written communication in the form of a memo, training manual, in-house newsletter or notice.

Horizontal information takes place between departments and individuals at the same level in an organization; the degree of interdependence between departments will determine the amount of information flow. The trend in organizations is towards greater cross-functional interaction, usually aided by computer-based technology such as electronic mail.

certain. del
definition *n.*
precise mea
distinct, cle:
definitive *a.* f
something;

DEFINITION 1.8

Diagonal communication occurs between departments in relation to specific tasks for which there is no obvious line of authority; in this case effective communication requires cooperation between the individuals involved.

Informal communication routes

A great deal of communication in organizations takes place informally through casual conversations, visits and gatherings, and so on. The informal network or grapevine can be a powerful instrument in shaping the culture of the organization and in passing on information, some of which may be incorrect. This network needs to be managed or nurtured as carefully as the formal systems of communication.

Figure 1.5 demonstrates the types of informal structure that can occur in a hierarchical organization.

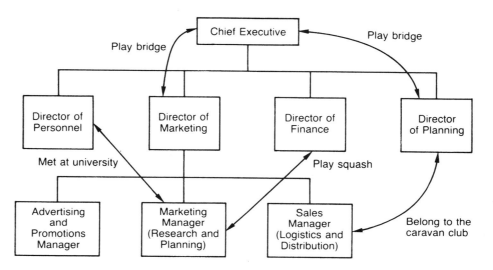

Figure 1.5 Organizational chart showing a typical hierarchical structure and informal systems of communication.

In conclusion to this section on formal and informal communication routes through organizations, you should have understood that an organization is basically a 'small world' in which effective and frequent communication is vital, whichever method(s) may be used. Indeed, it is 'the glue that holds the world together, enabling it to function' (J. V. Thill/ C. L. Bovée).

In your thoughts on business organizations (which you will get from personal experience and other CIM studies) you should reflect on an important fact which is that almost everything that a business does is based on some form of communication, written, verbal, nonverbal or visual. In particular, effective and efficient communication is the key to the whole planning process which includes setting organizational goals and objectives, developing strategies, establishing tactics/operations, implementing all these, effecting appropriate controls and finally engaging in the monitoring of results, carrying out a review and reporting the final conclusions. Needless to say, at each and every level of the business some one (indeed, groups and project teams too) will be involved and without efficient and effective communication (up, down and across) regularly issued, the task itself, is meaningless.

External communications

Communication must also take place with the outside world and does so using many of the channels described above – telephone calls, letters and so on. However, marketing has a particular role to play in managing corporate communications through a range of activities: public relations, publicity, advertising on television, radio, through poster campaigns and many other communication initiatives such as the creation and production of brochures, leaflets and flyers, catalogues and direct mail.

The majority of these communications are designed for the *mass market* and are therefore *impersonal*, i.e. there is a relatively informal level of communication between the sender and recipient of the communication.

Later in the workbook we will learn how to produce copy for advertisements, the rules for writing effective press releases and also how to plan a direct-mail letter, but the remainder of these marketing communications are beyond the scope of this text. However, as mentioned previously, whether a logo or letterhead is designed internally or by an agency, its consistency of use on all communications, internal and external, will benefit the organization as a whole because of the level of awareness that can be achieved and reinforce the values (hopefully positive!) that are associated with the corporate identity amongst the publics receiving the communications.

ACTIVITY 1.6

Organizational charts and formal and informal systems of communication
Draw an organizational chart of your company. Identify your position and those from whom you receive and send *formal and informal* communications, in the space below.

Communication networks

The process of communicating with managers, colleagues at the same level in the organizational structure and juniors, whether formally or informally, means that we establish communication networks around us. In most business organizations there are four types of communication network, which are described in the book on *Business Communication* by Norman B. Sigband (Harcourt Brace Jovanovich, New York). The simplest example is a communication chain, whereby information is passed from one individual to another along a line, and back again if feedback is solicited.

Chain 👤 – 👤 – 👤 – – – 👤 – 👤 – 👤 – 👤

This requires a great deal of *cooperation* amongst the individuals for the passing of information, backwards and forwards, and has the disadvantage that it is a relatively time-consuming and lengthy process, where information can easily become distorted.

Circle

In this situation communication flows from one individual or group to another systematically, reaching all in turn. Clearly the person at the 'end' of the chain will receive the information last and may only reflect his/her perspective in the feedback unless measures are taken in the process of communication to 'break out' of the cycle and provide individual feedback.

Wheel

This is the most structured of all the networks as communication flows directly from one source to all the others, individually and where feedback can be activated in return, saving valuable time.

Star

This is the least structured of all the networks as information flows from a number of sources directly to the others and therefore offers the greatest communication opportunities.

In conclusion, the more cohesive the network, the greater the chance of successfully transmitting information and receiving feedback.

Networking for communication

Which of these four types of network best describes the system of communication that is prevalent in your department (or organization) at work? Is this the most appropriate for your needs?

'Draw' your situation, in the space below.

In this unit we have seen that:

- Communication is an essential part of social and professional life and its success depends on the quality of information sent and received and the methods used in delivery. There are many barriers that can constrain the ability of the communicator to transmit messages and receive the desired feedback.
- Business organizations are set up to send and receive communication through formal channels which can be identified on organizational charts. However, a great deal of communication also takes place through informal channels which can be responsible for causing misrepresentation of official policy and rumours that disturb normal working practices. Both of these channels must be managed carefully so that the correct information is communicated to the appropriate recipient, using the most effective channel as efficiently as possible.
- Information flows vertically, horizontally and diagonally through the lines of authority which are depicted on organizational charts. These information flows also form the basis for establishing communication networks which are based on the cultural and structural norms of the organization and can enhance or constrain effective communication.

The successful business communicator

1 In your own words, briefly sum up the main criteria for successful communication in business.
2 Draw a simple diagram of the communication process and explain all five steps.
3 Identify and explain the main barriers to communication in business and underline those that directly affect your ability to be a successful communicator at work.
4 Draw a diagram that represents the type of communication network that you have in your department or organization and briefly explain its dimensions. Find out whether this network has always existed, evolved or been changed for a specific purpose. In the case of the last of these, find out when and why.

Successful business communication is:

1 The ability to transfer and receive information from within and outside the organization using the most appropriate channel.
2 The ability to eliminate the barriers to communication and proceed without prejudice, bias and unsuitable language in line with the needs of the recipient.
3 Using the formal and informal communication routes to best advantage in sending and receiving information.

You must be able to:

1 Define business communication.
2 Draw a diagram of the communication process and describe all five steps.
3 Describe the main barriers to effective communication and their significance when dealing with people both internally and outside the organization.
4 Explain the formal and informal channels of communication and how they can be enhanced within the organization.

5   Draw an organizational chart and indicate the lines of authority and chains of command, clearly understanding how communication takes place between people.

6   Draw and describe each of the four types of communication network.

Specimen examination question 1 (4 December 1995)

In a recent marketing article by Alan Mitchel he quotes from a recent Smythe Dorward Lambert report on internal communication that says that information and ideas can flow more quickly . . . *direct communication can improve morale . . . reduce costs and empower employees.* But at the same time, the new communication channels create a dilemma of directness *where there is greater accessibility to top managers via E-mail, there can be less face to face interaction and where there is communication overload.*

(a)   Illustrate in a diagram the process of internal communication which occurs in an organization, explain possible barriers to effective communication.

(12 marks)

(b)   Give examples of situations in organizations which accurately describe the points in italics mentioned above.

(8 marks)

(a)   The process of internal communication which occurs in an organization is both formal and informal.

Formal communication will usually take place along the formally designated channels, i.e. according to the organizational structure; this may be upwards, downwards, horizontally or diagonally. However, this implies a traditional hierarchical structure even in 'flatter' organizations, which may be inappropriate for an organization with a different type of culture, such as a power culture.

The formal methods of communication in business organizations are meetings, interviews, discussions, letters, memos, etc., sent and received either manually or through electronic mechanisms, such as E-mail, video conferencing, etc.

Informal communication knows no boundaries and can take place at any time, between any parties in the organization, or outside it! The usual methods are lunch-time conversations, social gatherings and so on.

A diagram to illustrate internal formal and informal communication in a hierarchical organization (possibly one with a 'role' culture (Charles Handy, *Understanding Organisations*) is shown in Fig. 1.6 below.

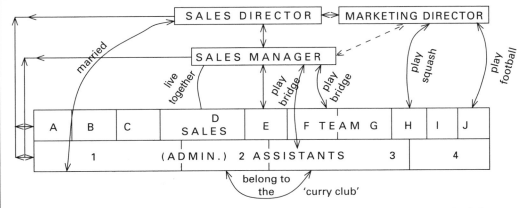

Formal communications will take place along the designated arrow routes, for example, information is received and passed from the Sales Manager to his/her sales team.
Informal communications will take place in a variety of ways, same examples are given above.

Figure 1.6   The marketing department of Superior Sales Ltd.

(b) Examples of situations which accurately describe the underlined points mentioned above are as follows:

(i) 'Direct communication can improve morale'. There is no doubt that employees like and wish to receive feedback on their performance. One example of a situation in which this happens in business organizations is when a senior manager holds an appraisal meeting with a lower level employee and not only 'thanks' him/her for effort during the (six-month/year) period, but also uses the opportunity to evaluate the employee's strengths and weaknesses and both make plans for the future.

(ii) 'Direct communication can . . . reduce costs and empower employees'. Even in hierarchical organizations, if communication takes place directly between individuals or groups, thus avoiding going through the layers and layers of people in between, this must speed up the communication process and therefore in the long run reduce costs. An example of a situation in which this process happens, and one that is frequently used, in particular by large manufacturing organizations, is quality circles. Quality circles draw individuals or small groups from all levels of the organization, in every or several functional areas in order to discuss matters affecting the organization and to make suitable plans for all concerned; they have been highly successful in reducing costs and empowering employees.

(iii) 'Where there is greater accessibility to top managers via E-mail, there can be less face to face interaction and where there is communication overload'. Face to face interaction has a number of major advantages that cannot be achieved through electronic communications such as using E-mail.

Firstly, information cannot be clarified on the spot and returned immediately.

Secondly, face to face interactions not only allow conversations, where information can be sent back and forth, but also observation of speech tone(s), body language, etc., all of which help to develop a complete picture of what is being communicated.

Finally, because of the relative ease with which E-mail can be used (relative to making appointments, physically transporting oneself to the senior manager's office, etc.), it is used more frequently, and there is the danger that this become an overload for all concerned. The majority of E-mails require a response which is time-consuming and takes away some of the cost-saving advantages.

EXAM QUESTION

Specimen examination question 2
You are a member of a group of six marketing consultants who have formed an association and occupy an office in a major capital city of the world.

(a) Explain the type of formal and informal communication systems that are likely to exist in this type of organization. (10 marks)

(b) Identify the main factors that each consultant has to take into consideration when preparing for a face-to-face interaction with clients in other countries. (10 marks)

ANSWER GUIDELINE

(a) The group is most likely to represent a power or people culture. In the case of the former it will be structured according to responsibility and status in the organization. The diagram below, as explained in Charles Handy's *Understanding Organisations*, demonstrates the communication system and relative power of the individual, which increases the closer one gets to the middle of the web. Communication tends to flow from the inside *out*. Informal communication will happen by the coffee machine or in other social interactions and be responsible mainly for sharing information of a range of personal and work-related issues.

As a people culture, these individuals will largely work independently of each other and engage in formal communication to discuss issues such as overheads or possibly professional aspects, such as the type of work coming in, its regularity and sources. Informal communication is likely to be a significant channel of communication and will happen in a number of ways – business lunches, travels abroad, sports or social interactions, etc.

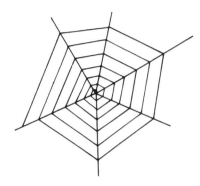

Figure 1.7 Web.

Figure 1.8 People culture.

(b) Face-to-face interactions with clients in other countries will require the consultant to consider factors such as language, cultural and subcultural factors, appearance, protocol, including gestures such as a handshake in a greeting, rather than kissing on both cheeks, as is the preferred method in some parts of Europe.

The *position* of the client in his/her organization may determine the style and level of language used and the time spent on the discussion or meeting, which in itself will partly be determined by whether it is an introductory information-gathering or -sending exercise or a final presentation of research and findings.

EXTENDING KNOWLEDGE

1 One of the most important aspects of the business communication process is feedback. Consider the alternative methods that may be used to facilitate feedback in both verbal and written communication and plan how and when to receive it.

Do you think that there are any situations in which feedback should be limited?

2 Communication in organizations must take place within the context of its culture and structures. Read Charles Handy's *Understanding Organisations* and evaluate whether the process and quality of communication that takes place in your organization are consistent with its culture and structures. Can you make recommendations for improvement?

Key factors in effective and successful communication

OBJECTIVES

In this second unit you will:

- Examine the variables in non-verbal communication and appreciate the importance of body language.
- Consider the importance of verbal communication and understand how vocal characteristics and speech can convey the type of message that you wish to express.
- Appreciate the skills in effective listening and reading.

By the end of this unit you will be able to:

- Appreciate the importance of body language in non-verbal communication.
- Understand how vocal characteristics, personal appearance and speech can convey the type of message that you wish to express.
- Use effective skills in listening and reading.

STUDY GUIDE

The objective of this unit is to establish that effective communication requires verbal, non-verbal and good listening skills, in face-to-face inter-actions and effectiveness in reading and interpreting written matter.

Marketing requires a great deal of face-to-face interaction and communication in a variety of contexts. It is therefore vitally important that you have the skills not only to send information which is clear, concise and capable of being understood but learn how to receive information by listening, watching for verbal cues and effectively reading and interpreting written matter.

This unit corresponds with parts 1.1.3 and 1.1.4 of the syllabus and will take about 3 hours of study time and another 3 hours to answer the set questions and to carry out the activities.

The ultimate aim is to enable you to produce a personal communication plan, based on an analysis of your level of performance in each of the skills described above and how you can set targets to improve your effectiveness as a business communicator.

You have already done a brief exercise in Activity 1.2 which will help towards the construction of a more formal personal communication plan.

Use your experience of professional and personal life to think about how you and others pass information and whether anything can be done to improve the quality of communication, particularly through written, verbal and non-verbal skills.

Passive observation is a very good way to learn how others communicate and can be used as a basis for assessing your own personal communication skills and therefore identifying the areas that need to be improved. If you are at work, this can be used in appraisals and interviews or by making informal requests for training and guidance which will help you to be a better business communicator.

The main areas to consider are use of body language, voice characteristics, personal appearance, use of time and personal space, speech characteristics and skill, listening skills, writing and reading skills. At the end of this unit there is an activity designed to help you produce a personal communication plan. You may therefore wish to approach superiors or colleagues in helping you to make an assessment of your present level of skill and training needs.

(a)   From the previous chapter and your own knowledge/experience how do you think that non-verbal communication takes place?

(b)   Are there any situations in which only non-verbal communication will do?

Jot down your thoughts below.

(a)

(b)

Non-verbal communication

The most basic form of communication to human beings is non-verbal, which is often unplanned and spontaneous but can have a greater impact than verbal communication.

Body language is the main medium for communicating non-verbally and takes place through facial expression, gestures and postures and physical contact; these all provide important clues as to our own and other people's behaviour and real feelings.

certain. **deh**
definition *n*.
precise mea
distinct, cle:
definitive *a*. f.
something;

John Thill and Courtland Bovée in *Excellence in Business Communication* (McGraw-Hill) argue that the following are the main types of non-verbal communication.

1 Facial expressions and eye movements, such as smiles and frowns, showing signs of anger or disbelief, reveal both the type and intensity of feeling and are particularly effective in communication.

2 Gestures and postures such as pointing, the way an individual moves, sits or stands can express a number of different feelings: friendliness, hostility, assertiveness, passiveness and power. In copying gestures and postures, our body language confirms that we are thinking and feeling the same way as the other person.

I stated in the previous unit that in an international business environment it is important to be aware of cultural traditions, which, if they are not observed, may cause a barrier to communication and therefore constrain your ability to transmit the desired message and to receive feedback. Gestures and postures must therefore be used to express important feelings and enhance the communication.

3 Physical contact such as shaking hands and holding another individual accounts for about 60% of all greetings and farewells and is an important method for conveying professionalism, for example from a sales executive to a client and warmth and reassurance amongst colleagues and friends. This may be an important way of breaking down initial barriers and therefore opening up the opportunity for effective communication.

ACTIVITY 2.1

Different types of non-verbal cues are used in visual communications such as advertisements to emphasize various 'feelings' of people and often to emphasize the attributes of a brand. Can you name any examples?

Channel of communication   *Example of non-verbal cue*

1 Television advertisement

_____

2 Magazine advertisement

_____

3 Newspaper advertisement

_____

4 Poster advertisement

_____

4 Voice characteristics form an important part of our personality and relay a great deal of information. They are extensively used in verbal marketing communications such as radio and television advertising. Accents and tones reflect psychological characteristics, seductive voices and tones increase our attention and research suggests that consumers of information find it difficult to listen to monotone voices. Successful speech is confident and positive, particularly in presentations to clients, or at conferences.

5 Personal appearance in terms of what you wear, when you wear it, hairstyle and make-up all express psychographic characteristics of lifestyle and personality, occupational and socioeconomic grouping, sexuality and even political orientation and religion. The image you wish to be projected in a visual communication such as a poster campaign can be achieved through combining clothes and styling, and are mostly used to reflect aspirational values of the target market. In your professional capacity, the type of clothing worn at formal functions such as an advertising pitch may differ to office clothes or when attending a training seminar.

6 The use of time and personal space is a rather more abstract concept in non-verbal communication but just as important, particularly in business situations. The size and type of office, its furnishing and equipment will usually reflect the status and position of an individual in a business organization.

In some cultures it is important to be late if you wish to demonstrate power and status. In other societies or business environments this would be considered disrespectful and even rude.

Non-verbal communication consists of:

- Body language +

  Gestures, postures, eye movements, type of physical contact and voice characteristics

- Personal appearance +

  Clothes, hair, make-up

- Use of time and personal space

  Manners, hospitality, respect, physical space

In short, when engaging in face-to-face interactions it is vital that the correct signals through suitable use of body language are conveyed in order to increase the chance of communicating a message which will be understood and interpreted as desired and achieve the communication objective. This can of course be measured by the positive or negative feedback which is received, as discussed in the previous unit.

Observe the non-verbal communication of colleagues or friends and make an assessment of what they are trying to communicate and the image they project in doing so. What conclusions can you draw from your observations?

Verbal communication

What proportion of time do you think managers spend on the various channels for sending and receiving information? Ring the answer below.

Speaking: 10%, 15%, 20%, 25%, 30%, 35%, 40%, 45%, 50%, 55%, 60%

Listening: 10%, 15%, 20%, 25%, 30%, 35%, 40%, 45%, 50%, 55%, 60%

Writing: 10%, 15%, 20%, 25%, 30%, 35%, 40%, 45%, 50%, 55%, 60%

Reading: 10%, 15%, 20%, 25%, 30%, 35%, 40%, 45%, 50%, 55%, 60%

From *Business Communication Today* by J. V. Thill and C. L. Bovée.

Figure 2.1 demonstrates that managers are increasingly using verbal communication to deliver information, but they do tend to put important messages in writing. However, 45% of a manager's time is spent *listening* and we shall be looking at developing effective listening skills later in the unit.

Although non-verbal communication is effective alone, it is most powerful when delivered with speech and, together with listening skills (discussed below), these are critical success factors in business for communication at all levels, including giving instruction and motivating employees, handling negotiations and conflict for the internal market and in demonstrating the benefits of products and services to the external market.

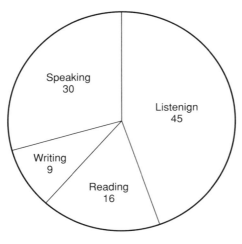

Figure 2.1 The percentage of time spent by managers on methods of communication. (J. V. Thill and C. L. Bovée)

Speaking is an important vehicle for effective communication in business. Planning what you wish to say and then delivering it by stressing positive words and phrases and tailoring remarks to suit the audience and situation will create a professional and lasting impression. Analysing the response of the receiver can help to identify whether the message is clear and understood.

J. V. Thill and C. L. Bovée argue that the essential skills required to be an effective speaker are as follows:

1   You must have a clear objective to the exercise and outcome, and complete familiarity with the subject, topic or key points to be communicated; this will also give confidence as you will be able to anticipate and answer questions.
2   You should present your argument logically, with a distinct beginning that introduces the main message; a middle that develops the points or arguments; and an end that states the action to be taken or follow-up required. This helps you to keep the attention and interest of the recipient as you will be better able to stay on track and move smoothly and swiftly through the presentation.
3   Style the message with appropriate gestures and eye contact that help you communicate the main message and reinforce the important points or arguments.
4   Speech characteristics, such as accent, pronunciation, enunciation, intonation and the choice of vocabulary and rate of delivery will all determine the quality of the communication, which is an important factor in the level of understanding capable of being achieved by the recipient.

5 Concepts and jargon that will be unfamiliar to the recipient of the communication can only be determined by carefully analysing the background of the individual or group. The most important concepts and phrases or jargon should be defined and explained either in the introduction or during the course of the presentation.

Effective listening

QUESTION 2.5

What do you think makes a good listener? Write down your thoughts below and compare the list made with the statements that follow.

J. V. Thill and C. L. Bovée argue that listening accounts for approximately 45% of the communication process and is increasingly recognized as an essential communication tool. There are three types of listening:

DEFINITION 2.3

certain. defi
definition *n*.
precise mea
distinct, clea
definitive *a*. f
something;

1 Attentive listening is required when receiving (new) information or instruction, e.g. by a sales person at a sales conference where intelligent information may be disseminated or new products demonstrated.

   It goes without saying that good practitioners of sales and marketing need to listen attentively to their customers and take suitable action as quickly as possible.
2 Empathetic listening occurs in situations such as appraisal/joint review interviews where it is important to get as much feedback as possible from the interviewee. On this basis an assessment of his/her needs can be made and valuable feedback in respect of his/her ability to cope with the role and tasks and general feelings about the organization can be recorded.
3 Critical listening, where the aim is to evaluate the strength and implications of the message. An example of a situation in which this type of listening is required would be in business negotiations, such as those between employees and management over working conditions and pay. The 'listeners', say management, will evaluate the level of concern and strength of feeling amongst the employees based on what is said and how it is expressed – short, sharp messages will usually indicate a great level of concern and 'high' strength of feeling which may result in industrial action if the situation is not addressed quickly.

Effective listening requires the following:

1 Concentrating on the key ideas being presented and finding areas of interest in the subject.
2 Remembering key words and concepts associated with the ideas helps to judge the content, not delivery.
3 Keeping an open mind through setting aside bias can help the learning process.
4 Working hard to listen through resisting distractions and using perpetual cues to facilitate the speaker, maintaining eye contact, reacting responsively and paying attention to body language.

ACTIVITY 2.3

Consider the essential characteristics of good listening and identify any areas in which you have a problem. Can you say why? Give examples of business situations where good listening is important and state the reasons for this.

Checklist of the essential characteristics of a good listener

1 _____
2 _____
3 _____
4 _____
5 _____
6 _____
7 _____
8 _____
9 _____
10 _____

A list of your problems/constraints in being a good listener

1 _____
2 _____
3 _____
4 _____
5 _____

Examples of where good listening is important in business

1 _____
2 _____
3 _____
4 _____
5 _____

In a later unit we shall be exploring business situations in which meetings, discussions and interviews take place. These are the main fields of face-to-face interaction where good speaking and listening skills are required. However, they are also very important when the other party cannot be seen and therefore body language signals cannot be used to help us understand the meaning of the message. This is particularly the case in verbal communication on the telephone.

Effective reading

Reading written communication effectively also requires a great deal of skill and practice. Below are a few basic guidelines to help you.

1 Minimize distractions and focus your complete attention on the reading matter.
2 Evaluate and interpret the information by deciding what is important. This is achieved through identifying the main ideas, concepts and issues and the relationships between them.
3 Look for appropriate material which is supportive and can help you to formulate conclusions.

SUMMARY

In this unit we have seen that:

- Successful business communication requires the use of both verbal and non-verbal skills such as effective speech characteristics, body language, personal appearance and use of time and personal space.
- Managers spend approximately 45% of their communication time listening. Therefore these skills are very important and essentially require the listener to concentrate, remember, keep an open mind, work to listen and to look for

verbal cues which will enable them to achieve a greater understanding of the message being delivered by the other party or parties to the dialogue.

- Receiving communication messages is as important as sending them. Therefore planning how to receive the information, interpreting and evaluating written material through initial careful reading and providing feedback are all important aspects of the basic functions of communication.

Analysing your personal communication skills

1 Use the chart below to rate your personal communication skills in terms of verbal and non-verbal characteristics discussed in this unit. Use a rating scale of 1–10, with 5 being the average for a person of your age or experience. Above 5 is a higher rating indicating stronger skill and below 5 a lower rating, indicating less ability and skill.

	Rating scale									
	1	2	3	4	5	6	7	8	9	10

Body language

Voice characteristics

Personal appearance

Use of time and space

Speech characteristics
and skill

Listening skills

Writing skills

Reading skills

2 Analyse the above information and draw conclusions about your personal effectiveness as a communicator. Use the information as the basis for a personal communication plan.

In order to produce a personal communication plan you must do the following:

(a) Identify what are the personal communication *objectives* that you would like to achieve, e.g. improving speech characteristics to a rating of 8 in the next 2 months and 10 in the following 2 months and so on.

(b) Identify which *strategy* will be used to achieve the objectives, e.g. training, asking for advice and guidance from experienced managers or colleagues and so on.

(c) Develop the *tactical* plans to implement the strategic proposals by recruiting a trainer or getting colleagues to set aside time every week or month to help you in acquiring or improving the skill.

(d) *Measure* the achievements made by asking an independent observer to make an assessment of the skill and use this to review and assess your future levels of performance until your objectives have been met.

This activity will undoubtedly require *resourcing* and you will need to use your existing skills to negotiate for the necessary resources to enable implementation of the plan. Use the pro forma below to present an analysis of your personal communication needs.

Personal communication plan

Name
Department
Position
Date

1   Executive summary (key points based on the above analysis and conclusions).

2   Objectives and actions:

Improve (e.g. speech)	By (e.g. next week, month or date)	Method (e.g. speech therapist)	Resources: cost and time needed
1			
2			
3			
4			

ACTIVITY DEBRIEF

The key skills needed to be an effective business communicator and therefore to foster good interpersonal relationships are speech and vocal characteristics, using body language correctly and having the appropriate personal appearance to suit the occasion. Listening, writing and reading skills are also critical in determining the ability to send and receive useful information which is fit for the purpose and needs of the parties.

Individuals are not born with these skills; they have to be learned through the process of social and professional socialization, therefore guidance and training can go a long way to improve the quality of an individual's communication ability.

REVISION TIPS

You must be able to:

1   Distinguish between the essential characteristics of verbal and non-verbal communication.
2   Analyse a situation and determine whether verbal, non-verbal or both will be most effective.
3   Understand and demonstrate the value of good speech characteristics and effective listening and reading skills.

EXAM HINT

The material in this unit is part of the foundation for your understanding the nature and importance of good communication skills, whether they are verbal, non-verbal or written. The examination will ask you to explain one or more of these skills in terms of their importance in facilitating the communication process and therefore you should know the basic rules that guide each one in greater effectiveness, and also the different business situations in which one or more may be significant.

Specimen examination question 1 (4 December 1995)
You are due to attend a second interview for a job as Customer Care Manager in a firm selling computers and computer software throughout the UK and Europe. You are required to deliver a short presentation on the importance of customer care and effective listening.

(a) Prepare the outline notes of your presention. (10 marks)
(b) Explain how positive body language may persuade your interviewers that you are a suitable candidate. (10 marks)

(a) The written presentation for this answer is not designated, and so candidates should use a straightforward note format. You should observe that it is a *short* presentation, and this should be reflected in the notes.

Customer care is most effective when the person dealing with a customer is responsive to his/her needs; this primarily takes place through attentive listening. Attentive listening allows an individual to fully absorb the message and therefore to find a suitable course of action for dealing with it.

A firm which sells computers and computer software is unlikely to interface directly with the end user, the consumer, but will interact frequently with the client, who is likely to be a retailer or distributor of their merchandise.

Business to business relationships require the same level of responsiveness, and, indeed, some passive listening in a client interaction can provide very useful feedback information which may be used by the organization.

Effective listening requires the listener to do the following:

- Concentrate on the key ideas and concepts being presented and find areas of interest in the subject of conversation.
- Remember key words and concepts associated with the ideas which will help to judge the content, not the delivery, of the message.
- Keep an open mind through setting aside bias.
- Work hard to listen through resisting distractions and using perceptual cues such as eye contact and other aspects of positive body language.

(b) There are many examples of how positive body language may persuade the interviews that you are a suitable candidate for the position.

Even before they have an opportunity to see you it is important to communicate a positive image by the way you dress, groom your appearance through hairstyle and, if appropriate, make-up.

If an appointment is made on the telephone to arrange a time or date/day for the interview, it is also wise to speak clearly, concisely and in an articulate manner. The tone of your voice and choice of vocabulary are important not just on the telephone (which you are likely to use frequently in this type of firm), but when you present yourself for interview.

Finally, when you do arrive for interview, observe that your body language will be critically important. You must sit or stand up straight but not rigid; it is useful to 'relax' as you are more likely to be 'natural' and therefore will not make mistakes in what is spoken or how it is spoken.

Remember protocol. In the UK most people will shake hands as a gesture of greeting. Use positive eye contact, smile and enjoy the event, you are more likely to get the job!

Specimen examination question 2

'Beside writing, reading and speaking, a fourth area of communication, listening, is now widely recognized as an essential management tool'. Explain why listening is important in good business communication and identify two business situations in which good listening skills would be particularly significant.

ANSWER GUIDELINE

Managers spend approximately 60–70% of their time actively communicating, approximately 45% of which is spent listening.

Listening skills are vitally important not only for understanding the information or feedback being received but also for fostering good interpersonal relationships both socially and professionally. Good listening skills can also help to stimulate the fruition and communication of new ideas and motivate others to improve their own personal listening skills.

There are three levels of listening: attentive listening for important information; empathetic listening to appreciate others' attitudes, feelings and emotions; and casual listening for pleasure.

Most people in business situations do not listen effectively for a number of reasons – we comprehend faster than we speak; external distractions compete for our attention; we do not take time to listen; we do not know how to listen effectively or we are biased or prejudiced, which affects our ability to listen.

Good listening skills include the following:

1 Concentrating on the key ideas presented and finding areas of interest in the subject.
2 Remembering key words and concepts associated with the ideas helps to judge the content, not delivery.
3 Keeping an open mind through setting aside bias can help the learning process.
4 Working hard to listen through resisting distractions and using perceptual cues to facilitate the speaker, maintaining eye contact, reacting responsively and paying attention to body language.

There are numerous business situations that call for good listening skills. First, in internal interviews and meetings, which are important face-to-face interactions when information is both transmitted and received, this will help both parties achieve a greater level of understanding and much faster than would be the case where constant interruptions took place. Examples include appraisals and team briefings. Second, in listening to the needs of clients, one is able to respond to their needs more effectively, for example in customer-related activity.

You should attempt to produce a personal communication plan every 6 months and use this as an opportunity for setting objectives that continually improve your skills as an effective communicator in a variety of different business situations, both internal and with external customers and clients.

Your abilities in communication can be improved over a period of time and through conducting this exercise you will learn which aspects of communication are most effective in different business situations at work, at meetings with your external market, nationally and internationally. In some situations it may be undesirable to engage in verbal and non-verbal communication. You will therefore need to have good skills in written and visual communication. We begin to analyse the former in the following unit.

Written communication 1

In this unit you will learn that:

- There are a number of considerations in the process of planning and composing messages for use in business communications. These are important in both written and verbal communications, and will be dealt with in this unit.
- There are a number of different vehicles used for transmitting written communications. The most commonly used are the business letter, the memorandum, briefs and reports; each will be dealt with separately in the unit.
- Each of these written communications is used in different business contexts, and you will appreciate the reasons why one may be used relative to another.
- Finally, each of these may be communicated through traditional methods such as the postal system (internal and external to the business organization), but increasingly are transmitted via electronic equipment such as facsimile machines, etc. These enable a number of advantages, which are discussed.

By the end of this unit you will:

- Know the difference between the main vehicles used for transmitting information either internally or externally.
- Appreciate the different situations, in which each would be appropriate.
- Be able to write a business letter, memo, brief or report with some confidence.
- Understand that transmission through electronic aids enables communications to be more efficient and can also save money in the long run.

In this unit I have combined the three main ways in which written material is communicated, i.e. business letters, memoranda and reports, together with a short emphasis on briefs, and information on planning and composing business messages.

The aim of the unit is therefore to give you a thorough grounding in the principles that underpin the successful preparation of letters, memos and reports in a business context. However, despite the many examples contained in this unit, you do need to supplement your experience of this area by looking at good and bad practice exhibited by professionals in the business environment.

Collectively, this unit represents about ten hours of private study together with another eight hours required for the various tasks, activities and questions.

In order to work through the text, study and carry out the tasks and activities and analyse the specimen questions and answers, this unit will take up approximately eighteen hours of your personal study time.

In order to become proficient in verbal and written communication you should do the following:

- Collect records of written communication sent by others. Analyse them against the rules established in this unit. You will be able to determine the skill of the sender and how the communication could have been improved; this is an effective way for you to learn.
- Keep records of written communication that you send and ask for a response from the recipient; this will help you to determine the effectiveness of your communication and will put you on the learning curve to improvement.
- Attempt to make recordings of verbal communication by tape or video so that they also can be analysed and used to improve your skill in planning and composing verbal messages.

Planning the communication message

QUESTION 3.1

What do you think are the important stages in *planning* a communication message? List them below.

1
2
3
4
5

The stages in planning a communication message

Understanding the purpose

The business communicator will have a number of reasons for sending a communication message.

In terms of the internal market, we briefly discussed in the first unit that this will be to:

1 Provide information on a range of general and specific organizational issues, possibly determined by the level of the relationship as established by the formal or informal structure of the organization and the routes used to send communication.
2 Motivate or commit staff and shareholders to organizational objectives or policy issues.
3 Create loyalty and therefore performance and productivity in their roles.

In terms of the external market this will be to:

1 Stimulate the interest of an inert or inept market and therefore to make attitudes more positive to the organization's product, service or specific communication message.
2 Motivate and persuade the target market to sample a product or service or to request further information from the organization.
3 Give information on organizational initiatives that may be important to individuals or groups with whom the organization has a relationship, such as customers and suppliers, the media or opinion leaders.

Acknowledge the audience

The background, interests, knowledge of the subject and relationship of the recipient to you will determine the depth of analysis, complexity of the message and choice of vocabulary used in your communication.

If you are a salesperson or employed in marketing and engage in regular correspondence with particular clients, you will have a good feel for their interest in the subject to be communicated and will be able to provide them with the information needed relatively easily.

However, when breaking new ground where no previous information exists on the person with whom you must correspond, the starting point will be to gain a profile of the organization (even if this is a mental picture, though extra caution must be exercised) and depending on the *status* of the person, you will be able to make some assumptions on the style of message and compose your verbal or written communication accordingly.

When dealing with audiences in verbal communication, such as speeches and presentations, large audiences cannot usually be involved in the effort and therefore to reach them all effectively, try to touch on areas in which the *majority* may have a *common* interest.

Smaller audiences tend to be less diverse in their profile and can be encouraged to participate in the exercise.

Create a conducive environment

Clearly, a quiet room for the team briefing or making sure that no building work is taking place whilst you are to deliver a keynote speech may seem obvious, but you need to plan that there are not likely to be distractions at a particular time.

Forming the main idea

Most notions are related to one central idea or theme, supported or demonstrated by the others. The main idea must achieve the objective of the message and ensure that the recipient responds in the desired manner. If you are trying to persuade the recipient, then establishing a rapport and method of agreement with your purpose is critical. It is less important to do so if you are simply responding to a request, where fulfilling that obligation is often enough.

Thill and Bovée suggest that unravelling your main idea is not always easy, but there are a number of approaches that can be taken:

1 Brainstorming all the points and then looking for relationships between them and determining the most important facts.
2 Using a journalistic method, where answering the six questions of who, what, where, when, how and why could provide the solution.
3 Taking the recipient's perspective, identifying the questions that he/she is most likely to ask and determining your responses.
4 Story-telling – make a tape of a conversation (between you and a fictitious individual) pertaining to the situation for which you wish to clarify the main idea. Critically evaluate the tape recording to identify the idea.

Style

Style is about presenting the message and allied information in such a way that it is both convenient to use and easy to understand. The choice of words is critical in evoking an image in the mind of the reader. The style of writing should also flow smoothly through a variety of sentences and phrases with the appropriate tone.

Coherence through the logical presentation of the ideas (including identifying those which are to be appendices, enclosures, etc.), emphasis through type styles, headings, summaries, lists and proportion and use of creativity which lets the reader 'feel' the message will all contribute to a high-quality communication.

Readability

Readability is an important factor in convenience and ease of understanding. Therefore written communication should comprise sentences which are mostly short, use simple language and familiar words and tie in with the reader's experience.

Produce an outline

This helps to identify whether the ideas will work together in a logical format and cover the main theme and completeness of the message. Outlines may be in the form of topics and subtopics, sentences or paragraphs, but must reflect the desired content, tone, style and format required.

Generally, routine messages require less planning and composition thought than complex messages, though the time taken and method used for writing the message can enhance or constrain the quality of the written communication.

Revision of the message

Finally, to ensure that the message is free from potential misinterpretation, revise, revise and revise again.

The channel of communication

Select the channel of communication, whether it is verbal, written or visual (Fig. 3.1).

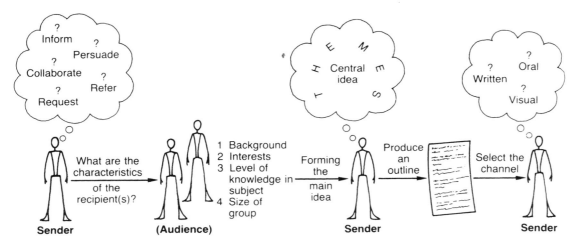

Figure 3.1 The process of planning the communication.

The main advantage of *verbal communication* is the interaction it allows between sender and receiver and the opportunity for immediate feedback. The verbal method of approach also allows you to judge the receiver's responses to the communication through his/her use of facial expressions, body language and vocabulary, allowing you to respond accordingly. The main types of verbal communication are face-to-face conversations, telephone calls, interview situations, meetings, speeches and presentations, all of which can be formal or informal.

The main advantage of *written communication* is the opportunity to plan and control the message. The main disadvantage is that immediate feedback is not available. Written communication is most likely to be used when the information is long and complex, a permanent record is needed for future reference and when immediate feedback is unnecessary or undesirable. The main types of written communication are letters, memos and reports for the internal market and advertising copy and press releases for the external market.

Visual communications have the ability to demonstrate the product or service to its best advantage through the use of graphics, colours and shades and, together with verbal communication, this is a particularly effective medium for a mass market, especially if the communication can stand out from the competing stimuli constantly being received by the audience.

ACTIVITY 3.1

Analyse six pieces of communication that you have received in the last week and answer the following questions:

1　Do you consider the general and specific purpose of the message to be clear?
2　Was the message delivered by the most appropriate person?
3　Do you think that the best medium for delivering the message was used?
4　Was the timing of delivery of the message suitable?

ACTIVITY 3.2

You have been invited to write a brief and give a talk on marketing fmcg (fast moving consumer goods) branded goods in the UK today. What are the main factors to consider in planning the message? How would the size and needs of your audience affect your composition and delivery if they are:

1　The 'top five' advertising agencies in the UK?
2　Product managers in your organization?
3　Undergraduate students of marketing at the local university?

Planning and composing business messages, whether written or verbal, requires the following to be addressed:

1   Determine the purpose.
    (a)   Is it to inform, persuade or to seek collaboration on the information that you are presenting?
    (b)   How do you expect the audience to respond?
2   Determine the audience and their needs.
    (a)   Who is the primary audience? Consider their size and profile.
    (b)   What level of understanding do they have and are capable of achieving?
    (c)   Consider your relationship and role you represent to the audience.
3   Determine your main idea.
    (a)   Undertake a process of planning, composing and revising that will critically evaluate your main message.
    (b)   Consider themes and tones that will stimulate interest and motivate the audience.
    (c)   Ensure that the length of delivery and timing are appropriate for you and the audience.
4   Determine the channel for communication.
    (a)   Written messages have the advantage that they are permanent records and particularly suitable for transmitting complex information, especially where immediate feedback is not required.
    (b)   Verbal messages are useful for communicating with small and large audiences, where feedback and further discussion are important and it is important to motivate the audience with verbal and non-verbal cues.

1   The advertising agencies will probably benefit most from a short verbal presentation backed by a report which is concise and articulate; the purpose is to inform.
2   The purpose of communicating with product managers is usually to collaborate and therefore an informal, loosely structured verbal presentation, preceded by a briefing document, are the most suitable channels.
3   The needs of the undergraduates is for information and, as they will probably be a large group, a structured, formal verbal presentation is the best medium for delivery. You may also wish to present them with a synopsis of your communication.

Give examples of the different types of message that might be used by business organizations in written communication for both the internal and external markets.

Types of written message

Business organizations have to send a variety of communications both internally and externally. Some of these will be routine, others non-routine and will generally convey either positive or negative messages.

1   Routine messages are used in business for a range of positive activities such as announcements to regular clients of changes in merchandise or prices, information on personnel changes to the internal market, etc.
2   Non-routine messages are specific to the purpose in hand. For example, you may wish to make an enquiry regarding the merchandise of a supplier or place a one-off order on behalf of a customer; these types of correspondence messages usually require a reply to the communication.

Positive messages are frequent occurrences in written communication, whether to the internal market through a memo or to the external market through a letter. Written communication which is designed to be positive should follow these guidelines:

1   The opening paragraph should be clear and concise, with a supportive tone that is positive and pleasing.
2   Subsequent paragraphs should contain increasing levels of detail that identify the reasons for the communication and any information that will be of significance to the recipient.
3   The closing paragraph should be polite and courteous, finally stating any action that may be required of the recipient.

Messages that are designed to convey bad news or negative messages require a great deal of tact and diplomacy in their composition and delivery. These types of written communication are usually used when refusing requests, for example for credit or information, or turning down applicants for positions in the organization. The following guidelines in planning a negative communication may be observed:

1   The opening paragraph should recognize the situation leading to the communication and explaining the nature of the negative message.
2   Subsequent paragraphs should give increasing levels of detail but remain clear and concise, firm, fair and positive.
3   The closing paragraph should have a polite and courteous tone. Avoid using clichés and make a suitable suggestion, if appropriate.

The communication messages described above may be used for the internal or external market but in respect of the latter, there are further initiatives that can be taken.

DEFINITION 3.1

certain. defin
lefinition *n.* s
precise mear
distinct, clea
lefinitive *a.* fi
something; r

The AIDA (attention, interest, desire and action) is a useful principle when planning written communication and, although it is usually used in communicating with a large, impersonal audience, its basic constructs can be used to guide the preparation of correspondence.

Attention arises from a bold headline or statement. In the case of a letterhead this is likely to be positioned in the logo or style of lettering used and therefore must be both immediately visible and stimulating. *Interest* will emerge from the content of the message which, as a general principle, should give an appropriate level of detail whilst remaining clear and concise. Good use of language and written communication skills (which varies for memos, letters, advertising copy, job descriptions etc.) are needed to successfully communicate the message. *Desire* will make the recipient 'read/listen' and want to know more. If you have requested specific *action*, the quality of the message should be such that it makes the recipient respond.

ACTIVITY 3.3

Consider the type of message (routine, non-routine, positive, negative, personal or impersonal) that would be most appropriate for the audiences in the following situations:

1   Internal audiences:

   (a)   Employees who need to be motivated on issues of change in the organization.
   (b)   Colleagues from other departments who need to support you on a new proposal for product development.
   (c)   Colleagues in the department who seek your support for proposing a budget increase in advertising expenditure.

2 External audiences:

(a) Retailers whom you wish to stock your brand of merchandise.
(b) Suppliers who need to be more flexible in responding to your business needs.
(c) Voluntary organizations that seek your support in the community.

The business letter

Undoubtedly you will have been already involved in writing business letters as millions are composed, produced and delivered daily. Every organization has its own style (which is important in reflecting image and efficiency) but there are a set of basic rules of layout that all will follow:

1 A blocked layout with all entries starting from the left-hand margin or an indented style where the main body of the letter is set to the left-hand margin and all other parts are centred; either method may be used but should be consistent throughout the organization or department (Fig. 3.2).

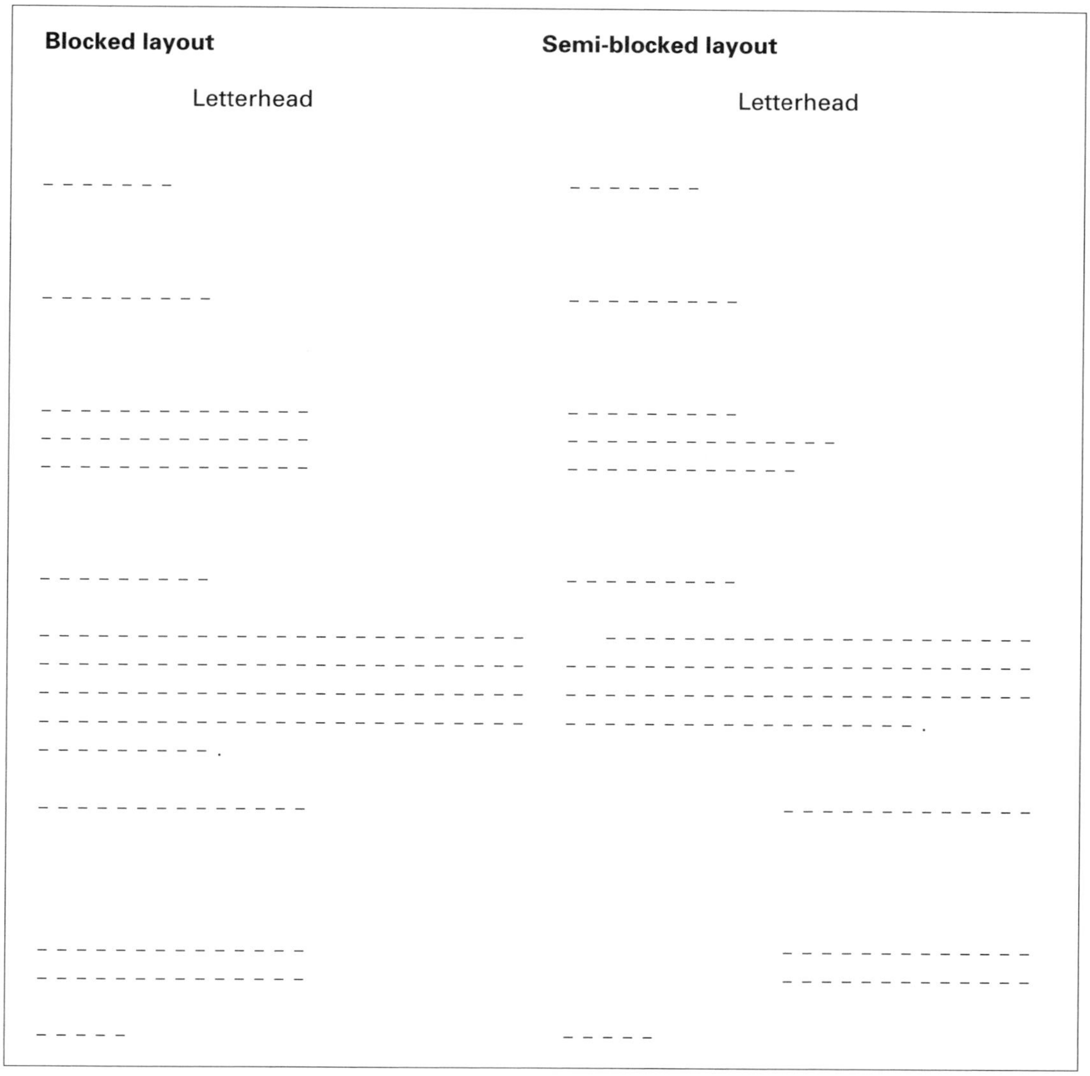

Figure 3.2 Layouts for business letters: (a) blocked; (b) semi-blocked.

2 Business letters are made up of the following parts:

(a) Letterhead and/or logo – communicates the corporate image through its graphic style and usually also contains the address, telephone, telex and fax numbers of the organization.

(b) Letter references – initials of the typist and author.
(c) Date – usually the month is placed first, fully written – not numerals, followed by the day.
(d) Recipient's title, name and address.
(e) Salutation – for example, Dear Sir, Dear Madam or Dear Mrs Jones.
(f) Subject heading – this is usually indented and underlined, for example, Conference on Marketing Communication, September 25th 1994, Queen Elizabeth's Hall, London.
(g) Body of the letter – short paragraphs centred on the page.
(h) Complimentary close – 'Yours sincerely' for named recipients, i.e. Dear Mr Brown; 'Yours faithfully' for formally addressed recipients, i.e. Dear Sir(s), Dear Madam; and 'Sincerely' or 'With kind regards' when the recipient is addressed by first name only, i.e. Dear Angela.
(i) Signature – usually in the sender's own handwriting.
(j) Position title of sender.
(k) References to enclosure and copies.

Figure 3.3 shows a model business letter.

LETTERHEAD

Letter references

Date

Inside address of recipient

Attention leader

Salutation

Subject heading

Body

Complimentary close

Signature
Name
Position

Enclosure reference

Figure 3.3 A model business letter.

Structuring business letters

1 The opening paragraph sums up the reason for the communication, and acknowledges any correspondence received and any other information which will provide a context for the rest of the letter.
2 The middle paragraphs set down the detail of the message and the sequence will either follow a direct approach (deductive), where the main idea comes first, followed by the supporting evidence or, where this is first, followed by the main idea, an indirect approach (inductive) is used. The method chosen will be determined by the likely reaction of the recipient: *deductive* for receptive audiences and *inductive* with those who may be displeased or harder to persuade.

3   The closing paragraph will summarize the main points of a complex communication and state any action that is needed from the recipient, and finally end on a courteous note with the suitable complimentary close.

Types of business letters

Writing order letters

Letters for placing orders are used infrequently because preprinted order forms are usually more convenient and efficient. However, if an order letter is written, state your needs clearly by presenting the information in column form, with double-spacing and totalling the balance of prices at the end, explaining to which account the balance should be charged. State the delivery address (it may be different from the address on the letterhead) and the mode of transport which should be used.

Figure 3.4 gives an example of an order letter.

MAKE-IT BUILDING SUPPLIERS
Churchyard Grove
Pickwick
Lancashire LU1 5TF
Tel: 0123 668791

Our ref: HBJ/abc

October 1st 199X

The Timber Merchants Ltd
Station Road
Ripon
Yorkshire YU8 TR3

For the attention of Deborah Jones

Dear Ms Jones,

Account Number: 5690   Special order under invoice 123

Further to our last order, would you supply the following additional items:

1	20 metres of extra hard-wearing timber for fencing.	£5.95 per metre excl. VAT	=	£119
2	5 litres of creosote liquid in natural colour.	£2.75 per litres excl. VAT	=	£ 13.75
3	24 litres of indoor wood varnish in antique pine.	£1.44 per litre excl. VAT	=	£ 34.56

Balance	£167.31
VAT on items	£ 29.28
Total balance	**£196.59**

The balance should be stated on the above invoice and charged to our existing account. I would appreciate delivery by November 15th, latest.

Yours sincerely,

Harold Jenkins
Purchasing Manager

Figure 3.4   An order letter.

Draw up an order letter based on the following information:

To: ABC Printers Ltd, Queen Street, Wolverhampton, Staffs, WV5 EL8
For the attention of Jonathan James. Account no. PC 123.

You wish to receive the following:

1   300 copies of the sales promotion literature for Brand Y, cost per copy: 20p.
2   2000 leaflets for the mail-drop campaign, cost per leaflet: 7p.
3   500 of your latest catalogues and price list, cost per catalogue: £1.50, cost per price list: 15p.

Answering order letters

If an order letter is received from a new customer, you should send a personal reply, which can also be used to state or clarify the terms of payment and other administrative procedures.

From time to time, you may also have to deal with non-routine order letters from customers, which will usually mean conveying some bad news about back orders, unfillable orders or having to make substitutions.

Your overall aim should be to keep instructions clear, remaining positive and confident in the tone of the letter so that the customer is pleased to respond, and attempting to ensure that the sale, as close to the original, is made and good will is maintained.

If a letter based on an unclear order is received, your first task is to get the information necessary to complete the order, which may be in writing if the order is long or complex and the customer needs time to restate the information, or by phone, if time is short and it is relatively easy for the customer to deal with the data required.

If the letter is written, begin by confirming the original order and emphasize again the positive features of your goods. In the next paragraph, state the nature of the problem and in the close, tell the customer how to solve the problem and how soon you expect to hear from him/her.

When dealing with back orders, you will either be able to fulfil some of the order, or none if the organization no longer makes the product and you are not able to offer a substitute. If some of the order can be fulfilled, this will convey some good news (see above), but if you cannot meet the customer's needs, then tact is necessary for conveying the negative message (see above).

Writing letters of enquiry or request

DEFINITION 3.3

certain. defi
lefinition n. s
precise mear
distinct, clea
lefinitive a. fi
something; i

Letters of enquiry or request can deal with a variety of questions, such as asking the reader to supply certain information, make a presentation or inviting him/her to attend a function. They almost always require a reply and some action to be taken, therefore they should be sent out in advance of the action date and be well-written and tactful.

The opening paragraph should state the nature of the enquiry or request clearly and simply with a personal tone that will make the reader want to respond.

If further explanation or justification is needed, explain the importance of the information required and the situation which prompted the inquiry or request and, if appropriate, the benefits to the reader. Next, specify the desired action in a positive manner and present the questions logically.

Close the letter with a courteous statement and explain the type of action needed, the deadline by which a reply should be made and assurance that the information will be treated as confidential (if appropriate).

Figure 3.5 gives an example of a letter of request.

Write a letter of request and inquiry based on the following information:

To: Jennifer Stevens, Sales Manager, Graphics Galore, The Hyde, Palmers Green, London N3 6TV, asking for the latest catalogue and price list of software packages for producing graphical visual aids. You are also interested to know whether they will have any packages available in 3-D in the near future.

Answering letters of inquiry and request

The *perception* of your organization is partly based on how efficiently, courteously and thoroughly enquiries and requests are handled, whether written or verbal, and the style in which they are expressed.

The majority of enquiries and requests are routine, so it helps to have preprepared information that can be sent out quickly (this may simply mean a brief covering letter, together with a catalogue, brochure or price list).

ULTIMATE COMPUTER COMPANY Ltd
3 The Gateway
Hounslow
Middlesex TW15 6TU
Tel: 0181 967 6345

TRJ/abc

October 1st 199X

Mr Andrew Collins
Marketing Communications Consultants
'The Nook'
Twinkle Lane
Beaconsfield
BUCKS DU18 74R

Dear Mr Collins

Ref: 'Computers of the World' Exhibition, London, 199X

I had the pleasure of using your professional services in helping us to prepare and present at the above last year.

We are now in the process of planning to exhibit our new product range again this year and would like to know whether you would offer us your services. I am pleased to enclose our latest catalogue.

Please contact me at the end of next week to arrange for a meeting at our offices.

I look forward to hearing from you.

Yours sincerely,

Timothy R. Jones
Marketing Manager

Enc. Catalogue of product range X.

Figure 3.5 A letter of request.

Non-routine enquiries and requests, especially those that may involve a potential sale, which require a specific letter should contain the following:

1 An opening statement acknowledging the enquiry or request.
2 A favourable response of key information regarding the enquiry or request, making references to enclosures (if appropriate).
3 A personal close leading towards a sale (if appropriate), but encouraging goodwill and appreciation.

Writing claim or adjustment letters

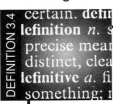

DEFINITION 3.4

In marketing, claim and adjustment letters are likely to deal with faulty, mishandled or lost merchandise and other types of customer complaint.

Your motive for communicating is to have the claim sorted out and therefore written documentation is better than verbal communication as there is evidence of action you have taken.

In writing a claim letter, you should contain the following:

1 Opening paragraph with a clear statement of the problem.
2 Further information that will verify the claim or adjustment needed.
3 Closing statement with a polite, non-threatening request for action, emphasizing that the business relationship need not be affected if the matter is resolved satisfactorily.

Figure 3.6 gives an example of a letter making a claim for adjustment.

BEAUTY POTIONS LTD
2–6 Staines Road
Windsor
Berkshire BK7 9LE
Tel: 01753 576423

JK/abc

October 1st 199X

Variety Fragrances
10 Harrow Road
Wembley
Middlesex 8TU 65R

For the attention of Mr Gardiner

Dear Mr Gardiner,

On September 5th 199X, we received your order 1112, together with the invoice, 2224.

You will note that the first item on the invoice is listed as 50 × Fragrance 'Irresistible', but unfortunately we received 50 × Fragrance 'Uncontrollable'. A copy of the invoice is attached.

Please be kind enough to collect the wrong items and have them replaced by 50 × Fragrance 'Irresistible' at the same time.

I look forward to receiving the correct order by November 1st 199X.

Sincerely,

Joanna Kemp
Sales and Purchasing Manager

Enc. Copy of invoice 2224

Figure 3.6 A letter making a claim for adjustment.

Write a letter making a claim for adjustment based on the following information:

To: The Sales Manager of Ladies Fashion Shoes Ltd, Northampton Business Park, Billings Road, Northampton NNE 5XT.

You are the manager of a retail shoe shop and ordered eight pairs of shoes in style 'Italian', but were sent size 5 instead of size 6. They were ordered on pro forma no. 876 and are urgently needed for a wedding in 2 weeks' time.

Answering letters for claims or adjustments

This type of letter will usually be most significant when a claim or adjustment is refused. In this situation, the following rules should be observed:

1   An opening statement with reference to the claim or adjustment but with a notable point on which both parties might be agreed.
2   An explanation which is tactful and maintains the goodwill of the organization, whilst ensuring that the claimant accepts (some) responsibility for the nature of the claim.
3   The refusal, possibly with the suggestion of an alternative course of action.
4   A pleasant close.

Writing letters of credit

In most organizations today, the process of buying and selling goods and services is facilitated by credit. The credit manager has responsibility for accepting or rejecting an application for credit, which is based on an assessment regarding the person or organization's financial viability and outstanding debts, in relation to the type and value of credit required.

Approving credit

1   A pleasant opening paragraph which grants the credit request.
2   Details of the terms and conditions under which credit is granted, addressing any specific points which may not be in line with company policy, but have been raised.
3   A courteous close.

Refusing credit

1   An opening statement appreciating the request for credit. Make the refusal, but with a notable point that both parties may agree.
2   Details for the refusal in positive terms which are specific to the reader, whilst maintaining a tactful tone to ensure goodwill.
3   A courteous close, with a sales pitch in relation to the correspondence, if appropriate.

Figure 3.7 gives an example of a letter approving credit.

Write a letter refusing credit to: Sonia Grant, Sales Manager of The Jewellery Store, Cirencester, stating that her establishment can continue to purchase on a 'cash-with-order' or 'cash-on-delivery' basis. You are a jewellery wholesaler with whom Sonia Grant has been a customer for 1 year and it is company policy to trade with customers for a minimum of 18 months before credit is made available.

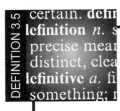

certain. deﬁr
lefinition *n.* s
precise meai
distinct, clea
lcfinitive *a.* fi
something; r

Sales letters are designed to motivate people in a variety of different ways – in making purchases, endorsing the activities of an organization, participating in campaigns and so on.

Before a sales letter can be written, the sender must be clear on the main idea and message he/she wishes to express, the target market or audience to whom the communication is directed and the appropriate format for the letter.

The main idea or message will usually be about a product or service: new, repackaged, relaunched, changes in price, distribution or marketing communication, i.e. new advertising campaign or different channel of communication, and so on.

The target market will be determined by identifying potential buyers of the product or service, based on traditional market segmentation variables such as age, sex, position in family life-cycle, socioeconomic group, etc. or psychographics and behavioural aspects of consumer behaviour. Clearly the size of the target market will determine the number of letters that need to be prepared and sent and the costs associated with this activity, which may exceed the designated budget; this may in turn lead to the need for sample coverage.

The format may be just a letter, or may include brochures, response cards and other (promotional) material; it may be (colour) printed or photocopied.

CATERING WHOLESALERS LTD
35 Redruth Avenue
Tunbridge
Kent TN15 UC1
Tel: 01932 57311

HB/abc

October 1st 199X

Mr R. Anderson
The Manager
'THE RESTAURANT'
76 Sevenoaks Road
Sevenoaks
KENT

Dear Mr Anderson,

Thank you very much for your recent application for credit. I am pleased to inform you that this has been approved.

Our terms and conditions are as follows:

1   A credit limit of £2000 is available for your establishment.
2   Invoices must be settled within 15 days of the date of issue, after which an interest charge of 5% will be levied on outstanding balances.

Yours sincerely,

Harry Bains
Credit Manager

Figure 3.7   A letter approving credit.

Composing the letter

The letter should follow the AIDA principle:

A Arouse the attention of the reader by having a personalized opening which responds to the reader's emotions, a surprise statement or a free sample.

ID Keep the interest and desire of the reader by highlighting benefits to the reader and unique selling points (USPs) or talking about the price.

A Motivate the reader through positive statements and challenges to undertake the desired course of action.

Figure 3.8 gives an example of a sales letter.

ACTIVITY 3.8

Write a sales letter based on the following information:

To: Dr Makhan Singh, 36 The Grove, Slough, Berks SL3 7TY, informing him about your new range of garden furniture and the special offer of a free bag of compost with the first order received by November 15th 199X.

You are also enclosing the new specialist catalogue and price list.

Sales letters and direct-mail

Sales letters tend to be sent as part of a direct-mail exercise, which has rapidly grown as an

---

WHOLESALE HOLIDAY Co. Ltd
26–28 Kensington High Street
London W14 XA5
Tel: 0171 635 2146

APJ/abc

October 1st 199X

Sally Kenkins
25 Rosemary Court
Ipswich IP7 14T

Dear Ms Kenkins,

A FREE CRUISE ON THE MEDITERRANEAN!

You are one of our most valued customers. As part of our fifth birthday celebrations we are offering you this unique opportunity to cruise on the Med for free.

We are also pleased to enclose our latest brochure of holidays for the discerning traveller and if a booking is made for yourself and one other person by November 15th 199X, a free cruise on the Mediterranean is yours.

Call or write for further information, but this special offer can only be made available on booking from our brochure.

I look forward to receiving your reservation in the next few weeks.

Yours sincerely,

Anthony P. Jones
Senior Marketing Executive

Enclosure: Wholesale Holiday Brochure

Figure 3.8   The sales letter.

important medium for both communicating and selling directly to a target market. A direct-mail package has four main components:

1　An outer envelope, which may show the organization's logo and name.
2　The (covering) sales letter, following the AIDA principle.
3　A brochure or catalogue, price list and order form as appropriate.
4　A (postage-paid) return envelope or order card.

In marketing activities today, mailing lists are frequently used to identify potential recipients of the communications. These are available through various sources such as ACORN (A classification of Residential Neighbourhood).

Writing letters of recommendation

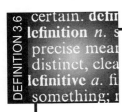

Letters of recommendation convey information about people, their characteristics and suitability for the position. Therefore they are usually confidential and must contain the following:

1　The name of the person.
2　The position that the candidate is seeking.
3　The nature of the relationship between you and the candidate.
4　Relevant details to the position being sought by the candidate.
5　Evaluation of the candidate by the correspondent.

If you feel unable to provide a letter of recommendation, be brief and factual in your reasons. Figure 3.9 gives an example of a letter of recommendation.

FINANCE and INSURANCE Co
The Causeway
Newcastle upon Tyne NN4 65T
Tel: 0191 35202

SB/abc

October 1st 199X

The Membership Secretary
Chartered Institute of Marketing
Moor Hall
Cookham
Berks

Dear Sir/Madam,

Re: Caroline Taylor

I am pleased to support Ms Taylor's application for membership of the Chartered Institute of Marketing.

Ms Taylor has been in our employment for 6 years working in the area of Direct Marketing.

I understand that she has passed all her CIM examinations and will be pleased to receive further benefit as a member of the CIM.

Yours faithfully,

Sheila Brown
Marketing Director

Figure 3.9　Letter of recommendation.

ACTIVITY 3.9

Write a letter of recommendation for a friend who wishes to join a social or professional club of which you are a member.

Memoranda

Memos are widely and routinely used by organizations, mainly for internal correspondence to convey short specific information such as the schedule of meetings, decisions made and the results of research; these can be stored for future reference and follow composition principles similar to that of writing business letters.

DEFINITION 3.7

Memo paper is often preprinted on A4 or A5, in the following format:

(Letterhead)

MEMO
To:
From:
Date:
Subject:

The sender and recipient of the memo are usually addressed by job title (e.g. sales manager), but may also include the full name. There may need to be circulation of the memo to other interested parties and this should be indicated here.

The subject title should be clear and concise and tell the recipient exactly what the memo is about.

The body of the memorandum should be in short paragraphs, with summary headings if appropriate.

Figure 3.10 gives an example of a memo.

MEMO
Medical Software Ltd

To: Carole Francis (Sales and Marketing Director)
From: Clare White (Marketing Manager)
Copy to: Hannah Craven (Secretary)
Subject: Software 199X Exhibition, Amsterdam, December 1st–3rd
Date: October 1st 199X

We have 8 weeks before the exhibition takes place and need to finalize the details of the follow-up campaign, particularly the role of our sales force.

Further to our meeting last week, we also need to discuss the sales promotion initiatives to push our products following the exhibition.

Please confirm that a meeting on October 5th at 3 pm in my office will be convenient.

Figure 3.10 A memo.

ACTIVITY 3.10

Write a memo to your superior asking for training in one of the areas identified in the personal communication plan from Unit 2.

Notices

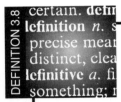

DEFINITION 3.8

Notices can play an important role in disseminating unconfidential information to a large number of employees who share a common interest. Effective notices should follow these rules:

1 The size of the paper should correspond to the amount of information to be conveyed and its effect when displayed on the noticeboard and possibly viewed from several feet away.
2 The AIDA principle can again be used with a large, bold heading which captures attention, detail which holds the reader's interest and desire, and clear instructions as to the action which should be taken.
3 The message should be simple and concise.

Figure 3.11 gives an example of a notice.

SAFETY FIRST!

A Special First-Aid Course designed to give you basic introduction will be available free to all employees on the following dates:

October 1st 5–6 pm
November 1st 5–6 pm
December 1st 5–6 pm

The number of places is limited to 20 per class so early booking is advisable.

Contact: Jane Slater, ext. 123

Figure 3.11   A notice.

ACTIVITY 3.11

Write a notice to all employees in your department or organization stating that a special course on body language will be available on two dates and free of charge, though places are limited to 10 per class.

Briefs

DEFINITION 3.9

The word 'brief' is commonly used in most countries (especially those based on the English legal system) to refer to documents 'carried' or given to a barrister which are the necessary details required to help him/her to prepare a case for trial.

Briefs do not have to be lengthy documents but can be presented to an audience in the form of a circular letter or memo. However, the common link is that they are another format for the dissemination of information to an audience – one that is usually large. For example, in the college where I lecture, the senior management team, notably the Principal and Vice-Principal, issue briefs on an irregular basis, which are circulated to *all* staff. The items discussed in the brief refer mostly to matters of college policy and, in particular, feedback from meetings held and decisions taken. Most recently, we have received information on equal opportunities, the status of the college in terms of funding from central government, etc.

In order to prepare a brief, try to have a 'systematic' approach to its written presentation. For example, you may want to use a chronological format, prioritize issues in terms of their relative importance or use some other criteria. However, whichever method is chosen, whenever possible try to use the same approach for *consistency*.

ACTIVITY 3.12

Think of several different business situations in which it would be more appropriate to use a brief than any other form of written communication, and state your reasons below.

EXAM QUESTION

1   Write a letter to Sharon Taylor, Purchasing Manager of Furniture Makers Ltd, 37 Station Road, Barnsley, West Yorkshire from John Perkins, Credit Control Manager of Timber Ltd, The Yard, Harrogate, approving their request for a credit limit up to £6000.

(12 marks)

2   Describe the main features of a letter of recommendation.   (8 marks)

ANSWER GUIDELINE

Timber Ltd
The Yard
Harrogate
Tel: 01234 98765

JP/abc

October 1st 199X

Ms Sharon Taylor
Purchasing Manager
Furniture Makers Ltd,
37 Station Road
Barnsley
West Yorkshire

Dear Ms Taylor

Thank you for your letter dated September 5th 199X, requesting credit in relation to orders for our timber. We are pleased that your business with us is growing and happy to extend our services to you.

I am pleased to inform you that your credit has been approved up to a limit of £6000 and the terms and conditions are as follows:

1. A minimum order of £1000 must be placed.
2. Invoices are sent out on the 25th of each month.
3. Payment is due 30 days after the date of the statement.
4. Interest charges for outstanding balances will be 5% above the basic bank rate.

I hope that this information conveys all the details you need and we look forward to continuing to work with you.

Yours sincerely

John Perkins
Credit Control Manager

Letters of recommendation have an important goal: to convince readers that the person being recommended has the characteristics required for the job or other benefit. It is therefore important that they contain all the relevant details:

1. The full name of the candidate.
2. The job or benefit that the candidate is seeking.
3. Whether the writer is answering a request or taking the initiative.
4. The nature of the relationship between the writer and the candidate.
5. Facts relevant to the position or benefit sought.
6. The writer's overall evaluation of the candidate's suitability for the job or benefit sought.

Recommendation letters are usually confidential, i.e. they are mailed directly to the person or committee who request them and are not shown to the candidate.

Reports

Introduction

Reports are factual documents, prepared to fulfil the needs of decision-makers in organizations. They are therefore used for a variety of purposes and can be short (such as progress reports) or long (such as investigative reports or the annual report), formal or informal, routine, occasional or specially commissioned. Before any report can be prepared, decisions about the exact nature and purpose of the report, the recipient, distribution and likely reaction all need to be addressed because these factors will determine the structure, length and style (i.e. the degree of formality) of the report.

Report preparation

There are four main steps in the preparation of a report:

1. Define the issue(s) – this helps to identify the information that will be needed to deal with the main points by asking the right questions and clarifying the exact purpose of the report.
2. Identify the main issues – this will break up the problem into specifics that can be easier to analyse and also help to develop a logical structure to the investigation.

3 Produce a plan of action – the steps you need to take and the sources to be used in conducting the research.
4 Draw conclusions and make recommendations based on the facts and findings, which will aid the decision-maker.

Types and structures of reports

QUESTION 3.3

What do you think is the difference between a formal report and an informal report?

Long formal reports

DEFINITION 3.11

Long reports are designed to achieve a number of goals (discussed below), but mainly to provide information and arguments based on an investigational problem or opportunity.

Structure

1 The title page (which may be preceded by an additional page with just the title of the report) shows the following:

   (a) The title of the report.
   (b) The name, title and address of the person or organization that prepared the report.
   (c) The submission date of the report.
   (d) The name of the person or organization to whom the report is submitted.

2 Letters of authorization and acceptance ('for the record') which directed the report to you or your organization and your subsequent reply may be included.
3 Letter of transmittal which introduces the report in a conversational tone to the reader and indicates the purpose, scope and limitations, important points or sections, sources used and helpful suggestions for follow-up or further study. The final paragraph should convey thanks and a willingness both to discuss the report and to offer further services in the future.

   A synopsis of the major findings, conclusions and recommendations may also be included, in particular if this is a short report.
4 The table of contents lists the text and supplementary parts of the report with page numbers and any other reference details.
5 The executive summary is a synopsis or overview which enables the reader to review and appreciate the contents of the report quickly. A summary of this type is either informative, where the main points of the report are presented in the same order or descriptive, where actual findings are omitted, but the main emphasis of the report is highlighted.
6 The body of most long reports is usually divided up as follows:

   (a) Introduction. This section provides a background to the discussion and findings of the report which have not been cited in detail in the letter of transmittal. Therefore, identifying the report's terms of reference and purpose, procedures and problem(s) which were tackled, scope and limitations, sources and methods, references and the organization of the report might be stated.
   (b) The discussion should be the largest part of the report, where analysis and interpretation of the findings are presented, supported by the conclusions and

recommendations. All additional tables, charts and figures are also presented to make the interpretation easier for the reader.

7 Conclusions and recommendations which are substantiated and justified need to be clearly stated. Conclusions are the analysis of what the findings mean and recommendations are opinions about what should be done, in light of the investigation.

8 The addendum is the final part of the report which includes all supplementary material, such as appendices, which have been used to support the arguments presented in the report.

9 Appendices will contain the statistical charts and graphs that have been referred to in the text or research and any other information which has been useful.

Short formal reports

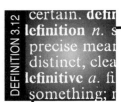

These are usually clear, concise statements pertaining to some organizational problem which can be solved, or a decision made relatively quickly, based on the facts which are presented.

Structure

1 The terms of reference deal with the scope and limitations of the report which has been investigated.
2 The procedures involved in carrying out the data-gathering process are identified.
3 Findings are the details that facilitate an understanding of the report's nature.
4 Conclusions present a final analysis of the findings.
5 Recommendations are the logical arguments about the course of action that should now be taken by the reader/organization.

Informal reports

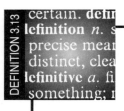

Informal reports are used where the information to be presented deals with relatively simple issues. An informal report has three main sections:

1 Opening section – this puts the report into context with an introduction and essential background that leads logically to the next section.
2 Middle section – this part presents the procedures and findings which have been highlighted in the opening section.
3 Final section – the main points are highlighted through a summary or conclusions and recommendations, which clearly stipulate any action required by the reader.

Information reports

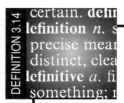

Information reports are designed primarily to provide information to others, for example, reports on conference activities or on sales training courses. They are mainly a summary of longer/complex material.

DEFINITION 3.15

certain. **deн**
definition *n.*
precise mea
distinct, cle:
definitive *a.* f
something;

Investigation reports are records of the investigation of a problem/situation or a proposal for change, for example a report on the changing working patterns or reorganization of a department layout. These types of report will usually offer recommendations and proposals for future action or consideration in the final sections.

SUMMARY

In this unit we have seen that:

* There are a number of important steps that should be followed in the planning and composing of messages to be used in business communications. However, it is also important to remember that not only should the message reflect the needs of the recipient and therefore contain enough information (not too much and not too little), but it must also be relevant, timely and written in both suitable format (presentation style, such as a letter or report) and with the appropriate use of tone and language.
* Written business communications must serve a direct purpose, whether this is to provide information, receive information or ask for information. In a business context, they cost time and money to produce and send and therefore must be cost-effective. They may be made more efficient and therefore cost-effective if sent through electronic aids such as facsimile machines.
* Written communications can be used in a number of different business contexts. For example, business letters are designed to communicate important and often sensitive information to the recipient(s), memos are often used in internal, mostly relatively informal communications, briefs provide an update on (business) activities that have taken place over a period of time or in response to a particular issue, and reports are usually designed to provide a decision-maker with information that is relatively complex and often long, compared with other forms of written communication.

UNIT ACTIVITY

Choose your own organization or one of which you have some knowledge and put yourself in the position of a marketing consultant to the business. Your task is to think about a marketing initiative that could be taken for the business, to carry out the appropriate primary and/or secondary research and to present your findings to the marketing director.

ACTIVITY DEBRIEF

You will have had a number of considerations in preparing this report, including in the final stages decisions on the length and format and the profile and needs of the recipient.

In terms of the purpose of the report, if it was analytical, it will have been organized around the conclusions and recommendations. Reports designed to provide information but little or no analysis are usually organized around a number of subtopics.

You must be able to:

- Explain the steps used in the planning and composition of business messages.
- Understand that the tone, language used and style of presentation will vary with each business situation, but in time common practice can be identified and used routinely, particularly in relation to the various formats available, memos, letters, etc.
- Identify in a given business scenario which format should be used, i.e. business letter, memo, brief or report.
- Structure each of these along the lines given in the study text in order to make them an effective vehicle of communication.
- Appreciate the relative costs associated with using these, particularly in large quantities, and the advantages of using electronic aids such as facsimile machines to make the communication more effective and cost-efficient.

From the information studied in this longer unit and also the study and revision tips above, you will have begun to appreciate that this is one of the most important areas in the syllabus and therefore likely to be frequently tested in the examination.

In most of the examination papers so far, there have been at least two or three questions relating to this unit, either as whole questions in Section B or as part questions in Section A, the compulsory question.

The examiner will probably expect you to identify the most suitable *format* for a written presentation. The choice will be to prepare a report, brief, memo or letter and will depend on factors such as amount of information, context or situation, sender and recipient relationship, etc. You will then be expected to use all the information given and to present it in this format – some creative thinking may be required if the information is incomplete.

Do not forget to use the rules regarding visual presentation referred to in Unit 7, as styles of lettering, making some statements 'bold' and so on can all have an influence in enhancing the written presentation.

Specimen examination question 1 (4 December 1995)
As Sales Manager, you are responsible for a sales team of 18 people who operate throughout the UK. They often have to make calls to head office and to their customers.

(a) You are becoming increasingly concerned about the high cost of their mobile phone bills. Write a memo advising your staff on efficiency and effectiveness when using the mobile phone. (13 marks)

(b) Write a memo to your finance department, explaining how you believe that mobile phone bills should be checked for cost and effective use. (7 marks)

(a)   MEMO

To: Sales Team
From: Candidate name (Sales Manager)
Date: December 4th 1995
Subject: Using your mobile phone

Recently, I have received a report from our accounts department regarding the cost of telephone calls associated with using the mobile telephone.

Whilst I appreciate that a number of calls have to be made both to customers and also head office, the cost of these is exceeding our budget allocation.

I must therefore ask you to both restrict the number of calls to those that are urgent and not routine and also cut down the time needed on the telephone; the latter can be achieved through careful planning of the call before it is made and also by having on hand any details that may be required.

Other calls should be made either through the 'non-mobile' telephone (you will be reimbursed for expenses) or by use of a facsimile machine.

I hope that we will all be able to cut costs and therefore retain the use of our mobile telephones.

(b)   MEMO

To: Jean Parker (Finance Department)
From: Candidate name (Sales Manager)
Date: December 4th 1995
Re: Cost and efficiency of mobile phones

I have recently communicated with my sales team of 18 people regarding the collective cost of using mobile telephones.

However, the situation does need to be carefully monitored, and although I would anticipate a reduction in the cost by the next monthly statement, please let me have a copy of the account as soon as it is available.

You may consider it appropriate to investigate a change to another provider, for example from Vodaphone (our current system) to Orange – please advise if there are any details that I should note.

Finally, I would be very pleased if my team could be given a short presentation or some training on the effective use of mobile telephones – I can advise on suitable dates and times.

Specimen examination question 2
Your organization is considering diversification into franchising its range of cosmetics and toiletries in the retail sector. Study Fig. 3.12 on the development of the Body Shop and write a short informal internal report to the Marketing Director, Ahmed al-Bayt.

PROFILE: Anita Roddick, founder of Body Shop
Anita Roddick was astonished by the ease of her success – which was due, she says, to breaking nearly all the rules. The following insight by Norma Wright, appeared in the magazine British Business.

The Body Shop International, named 'Company of the Year' at the 1987 Business Enterprise Awards, has a current annual turnover of more than £17.5m and almost 300 branches in 31 countries around the world. It has created almost 3000 new jobs – and 98 percent of its products are made in Britain. The inspiration for it all has been its livewire founder and managing director.

'Unemployable' is how Anita Roddick describes herself – but as head of the largest British-owned retail chain overseas, she needn't worry. A former student teacher and United Nations employee in Geneva, she is now the supreme entrepreneur – with a highly unorthodox view of what that means.

'I believe people are confusing entrepreneurship with opportunism', she said in a recent lecture at the City University Business School. 'They measure success by the profit and loss sheet.'

'In reality, entrepreneurship consists of three things: first, the idea one wants to get across; second, oneself – the person promoting it; third, the money that's necessary to make it happen. The third is the least important of all; the first is what matters – the integrity of the idea. You just have to believe in what you're doing so strongly that it becomes a reality.'

'Logically anybody who starts a small business with no money (as I did) can't succeed. But sometimes you do. Because you know if you don't succeed, you don't eat.'

Succeed she certainly did – and in an industry once described by Elizabeth Arden as 'the nastiest business in the world'.

Anita Roddick started her first shop in Brighton 11 years ago, with a loan of £4000 and some revolutionary ideas. She wanted to sell simple herbal and plant-based cosmetics, many of which she had seen used to great effect during her travels abroad; she intended to use the minimum amount of packaging and advertising; and she was determined to sell products that were developed with concern for the environment and were not tested on animals.

Inevitably the business had some teething troubles. The very first Body Shop had as neighbours a couple of funeral parlours who, not unnaturally, objected to its name; and her initial products 'looked and smelled peculiar' because the natural ingredients hadn't been prettified in any way. 'We had to explain to customers why our products looked revolting,' said Anita Roddick. And she only had 15 products in her range 'which looked pretty pathetic in the shop, because they only filled one shelf.'

She now has a range of over 300 products. The Body Shop still uses the cheapest bottles. 'The Sunday Times called them urine sample bottles, and perhaps they are' Mrs. Roddick said. There are now five sizes of each product. 'Because we had so few products at first, we originated the idea of five sizes; then we could fill a whole wall of the shop.' Customers have taken to the idea of a wide range of sizes; they can try the small one first, before splashing out on the more expensive sizes. Today's Body Shop is a franchise operation, each individual shop being 'almost a licence to print money' in Mrs. Roddick's words. The franchising came about almost by accident.

'All our "unique" marketing features happened because we had no money. Because it cost £3000–£4000 to open up a shop about a decade ago, my husband Gordon and I dreamed up what we called the "self-financing" idea; we didn't even know the word "franchising". Now we have a network of marvellous franchisees'.

Community project undertaking

She selects her franchisees with extreme care. Not for her is the man who wants to set up his wife in a little business, because it would be fun and should make a bit of money. She looks for franchisees who share her aims and ideals – and insists that each should undertake some kind of community project.

'This is not only altruism – it's survival. We have community projects which are riveting.' They range from running drug dependency groups and visiting elderly or handicapped people, to setting up street theatre. Most of our shops are run by women, who are enthusiastic about community work. And it's all done during working hours, not in their own time.

Anita Roddick has an enormous fund of ideas – 'drawers full of them', she said. And she's an expert communicator. The Body Shop publishes a bi-monthly 'Talksheet' for all members of staff, which contains – amongst others – a swop-a-job feature: staff are encouraged to exchange jobs for a few months, so a girl working in Bondi Beach can sample life in Aberdeen, and vice-versa.

Every month a video magazine, 'Talk Shop', is produced by the Body Shop's own video and film production company, and distributed to the franchisees worldwide. It includes reports on the various community projects and on Mrs. Roddick's overseas trips; she travels for two months of every year to find out how people in other cultures take care of their skin and hair, and to visit the various third world projects which produce products – for example cosmetic sponges – for her shops.

There is also a series of leaflets published for individual customers and for schools, containing detailed product information; and newsletters posted up in the shops. Customers' opinions are actively sought. 'Can you imagine,' said Anita Roddick, 'that we are the only high street retailer which has suggestion boxes in its shops? Why spend billions of pounds on market research if you can do it yourself?'

She sees customer education as a major role. 'We reckon that about 25 million people must pass our shops at one time or another, so we use our windows to promote environmental community issues. Every one of our shops is like a major poster site.'

She is super-confident about the future, predicting 'we will become a major communications company and within two years we plan to have a magazine.' She also hopes to open a Body Shop in Moscow in three years' time.

'We think following the route of promoting health is vital for the cosmetics industry – it will not suc-ceed by any other route. In the past it has often tried to create needs that don't really exist. We do things differently. It's so easy to break rules'.

Her advice to young potential entrepreneurs is simple: 'Never stop annoying people, and never stop asking questions. It is knowledge that gives you strength.'

Figure 3.12

REPORT ON THE PROFILE OF THE BODY SHOP

To: Ahmed al-Bayt
From: (Student name and title)
Date:
Reference: Diversification into franchising of our cosmetics and toiletries.

Introduction

The Body Shop International is in the business of producing and distributing cosmetics and toi-letries through its franchisees. In 1987 it had an annual turnover of more than £17.5m achieved through sales in some 300 branches operating in 31 countries.

Anita Roddick is the founder of this empire, having opened her first shop in Brighton in 1976 selling a few simple herbal and plant-based cosmetics. She has maintained a concern for the environment and that products should not be tested on animals, both concepts being used in her marketing strategy.

Findings

The product range has grown from 15 to 300, with five sizes of each, to satisfy the varying needs of customers from sample to bulk purchase.

The ownership of a Body Shop franchise is 'almost a licence to print money', but franchisees are picked only if they share the values of community involvement and are willing to engage in com-munity work.

The Body Shop also publishes a bi-monthly Talksheet for all members of staff and a video maga-zine every month for the franchisees. A series of leaflets is also published for customers and schools.

Finally, the founder states that 'the route of promoting health is vital for the cosmetics industry'.

Conclusions

Undoubtedly The Body Shop has been highly successful in creating a new market for cosmetics and toiletries which are cruelty-free, and have educated the buying public to want products that promote health whilst caring for the environment.

The establishment of the franchise system allows for flexibility in controlling the distribution of goods and marketing practice, whilst allowing franchisees the freedom to generate their own profits.

I recommend that we penetrate this lucrative market by setting up a system similar to that of The Body Shop.

Specimen examination question 3 (4 December 1995)
You are the Marketing Officer of a charity which raises awareness about issues relating to elderly people and funds for the cause.

(a)   Write to a contact you have at a local art college, asking if their students would take part in a competition to design a logo and letterhead for the charity.

(10 marks)

(b) Write a clear brief for the students, which should give sufficient details so that they understand the purpose of the logo and letterhead. You should include other essential details, such as the image/message you wish to communicate and the type of people you will be communicating with. (10 marks)

(a)

Concern for Age
The Strand
London W1 5XT
Tel: 0171 666 3434
Fax: 0171 665 3433

December 4th 1995

Miriam Khazem
London College of Art
The Strand
London WC1 3TU

Dear Ms Khazem,

I hope that my letter finds you well.

We are presently in the process of thinking about a redesign of the 'Concern for Age' logo and associated letterhead and would like to offer your students the opportunity to take part in a competition for this purpose.

The aim of your students should be to design and present (on A4-sized paper) an appropriate logo which reflects our continuing desire to raise greater awareness and funds for this worthy charity.

We have invited other colleges to take part and the winner will be given a prize of £100, together with having the logo go forward as our representative symbol for the forthcoming period.

I would be grateful if you would write back confirming that your students will be taking part and we can then discuss further details.

I look forward to hearing from you.

With kind regards,

Yours sincerely,

Candidate name
Marketing Officer

(b)

Concern for Age
Logo and Letterhead Design Competition Brief

Introduction
The purpose of this competition is to give college students the opportunity to design and present a logo and accompanying letterhead for our charity 'Concern for Age'.

Aims of the Charity
The main aims of this charitable organization are to raise greater awareness among the general public and corporations and to generate funds which enable us to carry out much needed work.

Themes

The competition is completely 'open' in terms of a suitable logo and letterhead; however, you must bear in mind the main purposes of our charity together with the fact that we are relatively new in a highly competitive market and do not have a 'traditional' (fuddy/duddy) image. A further point is that our main beneficiaries so far are large businesses which use support of the charity as a vehicle for communicating their commitment of the voluntary sector in terms of age-related charities. Sponsorship of events is also very important for our business, and organizations are increasingly interested in this type of venture.

The main message therefore is that our charity and business can work 'hand in hand' as a partnership for mutual benefit and that this should be the beginning of a long-standing relationship.

Written communication 2

In this unit you will be studying three further methods of written communication which are commonly used in external communications and also internally, in particular through business newsletters, circulars and notices.

You will:

- Learn the rules which guide the preparation of press releases, advertisements and job descriptions.
- Be able to distinguish between them and identify situations in which one or other would be appropriate.
- Appreciate the value of this type of written communication.

This unit deals with the latter parts of Section B in the syllabus for Business Communications and will take approximately 4 hours; another 3 to 4 hours will be required for the questions, tasks and activities.

The scope of this book cannot allow for a study of all the variables that would be associated with *promotion*, but the three main written communication vehicles for this activity have been selected. I would therefore recommend that you supplement your study and knowledge by referring (in tandem or prior to the study of this unit) to the other subjects in the CIM Marketing or Selling Certificate, in particular Marketing Fundamentals.

Introduction

In this section we are going to address how press releases, advertisements and job descriptions are written.

You will remember from the previous chapter that there are a number of rules which govern the preparation of messages namely, acknowledging the audience, creating a conducive environment for planning of the message, forming the main idea, paying attention to style (including the tone used), readability, producing a suitable outline and finally revising the message to ensure it is free from ambiguities that could lead to misinterpretations.

In parallel to these thoughts is the AIDA principle which provides us with a useful frame of reference in the preparation of successful messages and which is equally important (if not more so) in this chapter, so do practise its rules when preparing press releases, advertisements and job descriptions.

Another important aspect of writing messages in the context of this chapter is that each of these three written methods of communication are *persuasive* in nature, they are trying to attract the attention of 'customers' and prospective employees.

Persuasion is the process of influencing and changing people's attitudes and actions towards a goal set by the sender of the message. Therefore, the first steps in preparing a persuasive message consists of a series of questions that you should ask (*and answer*) yourself.

Firstly, ask yourself what exactly is the nature of the topic that you are writing about and how is this to be presented; secondly, what type of audience will you communicate this information to and how do you expect them to respond. Finally, what are the resourcing (whose responsibility is this to be, time considerations (how long is to be spent on this activity, planning implementation and control) and what is the size of the budget which will have implications both for the choices of medium to be used and the frequency of the activity).

The most important factors in successful persuasion messages are as follows:

1   They should satisfy a *need* that your audience has, or will have in the future; (think about Maslow's 'Hierarchy of Needs' which you will have studied in other CIM marketing modules and establish examples of the *different* needs which people have at every level). Not an easy task if people have different needs at each level, but a way forward is to identify themes or similarities that arise.

2   The communicator or sender of the message should have *credibility*. If you or the organization does not have a 'track record' in respect of this issue, identify (perhaps through the use of a research or advertising agency, someone otherwise known as a 'brand personality') who does.

People are persuaded by those they consider trustworthy, genuine, truthful and who have an affinity with the issue, brand, product or service they endorse.

Press releases

Public relations is the area of marketing largely responsible for producing a range of verbal and written communication which is published or demonstrated to both internal and external audiences.

The aim of press releases is to convey information which is topical and newsworthy for the purposes of publicity and generating feelings of goodwill amongst the public to whom it is directed. I will not discuss the background to public relations or advertising but present you with guidelines to provide copy for these two channels of written communication.

Effective press releases should follow these rules:

1   Have an embargo date, i.e. the date before which the news should not be printed or released. This should be displayed at the top of the copy.

2   The name, position, address and telephone number of the person responsible for the release should also appear at the top.

3   Either leave space for the editor's own heading or insert your title/headline, which should be clear and simple (see AIDA principle).

4   The opening paragraphs should consist of a brief summary of the main theme and the subject of the release should be clearly stated in the first few words.

5   Subsequent paragraphs should give increasing levels of details, but keep the release short (one side of A4, if possible) and avoid puffery language and style.

'THE BURGER CHAIN PLC'

For Immediate Release

Contact: Angela Davies
The Burger Chain PLC
Harlesden Green
London W16 4AB
Tel: 0181 253 6812

SUPPORTING THE NATIONAL OLYMPICS

We shall be giving a donation of 10p per burger sold between October 1st 199X and July 31st 199X, to support the National Olympics being held in Manchester during August 199X.

The Burger Chain PLC will also provide free food to all participants at the games and give away a complete range of merchandise to those attending.

Support the National Olympics by eating in or taking-away at the Burger Chain PLC.

Figure 4.1   The press release.

Advertising

Advertising copy tends to be more informative and less emotive than press releases, mainly because of the larger numbers to whom the information must be conveyed and the decisions made by these individuals and groups, which are more formal and methodical. A great deal of information about advertising and its perception has been documented, but producing copy is all that we shall concern ourselves with in this workbook.

Effective advertising copy should follow these rules:

1   Be logical in the development of the message (see planning a business message, and the AIDA principle).
2   State the benefits and features of the product or service, emphasizing what it can do for the consumer/user.
3   State and explain any unique selling points (USPs) which distinguish the product or service in terms of its uniqueness and exclusivity.
4   Translate the USP into a strong creative concept (big idea) which can be visually demonstrated and is both attention-grabbing and memorable.
5   Ensure that the advertisement fits logically with any campaign that is being launched or run.

ACTIVITY 4.1

Think of an advertisement you have seen recently on the TV or at the cinema, say for a bank. Take a look at any literature you have seen running parallel to the advertisement, such as a press campaign in the newspapers or brochures which are available in the bank's lobbies. Considering both answer the following questions:

1   What is the purpose of this type of business communication?
2   Who is the target audience?
3   What type of message is the business (e.g. book) sending?
4   How effectively is the message conveyed?
5   Is there a logical development of the message?
6   How does the language used in the advert differ from that on paper?
7   Do the advert and the press campaign or brochure complement each other?
8   List the benefits and features of the product or service.
9   Identify any USPs.
10   What sort of visual imagery is used to convey the concept?
11   What alterations could be made to appeal to a different target audience?

Write an advertisement for a product or service of your business organization or a suitable communication message for a social or professional group of which you are a member.

Job descriptions

Legally, only a written job title is required in the recruitment of staff, but the preparation of effective job descriptions is an important communication vehicle for determining at the outset the parties' rights and duties, to avoid liability in the future, and for creating an image of the organization and for the position advertised. Choosing a suitable medium, for example a specific type of newspaper (e.g. local, national, tabloid, broadsheet) or magazine, is also an important consideration, but you should also bear in mind factors such as cost, circulation and deadlines for copy.

Writing a job description

The following guidelines can be observed:

1 State the job title.
2 Date.
3 Department that wishes to recruit.
4 Location of job.
5 Responsible to:
6 Responsible for:
7 Principal activities, including any agreed liability to alternative duties.

Sales and Marketing Manager

A self-motivated, ambitious and experienced individual is required to head a sales and marketing function for a manufacturer of confectionery in Budapest.

You will report to the Marketing and Sales Director and be responsible for a team of 5 marketing assistants.

Challenges facing the individual include developing new brands, evaluating and developing strategic options, implementing tactical plans, including promotion and pricing, organizing the distribution network and logistical operations, in order to maximize sales revenue and raise the profile of both the organization and the portfolio of products.

You must have a minimum of 5 years experience in a similar role and will be rewarded with a competitive package. A knowledge of international business/marketing and Hungarian/German would be an advantage.

Applicants should send a full CV and written letter of application to: Ivan Kotnei, P.O. Box 46, Budapest I, Hungary not later than October 1st 199X, including details of current remuneration.

Figure 4.2 A job description (marketing job).

Write a job description based on the following information:

'Person-to-Person is a small business based at 59 Hazlewood Park, Sheffield which has a regional sales force of door-to-door salespeople offering beauty treatments, between the hours of 9 a.m. and 5 p.m. each week day. The company wishes to recruit additional salespeople for the busy period from October 1st 199X to December 31st 199X.

No previous experience is necessary as full training will be given. Remuneration is based on commission from treatments for which the individual will be solely responsible, but working under the supervision of the area manager.

Write a job description to appear internally as the company wants to attract relatives and friends of staff who may wish to work for this short period.

SUMMARY

In this unit we have seen that:

- Press releases convey information that is topical and newsworthy for the purposes of publicity.
- Advertising copy is more informative and less emotive, designed to help individuals and groups make decisions about products and services.
- Job descriptions are an important communication tool for the recruitment of staff and need to be carefully planned so that they evoke a professional and appealing image of the organization and give sufficient detail to the potential applicant.

REVISION TIPS

You must be able to:

1 Create and present a press release from information or a seminar that will be presented.
2 Create and present an advertisement suitable for a product, brand, service or message to be communicated.
3 Create and present a job description for a marketing or sales-related role at any given level.
4 Determine the rules that enable the above to be created effectively.

EXAM HINTS

You will either be asked to *interpret* a written communication such as an advertisement and determine the principle that underlies the information that is presented, or be asked to prepare this for a given situation.

The examiner will also ask you to identify the most suitable vehicles for communication for various types of advertisements, press releases and job descriptions and it would be useful for you to know whether a press release or advertisement would be suitable for a given communications need.

It would be a good idea to look at a variety of sales and marketing job descriptions for all levels in order to determine the type of information to be conveyed and the image of the organization to be communicated, i.e. established and traditional, dynamic, friendly, local, national or global.

With respect to press releases and advertisements, clearly they are designed to fulfil different communication functions. The former is largely intended to convey concise details regarding significant events or occasions, such as the launch of a new product/ service or a birthday celebration of the organization, etc.

Advertisements are designed to evoke an image of the organization, its people, products or services and will play a key role in keeping a high-profile interest/motivation for each of the topics.

You should keep abreast of external communication initiatives from within the organization and play an important part in their preparation and exposure to the outside world – this will enhance your skill and serve the needs of the organization.

Verbal communication 1

In this unit you will:

- Understand the basic skills needed for effective verbal communication.
- Learn the rules for planning effective speeches and presentations.
- Appreciate the essential techniques required in the delivery of verbal communication.
- Learn the skills for making and receiving telephone calls.

By the end of this unit you will be able to:

- Plan the steps in making speeches and presentations.
- Develop techniques for effective delivery of speeches and presentation.
- Make and receive telephone calls in a professional manner.

STUDY GUIDE

The communication skills that we most commonly use are speaking and listening, yet most people in business are far from proficient in either. Verbal communication offers opportunities not available in any other form, i.e. immediate feedback and social interaction. However, unless what you say is structured and logical and your body language helps expression, the message you wish to convey can be misconstrued and cause a breakdown in communication. Some of these aspects have already been discussed in earlier units and we are now to focus on the situations in which verbal communication takes place and analyse the important factors to consider in preparing and presenting ourselves where speech is an important medium for communication and interaction.

This unit represents 10% of the syllabus. It will take about 3 hours of study time to complete, with another 2 hours to carry out the activities.

STUDY TIPS

Effective verbal communication can only take place by learning, which is acquired through training and practice. In order to make an assessment of your strengths and weaknesses as an effective verbal communicator, use the personal communication plan from Unit 2. This is the basis against which you can make a review after having acquired the skills in this unit.

Similar rules for written communication also apply to the planning of verbal communication. First, think what you wish to say and how it will be said is important – try not to speak spontaneously. Second, delivering your words in an appropriate style (i.e. the degree of formality used) to suit the needs of the listener and the situation is also a key rule. Finally, use the opportunity to watch for cues from the recipient as to whether you are effectively communicating and he/she is clear about your message.

Use experienced colleagues to offer you constructive feedback as a verbal communicator in different situations where delivery in this medium is required.

In the following units we shall be focusing on meetings and interviews where good skills in verbal communication and listening are required in order to disseminate information, facilitate discussion and request answers to questions or feedback from the other party or parties.

Speeches and presentations

What do you consider to be the important requirements in the planning and delivery of a speech or presentation?

During your career in business, at some point you will need to make a speech or verbal presentation. The rules established in 'planning business messages' (see Unit 3) also apply here, but there are a few additional requirements. Before we embark on these, let us consider the use of language in verbal communication.

English is the language used by most nations in international business but, rather than making this assumption, check that it will be acceptable as a medium of exchange, especially if you are not conversant in the appropriate foreign language, when an interpreter may be required.

Some nationals and business people are conversant in English but choose not to express themselves in the language for nationalistic reasons. France has recently banned the use of English words where a French equivalent can be used – with heavy fines and jail sentences for offenders.

You must be aware in your everyday use of English or a foreign language that certain words or phrases can evoke a positive or negative reaction. Do use those words, but check that they have the *same meaning* abroad as they do at home.

In Unit 1, we discussed stereotyping and therefore expressing yourself at an unsuitable level or using the wrong style of language as potential for problems in communication. This is more likely to happen in verbal interactions due to slips of the tongue or where you are unable to have the time to plan what you wish to say. If possible, find out as much as you can about the individual or group with whom the interaction is to take place and, if you remain positive and reassuring, the chances of successfully transmitting your message will be higher.

Planning the speech or verbal presentation

In making an effective speech or verbal presentation, you need to appreciate how much *time* should be spent, the audience's *level* of understanding and how they will be encouraged to participate. Bearing this in mind, proceed to the planning process by following these steps:

1   Introduction. First, you need to arouse an interest in the subject that you are communicating and then clearly state your purpose and aims in making the speech or presentation and how it relates to the audience present. Your purpose will be to motivate, persuade, inform or entertain and this will determine the content, style and amount of audience participation that is possible.
2   The body is where the main ideas and arguments will be developed and presented logically. This stage requires you to hold the attention of the audience by relating the subject to their needs and being visual and clear in speech and characteristics.
3   The close is the point at which the audience attention is highest, so make it clear that you are about to finish and express your conclusion or summary succinctly. Identify any course of action to be taken, finally ending on a positive note.
4   The question-and-answer session (if appropriate) is an opportunity for immediate feedback and to clarify any misunderstandings that the audience may have. Encourage this at the end, as questions during the presentation can disrupt the flow.

Key issues in verbal communication

How much time should I spend on a speech or verbal presentation?

The amount of time will usually be allocated to you either formally, e.g. in a conference you may be asked to present a paper or make a keynote speech from 5 minutes to possibly 15 or more, or informally, in terms of the situation in which you find yourself.

For example, in a meeting with colleagues you may find that you are able to speak *at length* on some marketing research projects where researchers' background results have to be delivered before they can be discussed and decisions made for the team or client. Conversely, it may be appropriate to deliver the information concisely and present the findings in a report which also contains the necessary context.

Hearing from people involved in these types of communication activity and your own experience and common sense will indicate the best type of combination communication to use in a given interaction and the amount of time spent speaking.

How will I know the audience's level of understanding?

The larger the audience for a speech or presentation and the more informal the situation will inevitably mean a greater range of background in the audience and therefore variety in their level of understanding.

However, this can be controlled to a certain extent if you analyse the situation for which verbal communication is required and possibly use *visual aids* to enhance the communication process, which can help to make the *time* required for delivery shorter and the information clearer and therefore possibly easier to understand.

If you are communicating at different levels within the organization, for example, a presentation to the chief executive versus that junior colleague in your department, clearly you will have to use a style and tone to which both are likely to respond, as they will have different communication needs and levels of understanding. The chief executive is likely to require a brief statement, perhaps supplemented with a written communication, but junior colleagues can be spoken to at length with significant issues elaborated – they are likely to find this approach reassuring and helpful in their understanding.

The subject matter should also reflect the level of understanding, for example, a strategic marketing plan would not usually be communicated to junior trainee staff but rather to the senior management team, unless this was an important communication mission of the organization. It is more likely that tactical aspects would be stated with instructions for tasks to be completed. However, at the level of the junior trainee staff may be some of the salesforce, for whom it would be important to communicate the plan in order for a context to be established in which they are to meet targets and goals.

How can I encourage the audience to participate?

There are numerous ways in which this can be achieved.

First, a *question* can be asked which clearly requires an answer from anyone or a particular member or group in the audience, to which you may or may not give feedback.

Second, a question can be asked, with your own interpretation and answer, to which further feedback or the reaction of the audience is required.

Third, a provocative statement, phrase or word can be used which will evoke a response from the audience. This could be negative or positive and may not be as planned, so use this approach carefully. The less you know of your audience, the more risky it is likely to be.

This is similar to playing 'devil's advocate' and is best used in a small-group situation.

Delivering the speech or presentation

Effective delivery requires the following:

1 Knowledge – complete familiarity and confidence with the subject. This also helps to build the credibility of the speaker.
2 Organization – of the main points, which are logically presented and hold the attention of the audience.
3 Visual aids – such as text visuals (e.g. overhead projectors) and graphic visuals (e.g. charts and diagrams) help the speaker and audience to focus on, absorb and remember the important points.

4   Language – should be appropriate for the audience, defining any terms with which they may not be familiar and having a positive tone in speech.

5   Body language – movements of the body, smiling and eye contact all help to communicate your message.

6   Congeniality – the message must be such that it will benefit or satisfy the needs of the recipient or 'add-value' to their knowledge/learning.

ACTIVITY 5.1

Prepare script outlines for the following speech and presentation situations:

1   A 30-minute presentation to a small group of senior executives in which you and a colleague present the results of research carried out on studies of consumer behaviour in different shopping environments. Your objective for the presentation is to enable the executives to make a decision about the preferred location(s) for your range of alcoholic beverages.

2   A 20-minute sales presentation for a new workbook on business communication to a group of 15 delegates at the Marketing Education Group conference.

3   A 5-minute talk to 30 operatives who are struggling to meet a deadline for the completion of an order that needs to go out tomorrow.

Telephone tactics and techniques

Introduction

The telecommunications business has grown rapidly in the last few years to provide a range of electronic communication systems, enabling fast and effective verbal communication. However, the *telephone* remains the most powerful medium and is extensively used in business communication, internally within the organization and with its absent workforce, such as the salesforce, people working from home, away on business trips to touch base or to acquire quick information and feedback.

Effective use of the telephone

A telephone is only as good as its user. Therefore following these rules will make its use more effective:

1   Before making the call, jot down any notes or questions to cover important points which need to be raised and keep those and any supplementary material close by.

2   Check that the number to be called is correct – incorrect connections cost money!

3   Choose an appropriate time for making the call and plan to avoid possible distractions during the call.

4   Give a polite greeting and identify yourself.

5   If the person you wish to speak with is not available, leave your name, telephone number, briefly explain the purpose for the call and be specific about when you can be contacted.

6   At all times speak clearly and cheerfully, because the spoken word can easily be inaudible, misheard and therefore misinterpreted.

7   After the call, make any notes which are important to the message that has been communicated. You may need to refer to them later.

If you are taking the call, jot down important names, addresses, times, dates and points mentioned. Give your name and job title on answering the call and be cheerful and helpful at all times.

Telephones and telephone systems operated electronically through switchboards and computers have undoubtedly revolutionized the ability of businesspeople to communicate quickly locally, nationally and internationally.

However, the *cost* of making calls has steadily increased in real terms and relative to most written forms of communication remains an expensive channel. Before using the telephone for external calls, check rates and tariffs, as regards whether it is cheaper to call at certain times of day or to make calls from certain countries.

You should be clear that this is the best medium to use in a given situation.

Observe the telephone technique of colleagues or relatives and friends and ask them to observe you. Can you identify any bad habits that they or you have which makes the use of the telephone less effective as a medium of verbal communication?

In this unit we have seen that:

- Verbal communication is the interaction between sender and receiver with the distinct advantages of immediate feedback and allowing you to judge the receiver's responses to the communication through his/her use of body language.
- The main types of verbal communication are face-to-face conversations in interviews and meetings (discussed below), speeches and presentations and the making and receiving of telephone calls.
- Telephones are the most commonly used method of verbal communication in business, but they are hardly ever used efficiently.

In the personal communication plan established in Unit 2, you identified areas of strength and weakness in written and verbal communication. You should now make a new assessment of your qualities as a verbal communicator, given the skills acquired and practice undertaken in this unit and the rules of effective speaking and listening learned from Unit 2.

Effective verbal communication requires careful planning and thinking about the words and delivery to suit the purpose, level of understanding and the needs of the audience and also an appreciation of the business situation in which this activity is taking place.

You must be able to:

1 Identify the stages in planning a speech or presentation.
2 Explain how effective delivery of a speech or presentation should take place.
3 Demonstrate that you are capable of effectively using the telephone.

Because speaking is such a natural activity, we tend to do it without much thought, but this casual approach can be a problem in business. You must therefore learn that verbal communication is a very important vehicle for accomplishing a range of objectives and need to plan what to say, how to say it and manage the impression that you are trying to create.

The examination will usually require you to express the important factors in planning for verbal communication and the different types of business situation in which it is best used. Finally, you may be asked to explain the advantage of verbal communication relative to other channels and its disadvantages. Factors such as efficiency and the ability to receive immediate feedback are in its favour, especially in face-to-face interactions.

Explaining the procedure used in making and receiving a telephone call and the advantages and disadvantages of this device relative to other types of external correspondence locally, nationally and internationally is also likely to be addressed from time to time.

Specimen examination question 1 (4 December 1995)
You have been asked to participate in the induction training of a group of new sales staff. These new recruits have not had previous work experience, but will be rigorously trained in selling techniques. Your contribution to the induction is to deliver a presentation on presentation skills.

(a) Produce a set of guidelines on the topic of 'Effective Presentations' which could be given to the people attending your talk. Present the guidelines in such a way that it will be clear to your assistant how you require the layout of guidelines to appear in a desktop published format. (14 marks)
(b) Describe three presentation methods you might use and why. (7 marks)

ANSWER GUIDELINE

(a)   Effective Presentations

1. The audience
The first consideration is the audience, who they are and what is their level of understanding of this subject. Answering these questions will help to determine the type and complexity of language/vocabulary/terms that can be used and how much information should be disseminated in one presentation.

2. Method of presentation
The next important consideration is the method to be used in presenting the information, which will partly depend on the nature of the subject, size of audience, time available and other factors as appropriate.

The alternative choices in a business context are many, but may include the following: meeting, briefing session, demonstrations, formal or informal discussion, etc.

3. Other factors
Finally, other considerations are suitability of the room for the presentation, your dress code, use of visuals and therefore organizing equipment as appropriate, preparing (overhead) slides, etc.

(b) Three presentation methods that I would use are meetings, briefings and demonstrations.

(i) Meetings are very useful where it is important to discuss (often with a selected audience) the implications of the issues which are being presented. The format can be formal or informal, but will require either a paper to be delivered (perhaps circulated beforehand, particularly if it is lengthy or complex) or a verbal presentation which may take place in conjunction with visuals.

(ii) Briefings are very effective when communication must take place with a large audience because the information can be disseminated and then, if appropriate, a large (cross-section) number of views can be taken.

(iii) Demonstrations, particularly on a 'one to one' basis with a client or client group, can also be a very effective method of presenting information, especially if it is complex or must be put into context. These are commonly used at business/trade exhibitions where a new product is being launched or established.

Specimen examination question 2

You receive the following memo from the marketing manager in your organization:

To: Sonia Atkins (Marketing Director)
From: Nigel Jones
Date: December 1st 199X
Subject: Conference on Marketing Management in the Small Business, London, January 10th–13th 199X

I will be presenting a paper at the above conference but have never delivered a speech before. Please advise me on the main factors to consider when preparing my presentation, which is to last no longer than 10–12 minutes.

Reply to the memo in suitable written format.

(20 marks)

MEMO

To: Nigel Jones
From: Sonia Atkins
Date: December 13th 199X
Subject: The main rules in preparing for speeches and presentations

There are a number of major considerations and they are briefly discussed below. Do not hesitate to contact me for further assistance.

1 What is the purpose of giving the presentation? Since you are presenting a paper on a topic in your functional area of business (marketing management), you presumably have the subject matter in hand but need to address the likely reaction of the audience to the issue raised or points made during the presentation.

2 The audience. Who will they be and what will be their level of knowledge and understanding? This is a key question and your content, theme and style of presentation must reflect and satisfy their needs in attending the conference and listening to your paper.

3 What information do I need to collect? In preparing the paper you may wish to use primary data, in which case the collection, tabulation and presentation of

this must be planned as the acquisition of field research is a time-consuming activity. You may be using secondary data which is generally relatively easy to collect, but must also be planned as the data may not be available, or may be obsolete or irrelevant for your purposes.

4   What is the most logical sequence for presenting this information to my audience? Bearing in mind that you will be speaking in simple English for only 10–12 minutes, a brief introduction, followed by bullet points building a logical argument and presented on an overhead projector would be useful for delivering the message. A full report can then be distributed to the delegates after the presentation.

5   Finally, prepare the visual aids (overhead projector transparencies) in advance, practise your voice (with a microphone), expression and grammar and check your clothing (appearance) for the day.

EXTENDING KNOWLEDGE

Your personal communication plan and the review carried out on a basis of studying this unit should have confirmed the main areas of weakness in terms of your ability as an effective verbal communicator.

The action that you need to take will be determined by the conclusions you have drawn and the appreciation of your needs by the superior who can facilitate training and/or practice.

If resources or time at work are limited, you can improve your skills by practising at home and asking a friend or colleague to observe your technique or by using a tape recorder for self-analysis.

Clearly, different types of verbal communication are required in the range of business situations, from speeches and presentations to meetings and discussions and interviews. Indeed, in interviews, good listening rather than speaking may be the key to successful interaction and therefore you need to appreciate the significance of each situation. This can be achieved by observation and practice. Remember to use body language to enhance your communication in face-to-face interactions and refer to Robert T. Moran's *Cultural Guide to Doing Business in Europe* (Butterworth-Heinemann) for further tips on conducting yourself in the countries of Europe and *International Marketing – a cultural approach* by Jean-Claude Usunier (Prentice-Hall).

Verbal communication 2

In this unit you will:

- Learn about planning and arranging meetings.
- Acquire the skills necessary to prepare and conduct meetings.
- Recognize the appropriate terminology and documents needed for meetings.

In this unit you will achieve the following:

- Recognize the purpose of interviews.
- Learn how to plan an interview.
- Appreciate the different types of interviews used by business organizations.
- Consider the different types of questions that can be asked in interview situations.

By the end of this unit you will be able to:

- Prepare yourself for meetings.
- Understand all the terminology and documentation needed to conduct successful meetings in business.

STUDY GUIDE

Meetings fulfil the need of individuals in organizations to exchange views and information on a range of matters that affect decisions and plans and provide an opportunity to solve problems.

Meetings may be required because of statutory legislation or the constitution of the company, or may be held for a number of other reasons, formal and informal. In the marketing and sales functions the need for a meeting may arise for a number of reasons, to discuss tactical issues relating to one or more of the marketing mix variables in the context of a plan that is currently being actioned, or may be significant in respect of discussing strategic initiatives and so on.

Generally speaking, meetings should be constructive and productive, which means that they have to be carefully planned and should focus attention on one subject at a time or have a structured and logical agenda that provides a reasonable sequence for discussion.

In business organizations a considerable amount of time is spent in meetings, therefore group interactions which are unproductive lead to frustration, wasted time and effort and are not cost-effective.

Interviews are a distinct type of face-to-face interaction because they are primarily designed to solicit specific information from the interviewee. In marketing or sales, interviews may take place in a survey situation with respondents addressing a number of issues related to your marketing research – these are left to the marketing texts to discuss as we are concerned with *your* skills and needs in an internal interview situation.

One important field of discussion that usually takes place in an interview-style situation (i.e. relatively formal, usually with a pro forma that is completed prior to the interaction, additional notes made during the communication and follow-up sanctions thereafter) is the appraisal, which leads to recommendations by the interviewer (usually a line manager or superior in the department organization) for promotion or suitable training to help in your personal, professional or career development.

Obviously, your first face-to-face interaction with the organization will be when you attend for a job interview, and the impressions created (see Unit 2, body language, speech characteristics, etc.) will last for some time.

Interviews can also take place due to organizational problems, conflict, need for negotiation with certain parties or because of change factors – all these will be discussed in this unit, which requires about 2 hours of study time and a further 2 hours to complete the activities and address the questions.

The study of this unit, which represents a part of the 15% syllabus weighting for meetings, discussions and interviews, will take about 3 hours, as well as another 2–3 hours to complete the activities.

The route to understanding how to be effective in personal communication within the context of meetings, discussions and interviews is first to observe, second to listen and third to interact.

You should approach colleagues and superiors to participate in meetings, discussions and possibly interviews and also to ask them to give feedback on your performance in handling the above.

In terms of observation, you should look out for the way in which group norms develop, the roles played by members of the group and personal objectives that may constrain the ability of the group to reach a decision, or one that is in the best interests of the department or organization.

Listening skills were established in Unit 2 and these should be used to understand the content and level of discussion taking place.

If you have the opportunity to interact, do so in a constructive manner, using all the non-verbal skills established in Unit 2.

My main recommendation to you is observe the rules established in this unit and then aim to follow them in all internal and external interview situations, whether you are the interviewer or interviewee.

Another useful way of acquiring effective skills as an interviewer is to be present in interview situations and observe the verbal, non-verbal and written communication that takes place. If you are not allowed to be physically present, ask if a video- or tape-recording of different interview types and levels at which they take place can be made. You can then carry out an evaluation of the processes involved.

Meetings

What is the purpose of meetings?

Do you think that *personal goals* can affect the success of meetings?

The main factors that all business meetings have in common are the following:

1 An objective. There should be a clear purpose of holding the meeting, whether it is to inform, persuade, collaborate, provide counselling or solve problems.
2 An outcome. Some action should have arisen as the result of the meeting which can be resolved in time.

Types of meeting

There are numerous situations that may call for a meeting and I have narrowed them down to the following:

1 Making decisions on strategic and tactical issues. This requires that information relevant to the decision is on hand and that sufficient time is allowed for discussion that will enable a decision to be reached.
2 Solving problems on internal and external issues. The discussion needs to be relevant to the problem under consideration and opportunity needs to be given to all participants so that different perspectives and interpretation can be identified, which may throw significant light on the issue. This, however, must be controlled.
3 Informing and collaborating on a range of organizational issues. This may be achieved formally with a structured presentation or informally through a casual discussion.
4 Negotiating to resolve conflict. The discussion will invariably take place with a minimum of two parties who need to achieve an outcome to satisfy their objectives. The skills needed in handling negotiations are more sophisticated than in most personal communication and cannot be detailed here.

Meetings are usually face-to-face interactions and therefore have the following advantages:

1 Group discussion can take place.
2 Immediate feedback can be received and further information exchanged.
3 It is an opportunity for fast and efficient dissemination of information.

Meetings do not generally work well if the following factors prevail:

1 The purpose of the meeting is unclear or no background information to the meeting has been provided for the participants.
2 The meeting does not provide relevant facts and information to facilitate valid discussion and decision-making.
3 The leader/chair does not control the meeting effectively or is biased in some respect.
4 The participants do not wish to contribute or communicate ineffectively at the meeting.

Preparation for the meeting

In general, the following rules should be observed:

1 Be clear on the need for the meeting – what is its purpose and aim? The success of a meeting will depend on whether a clear aim has been established and the approach that will be taken in its conduct. Meetings will usually arise because of the need for information exchange, decision-making, problem-solving, brainstorming or training personnel.
2 Identify the main subjects or topics and subtopics for discussion, by having analysed the situation leading to the call for a meeting and any (superficial) observations you have made.
3 Select the participants, namely key personnel who can make a positive contribution to the subject under discussion, limiting the size to reflect the level and aim of the meeting, with a chairman/woman who is objective, tactful and patient and to whom the speeches should be directed.

4   Set and distribute the agenda. This is the prepared list of matters to be discussed at the meeting, which should be agreed in advance with the chairman/woman and secretary of the committee. A list of the participants, time, location of meeting and order of business are also included and the agenda should be distributed several days in advance, to allow preparation by the participants and a strategy by the leader. Preparation of the agenda is discussed below.

5   Prepare the location. The room chosen should reflect the number of participants that will be present and non-tangible factors such as acoustics, room temperature, lighting, timing and availability of refreshments, handouts and accessibility of visual aids (you may even use tele- or video-conferencing, discussed in Unit 12) to yourself and the participants.

6   If you are the leader, follow the agenda as set. Do not dominate or monopolize the meeting, but keep control, interest and a pace that will cover all the issues that need to be discussed, to ensure successful completion of the meeting.

7   A record of the proceedings needs to be made and someone will have to be designated for this task, from which the minutes (a record of what took place, discussed below) will be produced and distributed (within 24 hours, if possible).

8   Finally, summarize or conclude the essence or main points of the meeting which the participants are likely to agree (or at least to agree deferment of the point/discussion) and close with a review of action that is to be taken, by whom and dates, as appropriate.

Terminology of meetings

There are a number of vocabulary items that are often exclusive to meetings, such as the following:

1   Proposer – speaks about the statement/argument that he/she has proposed.
2   Seconder – supports the proposal.
3   Quorum – the minimum number of members that must be present at a meeting, according to the rules.
4   Motion – a proposal to be considered at the meeting.
5   Amendment – to the proposal which will have to be voted for and, if carried, accepted.
6   Collective responsibility – a rule by which all participants agree to be bound by a decision.
7   Casting vote – by the chairperson if there are an equal number of votes on either side of an argument.
8   Adjourn – this means that a meeting will be held over to another time or date.
9   Constitution – a set of rules by which the members of a group are expected to abide.
10 Ex officio – an individual given rights and powers by reason of the position he or she holds.
11 Mover – an individual who speaks on behalf of a motion.
12 Opposer – an individual who speaks against a motion.
13 Point of order – drawing attention to the breach of rules or procedures.
14 Proxy – this means on behalf of another person, e.g. proxy vote.
15 Resolution – a motion that has been carried.

Constituting a meeting

A meeting is only properly constituted if it is convened (called) according to a set of regulations (statutory or otherwise). The main issues are as follows:

1   A meeting must have a *chairperson* who oversees the conduct and progression of the meeting.
2   A meeting must have a *quorum,* i.e. a minimum number of persons who are physically present, as stated in the regulations.

Informal meetings which are called from time to time by a colleague or superior in the department or organization may follow simple procedures and be tantamount to a group discussion. In this situation some notes may be taken and possibly documented. After the meeting has concluded, a summary of the main issues raised and decisions made may be circulated to the participants.

Formal meetings are completely different in their organization and procedure. A set of strict rules and conventions is followed and formal documents are required before the meeting takes place. The main documents are described below.

Motions and resolutions

> Proposals put to a meeting and which require a decision, usually through a vote, are called *motions*.

Each motion must have a proposer and usually a seconder, i.e. a person who supports the proposal. Motions always begin with the word 'that', for example, 'it is proposed that we initiate a new sales campaign based only on below-the-line initiatives for the next financial year'.

The motion is then discussed at the meeting and if participants approve and agree to take this forward, it is known as being 'carried' and becomes a *resolution*.

Sometimes the motion is changed because of issues that have emerged during the debate, and if this is the case it is known as an 'amended' proposal, which must also be agreed before it can be carried.

The chairperson to a meeting can reject a motion if he/she feels that it will not slow down the progress of the meeting, it is against the regulations laid down for the meeting or that it will prevent a full and equal discussion from taking place, particularly if it represents the view of only a minority of people.

Adjournment

Sometimes it is necessary to 'put off' discussion of an agenda item and leave it until the next meeting. This is known as an *adjournment*. On rare occasions the whole meeting may also be adjourned.

There are many reasons why a meeting may be adjourned. One reason is that not enough data or information is available for consideration by the participants and therefore they are not in a position to make reasonable decisions.

(a) Can you think of a motion that would be a suitable proposal for a meeting in which you may be a participant in the near future?
(b) For what possible reasons could the meeting be adjourned?

You have been asked to chair a meeting on the past experience and future expectations of undergraduate students of marketing and management who have had work placements in your organization. The informal feedback received to date identifies that some departments are keen to continue with this activity, whilst others wish it to end. The decision will determine whether work placements will be made available next year.

Your task is to consider what type of meeting this should be, how it is to be conducted and suitable items for the agenda.

Meeting documents

The notice

The notice will be prepared and circulated before the date of the meeting, according to the constitution of the company and any other regulations with which the organization may have to comply.

If a large number of participants are to attend, it may be impractical to communicate with them all individually, therefore notices of the meeting may be placed on notice boards as a main channel of communication, especially if these are regularly accessed by potential participants.

Where individuals can be contacted directly, the following channels of written communication may be used:

1. An invitation printed on a card or note.
2. An internal memorandum.
3. A personal letter.

If the agenda (described below) is already drawn up and available for circulation, it is usually included with the notice to enable the participants to study its content before the meeting.

The minutes of the last meeting (also described below) may be attached to the notice so that any issues in respect to the points made can be stated in advance of the meeting, especially if the minutes of the previous meeting have to be approved as a matter of procedure. Figure 6.1 gives an example of a notice.

Friedman & Sons Ltd
Memorandum

To: Jenny Hamson (Sales Director)
         Andrew Stevens (Marketing Research)
         Alison Perkins (Advertising and Promotions)
From: Clare Simpkins (Marketing Director)
Subject: Notice of Marketing and Sales Group Meeting
Date: October 1st 199X

The next meeting of the Group will be held in the 'Oak Room' on the first floor of 'General Building' on Tuesday October 10th 199X at 11am.

I enclose a copy of the minutes from the last meeting and an agenda. Please bring any relevant documents with you or circulate beforehand.

Figure 6.1 A notice.

The agenda

This is the schedule of 'things to be done', i.e. the subjects to be discussed, which is prepared by the secretary after having enabled all participants to propose items for the agenda. Although an agenda is not an obligation for the conduct of a meeting, it is a useful tool for guiding the discussion and ensuring that the full scope of the meeting is covered.

Once the agenda has been set, it is then discussed with the chairperson in terms of suitability of subject matter and order of items which the meeting will follow.

The agenda will then be distributed to all the participants so that they are aware of the subject matter of the forthcoming meeting and the order of proceedings, together with any supplementary material that needs to be considered and the minutes of the last meeting. This communication process enables the participants to prepare themselves in advance and also to decide whether their presence is necessary for the full duration of the meeting.

Copies of the agenda are either sent out with the notice of the meeting or distributed to participants as they arrive at the designated location.

A special agenda is prepared for the chairperson, which contains more details than the document circulated to the participants and the names of any particular participants that will be making a special contribution (e.g. presenting a report), with space for the chairperson to make notes on the meeting for personal reference.

Agendas normally contain the following items:

1 Apologies for absence – announced by the chairperson once the meeting has been officially opened and the time and date recorded by the secretary.
2 Minutes of the previous meeting – the chairperson will ask members whether the minutes represent an accurate record of the previous meeting and if so, he/she will sign them as such.
3 Matters arising is an opportunity for participants to declare views or report back on developments since the last meeting.
4 Correspondence from parties outside the meeting may be read and considered.
5 The main agenda items are then opened and discussed in turn, with the chair trying to keep the meeting moving ahead (particularly if a time constraint was imposed at the start) and aiming to reach a consensus on the main points. The types of items discussed will reflect the nature of the meeting, which may be to produce plans, solve organizational problems, deliver reports or feedback, debate proposals or to reach decisions.
6 Any other business (AOB) is stated and discussed. If an item is of relevance to the general discussion or appropriate for the meeting, it may be raised under this section. If the issue is considered unimportant or unsuitable for the present meeting, it may be carried over to another or a separate meeting called.
7 Date of the next meeting is discussed and agreed and the chairperson closes the meeting by thanking the participants for attending the meeting.

Finally, agendas will vary from meeting to meeting and may be a reflection of the following:

1 Degree of formality required for the meeting, which will determine the style of layout in the agenda and state the procedures to be followed.
2 Length of the meeting, which will be determined by:
    (a) The number of subjects to be discussed.
    (b) The complexity of the subject matter.
    (c) The number of important items relative to routine – both may be postponed or made the subject of a further meeting if the time allocated for the present is insufficient to cover all the ground. Figure 6.2 gives an example of an agenda.

Brown & Co. Squash Club
Annual General Meeting
Wednesday October 31st 199X
at 7pm sharp
Venue: 'The Chinese Room', Building Annexe

AGENDA

1 Apologies for absence.
2 Minutes of the AGM held on Oct. 30th 199X.
3 Matters arising.
4 Report of the club committee for last year.
5 Annual accounts and Report of the Treasurer.
6 Election of officers.
7 AOB.
8 Date of next meeting.

Figure 6.2 An agenda.

The *chairperson's agenda* is different to the one described above in two respects:

1 Each item on the agenda has additional notes which are pertinent to the discussion that will take place in the meeting and for which the chairperson should be suitably

prepared with background information or sensitivity in handling material presented and discussed or points raised.

2   A right-hand margin, which is wide enough for the chairperson to make notes during the meeting, is incorporated into the layout of his/her personal agenda.

The *duties of the chairperson* are as follows:

1   Keep the meeting to the agenda and in good order so that the business can proceed smoothly.
2   Be unbiased and fair in allowing the members and participants to make their contribution without taking too much of the meeting's time.
3   Allow only one person at a time to address the meeting and take a decision on the sequence of speakers if more than one wishes to make a contribution.
4   Ensure that all issues and points of debate are addressed to the chairperson, thereby avoiding the deterioration of the meeting into fragmented groups or arguments.
5   Conduct the system of voting if this is deemed necessary during the meeting or at its conclusion.
6   Keep an overall sense of the meeting according to the original agenda and the logic of the discussion.

The minutes

These are a written record of the transactions that took place and should be as accurate as possible, reflecting the duration and general tone of the meeting.

The minutes are usually taken by the secretary, who should have them typed and distributed as quickly as possible after the meeting as they are an important channel of communication and source of reference.

The style or format used to present them, i.e. narrative or structured in some way, should reflect the type of meeting and needs of the participants.

There are three types of minutes:

1   Narrative minutes – these are a brief summary of the meeting which led up to the resolution (decisions) and include the comments made by the participants which have gone on record as their judgement of the arguments preceding the resolution.
2   Resolution minutes – these are minutes where only the resolutions are recorded and therefore do not reflect the tone of the meeting or specific points made leading to the resolution.
3   Action minutes – these minutes indicate the specific courses of action that need to be taken as a result of the resolutions made in the course of the meeting and the individuals responsible for the action items. Figure 6.3 (opposite) gives an example of a minutes document.

!

In this unit I have introduced you to the following:

1   The notion of meetings in business organizations, which are designed as an opportunity for a group of individuals to discuss issues that are significant to the organization in a face-to-face interaction that give immediate feedback and a convenient method for decision-making, solving problems, hearing presentations and debating facts. Clearly, the marketing and sales functions will hold meetings for all these reasons but as they cost both time and money they should be justified and the most appropriate participants invited to attend at a convenient and suitable location.
2   Good preparation for meetings requires the following:

   (a)   Being clear on the purpose for the meeting.
   (b)   Clearly identifying the main subjects and topics to be discussed.

     (c)   Selecting suitable participants who will make a valid contribution.

     (d)   Keeping the size of the meeting to a manageable level.

     (e)   Preparing the location suitable for the number of participants and their needs during the meeting and ensuring that the venue is convenient.

3   A complete range of vocabulary that may be used in a variety of meetings.

4   The constitution of meetings is made valid by having the following:

     (a)   A chairperson who carries out his/her duties according to the rules and regulations.

     (b)   A quorum of people, as stated in the regulations.

5   The documents that are required at meetings, in particular:

     (a)   The notice.

     (b)   The agenda.

     (c)   The chairperson's agenda.

     (d)   The minutes, whether they are narrative, resolution or action.

In this unit I have described that interviews are an opportunity for face-to-face interaction where information exchange, motivation and professional judgements of people can take place.

Interviews are conducted for a number of different reasons, such as to make policy decisions, recruit staff and judge performance levels.

The key to success in interviews is careful planning beforehand, professional conduct, which includes using the correct vocabulary, terminology and documentation, and appropriate follow-up, as soon as possible after the event has taken place.

In interview situations it is important to ask the right type of questions that reflect the relationship of the parties, purpose of the interview and nature of the discussion.

Research and Development Group
Minutes

Minutes of the Meeting held in the 'Panelled Room' at 'Building Headquarters', Bromley, Kent on October 15th 199X at 4 pm.

Present: T. Stones (Chair), A. Peters (Secretary), L. Simons, K. Andrews, J. Clarke

1   Apologies for absence.
    Apologies for absence were received from J. Thyme, L. Young and P. Ankers.

2   Minutes of the last meeting.
    The minutes of the last meeting were taken as read and signed as a true record.

3   Matters arising.
    Further to item 2, the Chairman has received a report of the new innovation currently in prototype stage and will circulate a copy to all members before the next meeting.

4   Proposal to cut the budget by £1 million to be phased in over a period of three years.
    All members present argued for a strong statement to be issued to the M.D. on the consequences for new and existing projects as a result of this budget cut and seek clarification if jobs are also to be lost in this process.

5   New Product Development.
    Len Simons and Ken Andrews presented a visual report on the new products to be commercialized by the end of the financial year.

6   AOB.
    Jane Clarke raised the need for a new laser printer. Angela Peters will receive literature and circulate this to members of the group before the next meeting.

7   Date of next meeting.
    The next meeting of the R&D group was scheduled for January 10th 199X at Building H.Q.

Signed X   T. Stones (Chair) Director R&D. Date Nov. 10th 199X

Figure 6.3   Minutes.

Interviews

DEFINITION 6.2

Interviews in business organizations tend to be planned formal face-to-face interactions which are used for a variety of purposes.

1 Information-gathering and dissemination for the purposes of giving instruction, planning or coordinating effort.
2 Changing attitudes or behaviour, particularly in the case of conflict.
3 Negotiating on policy matters or personal issues, either with the internal market or with customers and suppliers who are part of the external market.
4 Motivating personnel to achieve greater levels of performance or to maintain interest in their role.
5 To persuade people to behave in a particular way.
6 Selecting potential employees or those suitable for promotional opportunities.

Face-to-face interactions have a number of advantages:

1 Immediate exchange of information and feedback is possible. In this context questions can be raised and responses given.
2 The quality and understanding of the verbal communication are enhanced through the observation of non-verbal cues, such as body language and reactions to the issues discussed.
3 The parties to the communication can develop a better relationship through exploring their sensitivity, degree of trust, sharing cooperation, empathy and sympathy to the issues under review.
4 The opportunity to exercise good listening skills will better facilitate the interview process and aid the interviewer's understanding of the information being received than is the case in more distant verbal communication, such as through telephone calls.

Planning the interview

The key to success in conducting interviews that are efficient and constructive comes from being in control throughout the event and this is largely a function of careful planning.

1 Before the interview, spend a suitable amount of time thinking about the purpose and aims of the interview, whether this is to select an applicant, solve a problem or negotiate for a contract or pay claim and so on.

   You should reflect on the nature of the discussion to be facilitated in the interview process and draw up a list of tentative points which will help to guide the interview proceedings and ensure continuity and completeness.

   The discussion should largely go backwards and forwards from the interviewer to the interviewee so that the interviewer maintains the position of controlling the proceedings.

The interviewer also has the responsibility for setting the general tone of the interview, which will reflect the relationship of the parties and the nature of the discussion.

2   The interviewee will also have a general purpose for attending the interview, i.e. to obtain or pass information. However, he/she may also have a personal agenda in attending the interview which is not explicit and, whilst it may be wasted effort to speculate on this issue, it is useful to consider the possible reaction of the interviewee to the discussion that will take place during the interview and to plan further points of action, if appropriate.

3   Choose an appropriate location and time and collect all necessary background data that will set the structure for the interview.

4   During the interview, listen carefully for facts and feelings expressed by the interviewee. This will help you to make an assessment of the real issues under discussion and the personal qualities and judgement of the interviewee, which may be significant in appreciating the overall value of the interview.

   You should also make notes on critical issues during the course of the interview and close with a summary of the main points raised, highlighting any further action to be taken. If possible and suitable, finish on a positive note.

5   After the interview, spend a few minutes making additional notes that may be useful for reference later, whilst the meeting is still fresh in your mind. This may also be the best time to draft a short response in the form of a memo or letter to the interviewee, to thank him/her for attending the interview and enclose a summary of the discussion and outcome, if applicable.

Your final task is to put into action any items that needed to be resolved as a result of the interview.

Interview questions

The aim of the interview and the relationship of the parties will determine the type of questions that are set before the interview and asked when it takes place.

   Questions are asked for a number of different reasons:

1   To obtain information on the general or specific issues to be discussed.
2   To enable and stimulate the interviewee to answer honestly and suitably for the purposes of the interview.
3   To establish a rapport with the inteviewee, particularly in the early stages of the interview which helps him/her to relax and feel comfortable in the interview situation and therefore to express him/herself fully and openly.

Types of questions

1   Open-ended questions allow interviewees to express themselves in detail, as they are able to form opinions and explain these, for example asking a panel survey of customers: 'What do you think about our new products that were launched last week and you have tested in the home?'
2   Closed-ended questions require short answers or simple 'yes', 'no' or 'don't know' type responses. For example: 'Have you acquired our latest catalogue and price list?'
3   Restatement questions enable the interviewer to check that he/she has:

   (a)   Not misunderstood a piece of factual information given in response to a question.
   (b)   Informed the interviewee correctly.

   For example, 'You stated that you do not use our executive lounge because it is always overcrowded. Is that correct?'

Types of interviews

Interviews are usually controlled by a person or panel (interviewers), who will ask questions and expect responses from the interviewees on a range of issues.

If both parties achieve their goals through the interview process, then it will have been a success.

Each interview will have a specific purpose and require a particular type of approach:

1   Employment interviews are used by an interviewer/employer to learn about the skills, qualifications and experiences of a prospective employee. The interviewee/applicant must use the opportunity to obtain information about the organization as a whole, the functional area for which he/she has applied and the related conditions of service; he/she will also want to make a good impression, therefore appropriate choice of vocabulary, clear speech characteristics, listening skills and body language are all important to express what you wish to say.

2   Appraisal interviews or joint performance reviews are used by superiors/managers to the employee as an opportunity to provide feedback in terms of an evaluation of the role and tasks achieved and to identify future expectations and needs of the subordinate, both specific to the job and any general issues that he/she may wish to raise.

3   Counselling interviews are used for a variety of purposes, in particular to resolve personal or professional problems that constrain the ability of the employee, or to motivate individuals and groups to improve their performance at work.

4   Disciplinary interviews are used by superiors/managers to try to change the behaviour of an individual or group, because company policy or rules/procedures have not been followed. The exchange is likely to be hostile, which therefore requires a great deal of tact and diplomacy by the interviewer, whilst objectively explaining the context and stand to be taken.

5   Exit interviews are used as an information exchange opportunity, before the employee leaves the organization, voluntarily or by dismissal; they are also used for employees transferring to another department. The focus of the interview should be away from personal issues and on positive aspects of the employee's time at work.

ACTIVITY 6.2

In the situations below, think about the interview from the perspective of both parties and address the following:

1   For each party, what is the purpose of the interview?

2   How should the interview be staged so that the process is effective and an outcome achieved?

3   What is the type of information that needs to be presented and received?

(a)   You approach a senior in the organization to discuss an increase in the budget for the marketing department to achieve the targets that have been set for this year, though you are only at the end of the first quarter.

(b)   You have produced a job description of your current role and the evaluation indicates that you are carrying out a number of additional tasks, some of which are appropriate to the next grade. An interview has been arranged with your line manager/superior.

REVISION TIPS

You must be able to address the following:

1   What is a meeting in business? Give examples of business situations in which only a meeting will be suitable as a channel of communication.

2   What points should be considered when preparing for a meeting?

3 Identify some of the terminology that is used in meetings.
4 (a) What is meant by the term constitution in the context of meetings?
   (b) What are the two main requirements for a valid meeting?
5 Identify and briefly explain the main documents needed for a meeting.

You must also be able to address the following:

1 Explain the purpose of interviews in business organizations.
2 Identify the benefits of face-to-face interaction during the interview process.
3 Describe the steps in planning an interview.
4 Identify the different types of question that can be asked in an interview situation and give an example of each.
5 State and briefly describe the different types of interviews used in business organizations.

Clearly you will need to learn whether a meeting or informal discussion is required in a given situation. If it is the former, you may be asked to explain the steps that need to be taken to plan and hold the meeting. It is therefore important that you are conversant with all aspects of meetings, notably the issuing of a notice, setting the agenda and producing minutes.

You may be given a fictitious scenario and out of this asked to set an agenda and/or issue a suitable notice – all settings will have a marketing context and you may need to rely on your knowledge from other parts of the Certificate course to place suitable details in these documents.

You will be expected to know the general rules and guidelines in the planning of interviews and to explain these in the examination. You may also be given situations in which it is important to identify whether a meeting, discussion or interview needs to take place, the preparation involved and the approach to be taken. Clearly you need to be aware of the different types of interview that can take place in business and how the use of different questions can help you to solicit the required information. You should also expect to comment on any body language, speech and listening skills as important tools in interviews for successful communication.

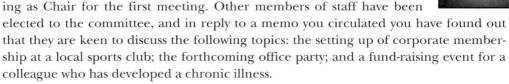

Specimen examination question 1 (4 December 1995)
A new Social Committee has been established at Datasend, the company you work for. You have been appointed Social Secretary and will be acting as Chair for the first meeting. Other members of staff have been elected to the committee, and in reply to a memo you circulated you have found out that they are keen to discuss the following topics: the setting up of corporate membership at a local sports club; the forthcoming office party; and a fund-raising event for a colleague who has developed a chronic illness.

(a) Draw up the agenda for the first meeting. Include one item of business in the form of a motion which is proposed and seconded.   (8 marks)
(b) Draw up a guide to meetings procedure for new staff and explain what the following terms mean. Give one example for each.
    (i)   a quorum
    (ii)   a procedural motion
    (iii) a point of order.   (12 marks)

(a)   Social Group Committee Meeting
4 December 1995 at 5.30 p.m.
Venue: Trinidad Conference Room, Datasend

AGENDA

1 Apologies for absence
2 Corporate membership at the Tobago Sports Club
3 Christmas Office Party
4 To propose a fund-raising event for John Ralphs, seconded by Helena May
5 AOB
6 DONM

(b)   *GUIDE FOR SUCCESSFUL MEETINGS*

The procedure for meetings is as follows, and should be observed for effective and successful mettings. It begins with a series of questions that you must address.

1 Decide on the nature of the meeting, i.e. is it solely to give or receive information or both? Is a facilitation of a discussion important?
2 Who should be invited to the meeting and what is to be each individual's relative contribution?
3 A notice of the meeting must be issued.
4 An agenda must be prepared.
5 Minutes should be taken and produced and circulated after the meeting has taken place.
6 A chair for the meeting must be appointed and his/her agenda drawn up.
7 Finally, a suitable room/location must be prepared and ready to receive the participants.
   (i) A quorum is the minimum number of members that must be present at a meeting, according to the rules of the firm.
   (ii) A procedural motion is a proposal to be considered at the meeting.
   (iii) A point of order is when participants have their attention drawn to a breach of the rules or procedures.

EXAM QUESTION

Specimen examination question 3

    1 Define the purpose of interviews.   (6 marks)
    2 You have been asked by the training manager to write a set of guidelines when planning interviews for all new junior employees joining the company from next month.   (14 marks)

ANSWER GUIDELINE

1 Interviews in business organizations tend to be planned, formal face-to-face interactions which are used for a variety of purposes:

    (a) Information-gathering and dissemination for the purposes of giving instruction, planning or coordinating effort.
(b) Changing attitudes or behaviour, particularly in the case of conflict.
(c) Negotiating on policy matters or personal issues, either with the internal market or with customers and suppliers who are part of the external market.

(d)   Motivating personnel to achieve greater levels of performance or to maintain interest in their role.

(e)   To persuade people to behave in a particular way.

(f)   Selecting potential employees or those suitable for promotional opportunities.

2   The key to success in planning interviews that are efficient and constructive comes from being in control.

(a)   Before the interview, spend a suitable amount of time thinking about the purpose and aims of the interview, whether this is to select an applicant, solve a problem or negotiate for a contract or pay claim, and so on.

You should reflect on the nature of the discussion to be facilitated in the interview process and draw up a list of tentative points which will help to guide the interview proceedings and ensure continuity and completeness.

The discussion should largely go backwards and forwards from the interviewer to the interviewee so that the interviewer maintains the position of controlling the proceedings.

The interviewer also has the responsibility for setting the general tone of the interview, which will reflect the relationship of the parties and the nature of the discussion.

(b)   The interviewee will also have a general purpose for attending the interview – to obtain or pass information. However, he/she may also have a personal agenda in attending the interview which is not explicit and, whilst it may be wasted effort to speculate on this issue, it is useful to consider the possible reaction of the interviewee to the discussion that will take place during the interview and to plan further points of action, if appropriate.

(c)   Choose an appropriate location and time and collect all necessary background data that will set the structure for the interview.

(d)   During the interview, listen carefully for facts and feelings expressed by the interviewee. This will help you to make an assessment of the real issues under discussion and the personal qualities and judgement of the interviewee, which may be significant in appreciating the overall value of the interview.

(e)   You should also make notes on critical issues during the course of the interview and close with a summary of the main points raised, highlighting any further action to be taken. If possible and suitable, finish on a positive note.

(f)   After the interview, spend a few minutes making additional notes that may be useful for reference later, whilst the meeting is still fresh in your mind. This may also be the best time to draft a short response in the form of a memo or letter to the interviewee, to thank him/her for attending the interview and enclose a summary of the discussion and outcome.

EXTENDING KNOWLEDGE

If you have access to minutes from meetings held at different levels in the organization, make an attempt to retrieve these and analyse them. You are trying to determine how the meeting was conducted, the number and position of participants and the type and level of decision reached.

Meetings are relatively formal settings for group interactions as they require both planning and following a set of rules. Many departments in organizations hold discussions, both formal and informal, and you may like to analyse which of these are the most suitable in different situations and whether they save time and are considered valuable by the participants. A systematic analysis over a period of time may reveal some interesting results for your department or organization.

For a humorous look at face-to-face interaction in the process of conducting meetings, refer to the text *The Secrets of Successful Business Meetings* by Gordon Bell, published by Butterworth-Heinemann.

Interview skills are not difficult to acquire, especially if you have the opportunity to practise them, which I recommend forms part of your training in management. Although good basic communication skills are general to all interview situations, your sensitivity, personality, preparation and conduct of the interaction may play a significant part in the eventual outcome and you should plan for these aspects as well as the formal research needed before the event takes place.

Visual communications

In this unit you will:

- Be introduced to the concept of visual aids in business communication.
- Learn about the purpose and nature of visual aids.
- Appreciate the important elements in designing visual aids.
- Consider the different types of visual aids that may be used in presentations.

By the end of this unit you will be able to:

- Understand the importance of visual aids in business communication.
- Learn the theory and skills needed for successful planning, designing and presenting of visuals.

Visual aids are useful tools for conveying information in a manner that makes the data and any relationships between variables clearer and easier for the receiver to follow. However, they should be used selectively, not as a substitute for verbal or written communication, but as a complement and enhancer of the main message because they are capable of attracting and holding attention usually better than speech or written words.

There are some visual aids that are particularly useful for the presentation of certain types of information, therefore an appreciation of the correct balance of words, pictures and colour and their timing in the presentation is crucial to success with visuals and your skill as a business communicator that can effectively use visual aids.

This unit will focus on the types of visual aids that are used by most organizations, how they can be used effectively and the process involved in the design and production of effective visuals. In Unit 8 we shall be looking at how to provide tables, charts, graphs and diagrams, all of which are often used in marketing and sales presentations and serve an important communication function in representing complex (interrelated) variables which are easier for the eye to follow and the brain to appreciate, relative to a mass of spoken or written words. But visuals are also used extensively to provide logos and letterheads which create an image of the organization, in turn these are used for a complete variety of written communications, from letters and memos to catalogues, brochures and annual reports, not least as trademarks on packaging and other forms of marketing communication. Unit 9 looks at how the production and transmission of information (including graphical visuals) has been revolutionized and the whole business communication field is now much more efficient.

Together, these three units and the lessons learned previously will enable you to make verbal or written presentations that are of a high quality because they will appear articulate, concise and clear.

This unit will take about 3 hours to complete. A further 2 hours are required for the activities.

You should make an attempt to use both manually and electronically produced visual aids in a variety of presentation situations, both verbal and written.

In planning the presentation using visuals, think about how it will benefit the overall quality and timing of the presentation and the needs of the audience.

Participate in business situations where visual aids are to be used and observe, listen and interact to achieve a better understanding of the value of visuals as a communication tool.

Introduction

Using visuals

In marketing and sales the need to use visuals will arise for a large number of reasons, ranging from the presentation of statistics on aspects of market or marketing research through to internal communication on issues such as budgets, recruitment of staff or policy matters.

Visuals can be used in both verbal and written communications, but should not replace significant aspects of the message. Rather they should be used to complement the main ideas and make these easier for the recipient to appreciate and follow.

In verbal communication a complete range of visual aids can be used, from a drawing on a flipchart to the use of videos, projection on screens and computers. It is clearly important to use the most appropriate medium given factors such as cost, time (both preparation and transmission), convenience and the likely reaction of the audience.

Designing visuals

The design of any visual requires some creativity on the part of the producer but must reflect the style and content of the message, the needs of the recipient and the channel to be used – these factors were discussed in Unit 1 in the context of the communication chain, especially the functions of encoding and decoding.

Today, the extensive market of computer software to facilitate the design and production of graphs and visuals which are aesthetic and symbolic, including three-/multidimensional pictures, has made the process for anyone simple and fast.

However, whether they are produced through a computer-based package or by hand, they should emphasize the *key points* to be made, from the use of simple underlining, boldening, enlargement of keywords/phrases or the use of colour and symbols, or contrast to enable differentiation between variables.

Using colour

Paul Zelanski and Mary Fisher in *Colour*, published by the Herbert Press, argue that colour is the most powerful tool at our disposal as it affects emotions and can convey any mood, from delight to despair. It can be subtle or dramatic, capture attention or stimulate desire.

The use of colour in visual communication is endless but a few basic rules could be used as a guide in planning a logo, letterhead or graph:

1 Colours that make us feel warm are those of fire – red, yellow and orange – which cause our adrenaline to increase and raise both our blood pressure and temperature.
2 At the opposite end of the spectrum are colours that make us feel cool, such as blue and green. These slow down our rate of breathing and cause us to relax.
3 You should also be aware in planning visuals and written corporate communications that colour is not necessarily perceived in the same way across all cultures and, whilst black may be used, some cultures (such as Jamaican, West African) respond more positively to the use of bright colours rather than neutral ones.
4 Colour can of course also influence our special perceptions of a shape to make an item seem larger than it actually is or stand out relative to others; this can also be achieved in a contrast situation using shades of colours.

Finally, the use of colour has endless possibilities to convey meaning through a visual, but when this artwork goes to print the desired effect may not be achieved. One technique to overcome this potential problem is to use the Pantone matching system which is based on nine colours used by printers but can be mixed to produce a range of 747 colours.

Reflect on catalogues, brochures and magazines/newspapers used by your organization to communicate both internally and with its external public. How effective do you feel has been the use of colour, lettering and overall style of presentation in evoking a suitable image for the organization and the communication contained within the medium?

Do you know whether any research has been carried out to investigate the perception of internal and external audiences to the communication they receive? If not, could you design a marketing research brief and either implement it yourself or find someone to do so on behalf of the organization?

Designing visual aids

This is the creative element in planning the use of visual aids. These days, the availability of computer software in graphics can offer a range of both aesthetic and symbolic (three-/multidimensional) pictures that greatly enhance the development and presentation of visuals. However, whether visuals are produced by hand or computer, they must:

1   Emphasize the key points to be made, from the use of simple underlining, boldening, enlargements, or the sophisticated use of colours and symbolic features, which are continuous throughout the presentation.
2   Use contrast to distinguish similarities or differences between variables.

Computer graphics

A complete range of pictures, diagrams, graphs, drawings, animations and so on can be produced for use in business communications through computer software packages.

There are two main ways of producing images on a computer:

Block-based images use graphic, alphabetic and numerical characters which can be displayed on the VDU (visual display unit) and then printed as required. Block-based images are relatively simple but effective visuals.

Pixel-based images are usually a higher quality visual than block-based images. In contrast to block-based images, these are 'built up' from a large number of black dots which are achieved through a computer screen that is made up of rows and columns – the dot positions on these are called pixels. The greater the number of pixels, the better quality of visual that can be achieved.

On the computer networks available today, together with easily available software such as desktop publishing packages, these images can be created at a touch.

Types of visual aids

What types of visual aids are available in your organization?

The majority of business organizations have the basic visual aids described below, which are all relatively easy to use. However, the market in electronic business communication is ever-increasing and many new products are rapidly entering the market to make the communicator more successful in his/her role.

1   Boards, chalk and white can be used for simple words and drawings that take minimal time to demonstrate, but are important in revealing the method by which they are completed. The main advantage of boards is that they can be easily erased and immediately reused and are the cheapest method of visual communication; in meetings and discussions they could prove to be a useful method to structure brainstorming and planning.

2   Acetate sheets (transparencies) can be preprepared and projected on to a large screen, appropriately positioned in the room, via an overhead projector. The characteristics of flipcharts are similar to acetates, except that they can be taken apart and posted around the room for further future viewing; both are particularly useful where planning complex aspects of the presentation is required before the event.

3   Slides can demonstrate both pictures and words and are easy to use once set up; however, for maximum effect the lights need to be dimmed, which makes note-taking impractical.

4   Videos can be used to educate and inform on a complete range of marketing or sales issues. This medium of communication is used extensively for training and is particularly useful for updating salespeople who spend much of their time outside the office environment. Videos are of course expensive to produce and, if it is not important for the demonstrator/presenter to be seen, a cheaper alternative is the use of a cassette in transmitting information.

The exhibition is an important medium for using videos as they can be used continuously and reach a large number of people simultaneously.

Logos and letterheads

Organizations can obtain exclusive rights to a name or symbol under trademark laws and communicate their corporate image through the use of logotypes (logos) and letterheads.

A logo is a unique and distinctive graphic presentation of the word or visual image, designed to focus attention and create an impression and which should be easily recognized when seen. They are often used on letterheads and other written media to identify the status/position of the organization and to communicate its characteristics.

Letterheads are official printed matter on letter paper and contain the trading name, registered address, telephone, telex and fax numbers, the names of company directors (and nationalities if they are non-EC), legal status of the organization, business activities of the organization and the logo. They communicate the desired image of the organization through the use of words and symbols, layout, letter styling, use of colour and size of print.

Marketers use techniques of word association and sentence completion to test names that are most easily understood and perceived in terms of the desired characteristics.

Look at the logos and trademarks used by your business organization. Explain what image they are trying to project with the symbolic aspects of the logo and style of the lettering. Is there evidence that the desired effect of the visual communication is perceived as the organization planned by the internal and external markets whom they wish to serve and influence?

In this unit we have seen that:

1   There is no question that visual aids which are carefully planned, designed, chosen and presented can greatly complement and enhance important aspects of a business communication, whether verbal or written.
2   The purpose of visual aids is to:

    (a)   Describe and clarify information to be presented.
    (b)   Emphasize and reinforce the important points.
    (c)   Make the information more attractive.
    (d)   Summarize the key issues or points through any one of a vast range of techniques.

3   The use of computer graphics has made the creation and production of most visuals faster, more sophisticated and cost-effective and also increased the opportunities for multidimensional visuals and the greater use of colour for maximum effect.

You have been asked to design a draft for the following and briefly need to discuss the main factors to consider in your planning.

1   A new brochure to demonstrate a range of adventure holidays around the world for the 18–25-year-old target market.
2   A supplement for shareholders to show the profitability of the organization this year against that of the previous 5 years and the predictions for the following year.
3   A visual to be used in a verbal presentation of a report which highlights new regional locations for retail outlets in the UK and Europe.

The types of visuals used will be determined by factors such as the needs and profile of the audience, the purpose of the communication, length of presentation and accessibility to electronic equipment.

Brochures should contain information on locations (using maps, for example), prices (using tables) and weather temperatures (using graphs). In general they should be eye-catching, informative, interesting and motivational, with good use of colours to evoke a range of emotions.

Shareholders are interested in concise and accurate information that clearly demonstrates the profitability trends. Graphs would be suitable, together with an appropriate level of detail. They would also be interested in the way in which the logo of the organization is presented.

A graph used in verbal presentations should be large so that it can be seen by all representatives and simple so that it can be followed easily. If two countries are being demonstrated and contrasted, it may be suitable to use maps and pictograms.

REVISION TIPS

You should be able to:

1   Determine the type of visual aid to be used in different situations.
2   Explain the key elements in the design of visuals, including the use of colour.
3   Explain the value of logos and letterheads in business communication.

In the examination you are likely to be asked to comment on the types of visual aid that are accommodated by most business organizations and the different communication situations in which they are likely to be used. For example, in an informal group discussion/brainstorming session of 4–6 colleagues it may be easiest to use a flipchart or white board, but in a more formal interaction where some preparation has taken place, an overhead projector may be used, especially if graphs or charts are to be presented.

The marketing function usually has a role in preparing the brief to a consultant or direct design and production of a range of visuals, from logos and letterheads through to covers for brochures and catalogues and the in-house magazine or newspaper.

You may be presented with a brief and asked to select a target audience, which means determining their communication needs, leading to the selection of a suitable vehicle and the factors to consider in its design, including use of lettering styles and colour. The value of logos and letterheads to corporate communication and customer perception may also be addressed.

Alternatively, you may be tested on the preparation of a graphical visual, based on the type of statistical information discussed in Unit 8, and asked how the use of colour would enhance its presentation and appeal.

EXAM QUESTION

Specimen examination question
You have been asked to prepare a list and brief description of each piece of visual-aid equipment that can be used in business presentations and which would be available in most business organizations. The information is to be used by the sales managers as a checklist when they are calling on customers and may need to make visual presentations. However, they also need to be convinced that visuals can be more advantageous than written or verbal communications in certain situations.

1   Explain the value of visual communications in making presentations and provide a suitable checklist.   (10 marks)

2   Evaluate the relative merits of written, verbal and visual communication.
                                                                (10 marks)

1   The type of visual aid that you may choose to use will depend on the purpose for the presentation, profile of the audience and type of message to be communicated.

   If the purpose of the presentation is to communicate information rather than to facilitate discussion, it will be important to use graphical tools for hard data and concise statements for communication that is presented verbally or in written format.

   The needs of the audience will determine the type of information to be presented, its breadth and also its depth. You will also need to consider factors such as familiarity with technical language and the most appropriate tone.

   For the purposes of physical presentations, most organizations have a number of typical visual aids that can be used; these are listed below.

   White boards can be used for simple words and drawings where during the communication process it is important to demonstrate how the diagram is compiled or statements and sentences constructed. Since boards can be easily reused, they are also cost-effective and time-saving in terms of reproducing material for distribution to the participants.

   Overhead projector transparency sheets can be preprepared, which is a major advantage during the presentation. These sheets are capable of being viewed over a large distance in a room.

   Flipcharts have the advantage that individual pieces can be placed around the room once they have been used. They are therefore a good method for producing temporary reference material.

   Slide projectors are useful for showing slides, but require the use of a room that can be sufficiently darkened to make them visible.

   Videos and audio tape recording and playback facilities may also be available.

2   The advantages of written communication are as follows:

   (a)   A permanent record of the communication can be stored for future reference.
   (b)   The communication message need not be spontaneous but can be carefully planned and composed.
   (c)   The communication can be delivered in a number of ways, either through the postal system or through electronic means such as E-mail.
   (d)   There is more security with written communication as it can be sent through special postal services and therefore will only be received by the person to whom it is addressed.
   (e)   Feedback can be solicited, either in writing or verbally.

Written communication, such as a sales letter, can be composed and written and sent to a large audience, all of whom have the same communication needs, for example to be told about a promotional campaign or sent a catalogue of the firm's latest merchandise with accompanying letter.

The advantages of *verbal communication* are as follows:

   (a)   It is fast, convenient and efficient as a medium of communication relative to other methods.
   (b)   Immediate feedback can be received – this is particularly important when a point or issue needs to be clarified.
   (c)   In face-to-face interactions, non-verbal clues can be used to emphasize points made and further information received from the observed actions of the recipient.

Verbal communication is particularly important in face-to-face interactions such as interview situations where the parties can discuss, clarify and agree issues raised or negotiated. This saves both time and money in the future.

The main advantages of *visual communication* are as follows:

(a) It is a stimulus that can be directed to a large or small audience, particularly if demonstrations are made or graphs used during the presentation.

(b) Visual communication can use a range of colours and shades to emphasize the attributes of products or communication messages that cannot be achieved through other media.

(c) Visual communication can use large and small letters, different styles of lettering and many other graphic techniques to add value to the communication of a message or product.

Visual communications are particularly effective as graphs, models or demonstrations in marketing, particularly if competitor organizations tend to use the more traditional methods of written and verbal communications.

EXTENDING KNOWLEDGE

Undoubtedly, the use of visuals and visual aids can add value to verbal or written presentations and communications. Find out the facilities that are available in your organization to produce visuals and the aids that have been acquired. Experiment in your use of visuals and visual aids to enhance your effectiveness as a business communicator. Try to use the skills for preparing graphs, tables, charts and pictograms from the last unit in this workbook as often as you can. Practice will make you faster and enable you to distinguish the most suitable visuals for the variety of presentations in which you are likely to be engaged.

Statistical information

OBJECTIVES

In this unit you will:

- Begin to appreciate the value of using graphs, tables and charts in the visual communication of business data.
- Study a range of graphs, tables and charts and learn which is/are the most appropriate in the communication of different business data.
- Learn the difference between primary and secondary data.
- Learn the definitions of all the graphs, tables and charts covered in the unit.
- Have an opportunity to practise producing all these for yourself.

By the end of this unit you will be able to:

- Produce a range of graphs, tables and charts from raw data, demonstrating a high level of skill and competence.
- Present them in such a way that they are both easy to understand and visually appealing in the information that they are trying to communicate.
- Understand that each one has a role to play in both verbal and written communications.

STUDY GUIDE

In the previous unit on visual communications we began to appreciate that, although the most commonly used methods of communication in a business context are verbal or written, visuals have a number of advantages that can enhance or replace the written or spoken word.

In this context, we can now study how to produce a range of graphs, tables and charts which are very effective visuals in both written and verbal communications.

A number of students will have learned how to produce these in a previous course. If that is the case, you have an advantage! In this unit I have assumed no prior knowledge and therefore provide a step by step guide; this is why, despite representing only 10% of the total syllabus, this unit is one of the longest.

I have also been fairly comprehensive in the presentation of a range of graphs, tables and charts, leaving you to select those which are most suitable for the examination question(s) on the day.

In Unit 1 I explained the nature of the compulsory question which appears in Section A of the paper and which has a 40% weighting. Whilst it will not be the case that on every occasion you will be expected to produce a graphically based visual, current trends indicate that this is the case, together with a further opportunity in Section B of the paper. An example of this type of question appears at the back of the book, together with a complete model answer.

The complete study of this unit will take 8–10 hours and you will need to allocate a further minimum of 8 to complete the tasks and to analyse the specimen examination question.

The first step is to read through the unit and familiarize yourself with the range of graphically based visuals that can be used in business communications.

During the next reading, keep a calculator to hand (unless you are particularly adept at mathematics!) so that you can follow through how the graphs, tables and charts have been created (they mainly use numerical date). Do make sure that you understand how each one is calculated and created. Try also to think about a suitable verbal or written business communication topic in which each one might be used.

Introduction

In Unit 9 we will look at the value of information technology in enhancing the process of business communication to make it faster and more accurate for managers to take decisions on a range of business issues.

Clearly, *factual* information is the key to the whole process of making decisions and solving problems and essentially there are two types of facts that can be gathered: primary and secondary.

Primary data is collected specifically for the investigation or survey being carried out by using observation, experimental techniques, depth interviews and panel surveys or questionnaires. These are frequently used in marketing as the basis for planning a complete range of initiatives.

In collecting information through primary techniques, it is unlikely that the entire universe or population can be surveyed, therefore a representative sample will have to be selected and tested. A number of sampling techniques are available and will be chosen to reflect the purposes of the research brief and time available to carry out the survey. These are discussed more fully in *Understanding Customers*.

Secondary data is information that has already been collected and published elsewhere, such as internal customer records, sales reports or external HMSO publications, periodicals and newspapers, which can be used for the research.

Primary data has the advantage of being up-to-date and tailored specifically to the research in hand, but is expensive and time-consuming to collect. Secondary data is usually relatively cheap to obtain, but may be out-of-date or unreliable.

Most data, particularly primary data, is usually collected in the *raw form* and then transformed into *statistics* to make the numbers more meaningful.

Statistics are a group of figures which relate to some important attribute or variable, e.g. market share or sales turnover, which are presented through a statistical method, e.g. tables, charts, diagrams, etc., allowing interpretation of the information more easily than would be the case if a mass of numbers were shown.

However, statistics prove nothing in themselves – they are merely indicators of what is likely to happen, based on past experience, and also used as forecasting models for the future.

The type of statistical data used and its visual presentation must reflect the business situation, the needs of the audience and the level of understanding and time available. Different types of graphical presentation lend themselves to different types of data and the needs of an audience will depend on their familiarity with the data and/or ability to interpret the information; some graphs are more complex than others in their presentation of data and interpretation.

Once data has been collected, it is usually divided into groups and recorded in a frequency table (frequency is the number of times a value occurs). The system of recording the data is called a tally.

Example

The number of brands managed by each of the 15 brand managers in a confectionery company are as follows:

Brand manager	A	B	C	D	E	F	G	H	I	J	K	L	M	N	O
No. of brands	4,	6,	3,	6,	7,	2,	4,	6,	7,	3,	6,	6,	6,	7,	6,

The raw data which has been tallied and identified in terms of its *frequency* of occurrence can now be presented as a table (Table 8.1). The table makes it much easier to 'visualize' the raw data.

No. of brands	1	2	3	4	5	6	7
No. of managers and managing brands	0	1	2	3	0	6	3

The table can now be used to produce a range of graphs. A couple of the most commonly used ones have been presented below; these are also the quickest to produce and present.

Figure 8.1 is a line graph/chart and Figure 8.2 is a stacked bar chart. You will be shown how to prepare and present these later in the unit.

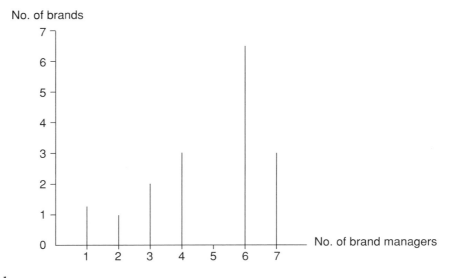

Figure 8.1

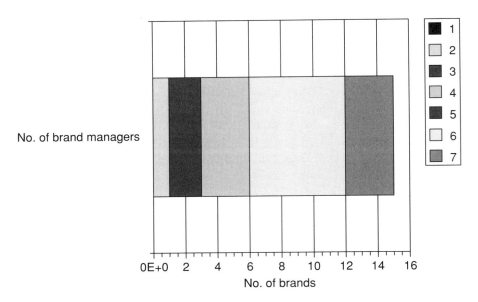

Figure 8.2

We can begin to see that the presentation of raw data can be made more effective when it is used visually through a table or graph/chart.

Other attributes of graphical presentation are detailed below.

Graphical presentation

Graphical presentation can cut the time needed to present long and complex sets of statistics and data on all aspects of marketing (e.g. costs, value and number of sales, profits, market shares), but will only be appropriate if the audience is able to follow the trends identified and understand the logic of the message, which will enable them to make sound business decisions. However, statistics prove nothing in themselves – they are merely indicators of what is likely to happen, based on past experience.

Graphs show the relationships between two variables – discrete (where only certain values are possible) or continuous (where any value over a certain range is possible) – by means of either a straight line or curve; they particularly demonstrate how the magnitude value of one variable changes, given a change in the other.

There are two axes on each graph, a horizontal axis (the *x* axis) and a vertical axis (the *y* axis). The horizontal axis is used to represent the independent variable (e.g. month or years) and the vertical axis to show the dependent variable (e.g. changes in sales figures), whose value depends on the independent variable (e.g. when demonstrating figures of promotional expenditure relative to sales turnover, promotional spend would be the independent variable and any changes shown in the sales figure would be dependent on the spend that had taken place).

Analysing data

Once the research process has been completed and the raw data made available, it must be analysed to provide significant meaning. You are looking for any patterns in the relationships between attributes or variables in order to form initial conclusions, on which you, or the recipient of the information, will base recommendations or decisions at a later stage.

The first step is to manipulate the data so that its significance can be determined. There are several ways to do this:

DEFINITION 8.5

1 Averages are measures of *central tendency* and, through the use of mean (most frequently used), median or mode, are used to find the number which is representative of a group of numbers, i.e. the middle value.

DEFINITION 8.6

(a) The arithmetic mean is found by totalling the sum of all the numbers in the group and then dividing by the number, in that group. This gives the average and the other numbers in the group can then be established relative to this average, i.e. either above or below.

$$\text{The arithmetic mean} = \frac{\text{sum of the observations}}{\text{number of observations}}$$

DEFINITION 8.7

(b) The median is the value of the middle number and is particularly useful when analysing extreme values in a distribution of numbers. The median is found by arranging the items in ascending or descending order of value and then selecting the number in the middle of the list.

$$\text{The position of the median} = \frac{n+1}{2}$$

DEFINITION 8.8

(c) The mode is the most frequently occurring item in a list of numbers. For example, if the following organizations had market shares of 20%, 13%, 15%, 8%, 13%, the mode would be 13%. If a list has two lots of items with the same frequency, the mode would be the average of those two values. The mode is useful when a frequency from a list can be commonly and easily identified.

Figure 8.3 calculates the averages of mean, median and mode.

SKINCARE UNLIMITED PLC

Location of branch retailer	Annual turnover
Appleby	£ 125 000
Barchester	£ 230 000
Collingwood	£ 216 000
Dedworth	£ 129 500
Eastling	£ 230 000
Fordingham	£ 215 500
Grange Town	£ 230 000
Harlington	£ 130 000
Jankley	£ 250 000
Total	£1 756 000

(i) The mean is £195 111.
(ii) The median is £216 000.
(iii) The mode is £230 000.

Figure 8.3 Calculates the averages of mean, median and mode.

Finally, consider the *range* of numbers that are being analysed in the list of data and use the opportunity to look closely at the relative values to identify any significant variations, which could be the basis for further research or investigation.

2 Trends are patterns and relationships that can be identified using data over a period of time (including the use of past information). However, be prepared for the fact that this analysis may raise more questions than provide answers.

3 Causal relationships can often be established based on trend analysis, i.e. if we manipulated *x* variable, what would be the effect on y variable? Correlations are often used in business and are particularly useful in planning for the effect on variables; when another is changed, what would be the effect on quantity demanded as a result of an increase in price?

ACTIVITY 8.1

Based on the following information, calculate the mean, median and mode and briefly conclude from the observations made from the data.

Competitor	Brand X Market share (£000s)
Competitor A	30 000
Competitor B	12 000
Competitor C	15 000
Competitor D	14 000
Competitor E	12 000
Competitor F	14 000
Competitor G	19 000
Competitor H	7 000

ACTIVITY 8.2

From your knowledge of marketing, think of the effect on some variables, if another is changed. Make a list below, using the marketing mix as a guide to your thinking.

We have just studied averages which help us to understand data better. The information which follows is a detailed account of how to produce tables, charts and graphs, some of which have been used and described briefly above.

Tables

DEFINITION 8.9

certain. defu
lefinition *n*. s
precise mea
distinct, clea
lefinitive *a*. fi
something; i

A table is a matrix structure where data is placed in titled rows and columns.

Tables are particularly useful for the presentation of detailed, specific information and, although only two variables can be demonstrated simultaneously, they do permit the reader to compare and contrast this information, particularly at points of intersection, from which similarities and differences can be observed. Tables can be used within the text to present the facts being considered and are introduced with a preceding sentence, or set apart as an independent piece of information, possibly in the appendices of a report, to which reference is made in the main text. Tables can be complex, such as reference tables, or relatively simple, such as spot tables, where only a few items are presented. Both figures and words can work equally well in tabular form.

Example

Salesperson name	Product line sales turnover (£000s) 1996–7					Total(£)
	A	B	C	D	E	
Helen Jenkins	13	15	8	12	10	58
Jane Atkinson	8	10	9	6	5	38
Andrew Salter	16	12	10	12	14	64
Luigi Romero	23	26	13	28	22	112
Karen Mann	33	34	24	22	30	143
Sunil Singh	12	16	11	17	15	71
George Vassiliades	4	7	3	8	11	33
Alan Bennett	11	12	12	12	11	58
Tony Taylor	15	7	7	9	8	46
Christine James	22	13	21	10	15	81
Total (£)	157	152	99	136	141	704

Guidelines for producing tables

1. Analyse the audience to whom this information will be presented and reflect their needs in terms of the amount and level of data used.
2. Keep the table simple, uncrowded and easy to handle, not tedious or difficult.
3. Label the table clearly, with a suitable brief introduction as appropriate.
4. Provide a key for complex headings or clearly label the columns and rows.
5. Use comfortable figures, such as decimals and percentages, rounded up, not fractions.
6. Label and number reference tables so that they can be easily identified and found.
7. Briefly explain any significant differences in the data by using a footnote to the table.
8. If appropriate, present a total column on the right-hand side and a total figure at the bottom of each column.
9. Use shading to highlight titles or significant features – this enhances the appearance of the table whilst drawing attention to important aspects of the information being presented.
10. In figure tables, clearly identify the units that will be used, e.g. percentages, £s, thousands, etc.

Observe the raw data below and manipulate it such that you can produce an effective table. In order to turn the data into information for decision-making, identify what further data or information might be required.

The brands listed below achieved a decrease or increase in sales during and up to 1996, compared with previous years:

Brand X: 1990: £120,000; 1991: £130,000; 1992: £120,000; 1993: £50,000; 1994: £145,000; 1995: £113,000; 1996: £189,000

Brand X1: 1990: £115,000; 1991: £131,000; 1992: £200,000; 1993: £500,000; 1994: £150,000; 1995: £131,000; 1996: £180,000

Brand Y: 1990: £11,000; 1991: £13,000; 1992: £12,000; 1993: £30,000; 1994: £14,000; 1995: £13,000; 1996: £18,000

Brand Y1: 1990: £200,000; 1991: £100,000; 1992: £100,000; 1993: £100,000; 1994: £140,000; 1995: £100,000; 1996: £100,000

ACTIVITY 8.3

Charts

Charts are usually used to convey a few main points (and possibly relationships between them) clearly, rather than the more detailed information which is used in tables. There are many different types of chart that can be used in the graphical presentation of data:

1 Column/bar charts.
2 Pie charts.
3 Line and surface charts.
4 Flow and organization charts and maps.
5 Diagrams, photographs, pictograms and drawings.

We will consider each in turn.

Column/bar charts

Column/bar charts demonstrate relationships and differences in variables by the respective heights of the columns/bars, which can be displayed vertically or horizontally, with the data on or near the bars. They are particularly useful when you want to:

1 Compare the size of several variables in one presentation.
2 Demonstrate important differences between the variables.
3 Demonstrate changes over a period of time.
4 Demonstrate the composition of variables.

Therefore, there are three types of column/bar chart that can be presented:

1 Simple column/bar charts.
2 Multiple column/bar charts.
3 Component (stacked) column/bar charts.

Guidelines for producing simple column/bar charts

Simple column/bar charts demonstrate the value of one piece of data by the respective length of the column/bar(s) on the chart. They are particularly useful for demonstrating the changes in the variable and for making comparisons based on the lengths of the columns/bars.

1 The chart must be titled and each axis of the graph must be labelled.
2 There must be a scale to indicate values on the corresponding axis (as on the y axis, where market share percentages are shown, below).
3 The vertical axis must always start at 0, so that the relative values can be accurately demonstrated, or indicate with a staggered line that the data does not begin at 0.
4 If possible, the data should be presented in some order of value, i.e. lowest to highest or vice versa; this is usually not possible if time comparisons are made.
5 Use spaces between columns/bars for ease of interpretation.
6 Use shading to highlight the columns/bars, making them easier to view.

Figure 8.4 demonstrates how to draw a simple column/bar chart based on the data below.

The following data can be shown as a simple column/bar chart:

Year	Market share of Brand A
1988	0.4%
1989	0.7%
1990	1.9%
1991	2.6%
1992	3.0%
1993	3.0%
1994	2.8%
1995	1.4%
1996	1.0%
1997	0.2%

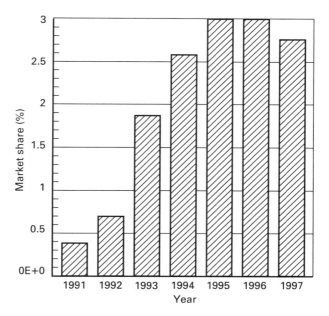

Figure 8.4 Market share of Brand A for the years 1991–97 inclusive.

Based on the following data, draw up your own simple column/bar chart and briefly conclude from the observations made.

Month	Turnover of Brand A (£m)
January 199X	4.4
March	5.7
May	5.3
July	5.8
September	6.6
November	7.5
December	9.0

Multiple column/bar charts

Multiple column/bar charts use several columns/bars for each variable, each column/bar demonstrating a particular aspect of the overall data.

Guidelines for producing multiple column/bar charts

1   Two or more columns/bars are used to present aspects/divisions of the data.
2   Shading must be used to distinguish the columns/bars representing different data.
3   Use spaces appropriately to draw attention to similarities, differences or trends, either in the columns/bars separately or groups of data.
4   Columns/bars can be drawn horizontally or vertically.

	Market competition for Brand A		
	1995 Sales (000s units)	1996 Sales (000s units)	1997 Sales (000s units)
Competitor B1	150	170	220
Competitor B2	230	240	210
Competitor B3	340	560	480

Figure 8.5 demonstrates how to draw a multiple column/bar chart based on the data below.

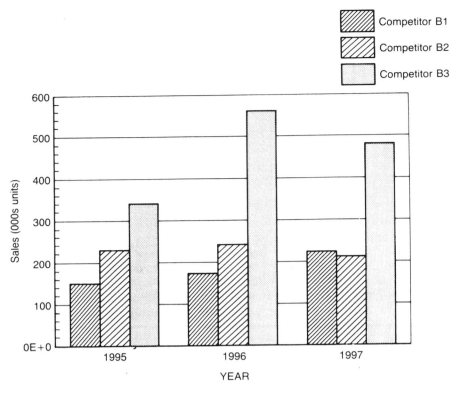

Figure 8.5 A multiple column/bar chart of market competition for Brand A.

Based on the following data, draw up your own multiple column/bar chart and conclude from the observations you have made.

	1995 Sales (000s units)	1996 Sales (000s units)	1997 Sales (000s units)
Brand X	120	140	110
Brand X1	125	185	199
Brand Y	85	100	90
Brand Y1	230	270	290
Brand Z	55	140	230

Component (stacked) column/bar charts

Component (stacked) column/bar charts can be segmented or broken lengthwise to show the relative size of components of an overall total. An example is presented in Figure 8.6 using the following data:

The launch of Brand X in 1997 was made up of the following promotional expenditure:

Media advertising 40%, public relations 10%, sales/promotional incentives 20%, demonstrations/exhibitions 10%, sales force training and special conference 15%, press releases 5%.

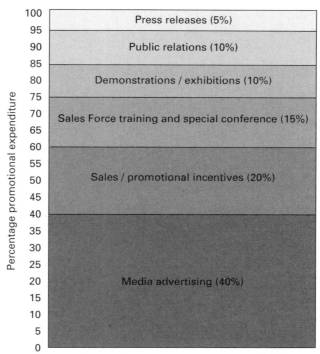

Figure 8.6 A component column/bar chart.

Guidelines for producing component column/bar charts

1 The components can be ordered in any way on the column/bar, but must remain consistent if more than one column/bar is demonstrated.
2 The relative values should be kept in order, with either the highest or lowest at the top, and then presented in ascending or descending order.
3 Use shading and/or a key if the components cannot be labelled directly.

The following are costs associated with the development of Brand F. Produce a component column/bar chart and briefly note the observations made.

Labour 50%, raw materials 25%, fixed costs 5%, test marketing 10%, commercialization activities 10%.

ACTIVITY 8.6

Histograms

Histograms are column/bar charts which show a continuous distribution of data and can demonstrate the basic shape of the distribution with the display of their columns/bars. They are particularly useful for identifying the comparative frequency in occurrence of data values within each class interval and therefore demonstrate those class intervals that are the most and least frequently occurring in a group of data.

certain. defi
definition *n.*
precise mea
distinct, clea
definitive *a.* f
something;

DEFINITION 8.10

Guidelines for producing histograms

1 The horizontal axis must show the intervals of the distribution.
2 The vertical axis must show the frequency of the intervals (if the intervals have different widths, it will show the frequency density).

3   The height of each rectangle (bar) must be proportionate to the frequency (or frequency density) of the base interval.
4   The mode must be calculated.
5   The class interval, class boundaries, lower and upper class limits must be established.

Figure 8.7 demonstrates how to draw up a histogram.

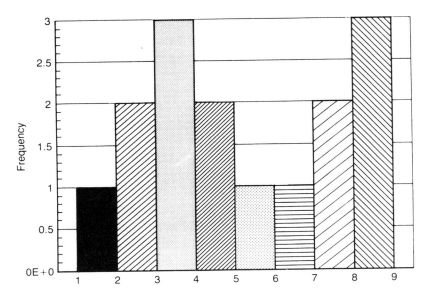

Figure 8.7   A histogram of chocolate bar rejects based on the data below.

The size of 15 rejects in a chocolate-bar manufacturing plant were measured in centimetres and are as follows:

3.98,   2.45,   1.33,   5.66,   4.75,   8.78,   8.76,   4.61,   3.43,   3.56,   2.45,   6.30,   7.45, 7.23,   8.10

The data is now grouped into classes.
The smallest value is 1.33 cm.
The largest value is 8.78 cm.

A class width of 0.99 cm gives the following (eight) classes:

Class (cm)	Tally	Frequency
1.0–1.99	1	1
2.0–2.99	11	2
3.0–3.99	111	3
4.0–4.99	11	2
5.0–5.99	1	1
6.0–6.99	1	1
7.0–7.99	11	2
8.0–8.99	111	3

In the above table, 1.0–1.99 cm is the class interval, with 1.0 cm the lower class limit and 1.99 cm the upper class limit.
The class boundaries are 1.0, 2.0, 3.0, 4.0 cm, etc.
The class width is the difference between the upper class boundary and the lower class boundary, i.e. 1.99 – 1.0 = 0.99 cm.

Pie charts
Pie charts are circular diagrams that are particularly useful for showing the composition of all the data, with the segments demonstrating the relative values of the data.

Guidelines for producing pie charts

1 Pie charts should be drawn accurately with a compass to represent the 360° of a circle and divided up equally into segments.

2 The component parts must represent 100%.

3 To draw the segment sizes accurately, use a protractor by putting the base line across the middle of the circle and mark off degrees to represent percentages (which must be worked out, based on numerical values). For example, 180° represents 50%, 90° 25%, etc.

4 Keep the maximum number of segments to seven, otherwise the chart will look too congested and be more difficult to interpret.

5 Place the most important (largest) segment at the 12 o'clock position and the others relative to it in some logical order.

6 Use shading to draw attention to salient features, usually largest and/or smallest segments, as discussed in Unit 7.

7 Label all the segments and show their relative values either on the segments or beside the graph. A key will be necessary for this.

Figure 8.8 demonstrates a pie chart based on the data below.

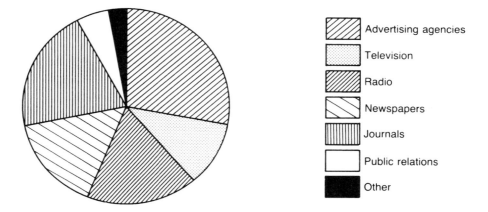

Figure 8.8   A pie chart.

In 1997, these graduates in media studies found jobs in the following sectors:

Sector	Number of graduates	Percentage
Advertising agencies	3 400	28
Television	1 300	11
Radio	2 100	18
Newspapers	1 900	16
Magazines/journals	2 500	21
Public relations	600	4
Other media	350	2
Total	12 150	100

Based on the following data, draw up your own pie chart and briefly conclude from the observations made. Can you identify the limitations of using pie charts?

The following are statistics on the socioeconomic profiles of daily consumers of wine in the UK:

Socioeconomic group	Relative amount of wine consumed (%)
A	76
B	67
C1	33
C2	21
D	13
E	4

Line charts

Line charts are a series of points joined together to form a straight or curved line and are usually used to reflect a trend over a period of time, or the interaction of two variables. They are similar to column/bar charts, but with lines instead of columns/bars, to represent the value of the variables, and in many cases several lines will be used to show comparisons between the data.

Guidelines for producing line charts

1   The horizontal axis should show the time period (years, months, hours, etc.).
2   The vertical axis should show the amount or value being measured.
3   Both scales should begin at 0 and increase in equal amounts, or indicate with a staggered line that the data does not begin at 0.
4   Both negative and positive values can be shown on line charts.
5   Use different colours for more than one line on the same graph, to distinguish between them; refer back to the topic on using colour in Unit 10 for further advice.
6   Use solid lines or broken lines to distinguish between different data or to draw attention to significant features of the data.
7   In order to avoid clutter and to make observation of the chart easier, a maximum of three lines on any graph should be used, especially if they are likely to cross over.

Figure 8.6a demonstrates a simple line chart, based on the data below.

Product line (XYZ)	Turnover 1997 (£)
Brand X	150 000
Brand X1	225 000
Brand Y	130 000
Brand Y1	195 000
Brand Z	85 000

ACTIVITY 8.8

Based on the following data, draw up your own simple line chart and briefly conclude from the observations made.

Year	Total advertising spend (£m) of Company Z
1991	5
1992	7
1993	7.5
1994	7.5
1995	8.3
1996	8.5

Figure 8.6b demonstrates a multiple line chart, based on the following data:

Year	Product lines (XYZ)	Advertising spend (£m)
1993	Brand X	0.5
	Brand Y	0.7
	Brand Z	2.4
1994	Brand X	0.7
	Brand Y	1.0
	Brand Z	1.9
1995	Brand X	0.9
	Brand Y	2.3
	Brand Z	2.5
1996	Brand X	0.9
	Brand Y	2.3
	Brand Z	2.5
1997	Brand X	1.4
	Brand Y	2.7
	Brand Z	2.5

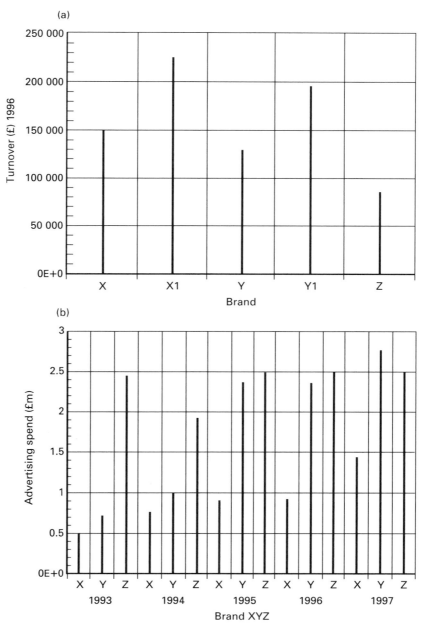

Figure 8.9 Line charts: (a) simple line chart; (b) multiple line chart.

Surface charts are a type of line chart, but which show the cumulative effect of all the different values depicted on the other lines, with the top line reflecting the overall cumulative total. They are particularly useful for demonstrating the values of data and how these have changed over time, relative to the total.

Based on the following data, produce your own multiple line chart and draw brief conclusions from the observations made.

Year	Total advertising spend for product line (XYZ) (£)	Medium
1992	450 000	Newspapers/magazines
	200 000	Radio
	500 000	Direct mail
	2 450 000	Television
1993	550 000	Newspapers/magazines
	400 000	Radio
	300 000	Direct mail
	2 350 000	Television
1994	750 000	Newspapers/magazines
	650 000	Radio
	600 000	Direct mail
	3 700 000	Television
1995	500 000	Newspapers/magazines
	650 000	Radio
	800 000	Direct mail
	3 750 000	Television
1996	700 000	Newspapers/magazines
	900 000	Radio
	500 000	Direct mail
	4 500 000	Television

Gantt charts

Gantt charts are a type of column/bar chart which show dimensions of a variable over a period of time and can be used to measure a number of different aspects of business activity in terms of actual, planned and cumulative. They are often found in marketing plans to show how the plan will be 'phased in' over a period of time.

Figure 8.10 demonstrates a simple Gantt chart.

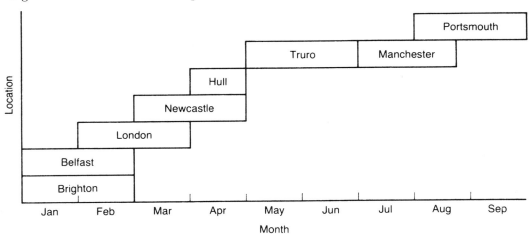

Figure 8.10 Gantt chart. Rolling national launch of Brand Q in different regional cities in the UK from January to September 199X.

Draw up your own Gantt chart based on communication needs to be actioned that you have identified from the personal communication plan in Unit 2.

Pictograms

Pictograms are charts in which the data is represented by a line of symbols or pictures. They are usually used for presenting information in a novel format and are often used in the transmission of simple messages, such as in some types of advertising. They can enhance the presentation of data by making it easy to view.

Guidelines for producing pictograms

1 Use a symbol which will be clearly representative of the subject matter, eye-catching and appealing.
2 The number of pictures or symbols must reflect the values they represent.
3 Use a key to indicate the value of one picture or symbol.
4 Keep the size of the pictures and graph consistent with the overall presentation.

Based on the following data, draw up your own pictogram and briefly conclude from the observations made.

Volume sales of Widgets by Company A1.

Year	Volume sales (000s)
1993	5
1994	6.5
1995	7
1996	9.5
1997	10

Figure 8.11 demonstrates some pictograms.

🧍 = 10 000, 🧍 = 5 000

Number of people in the UK who regularly eat (three bars a week) chocolate

1993 🧍🧍🧍🧍🧍
1994 🧍🧍🧍🧍🧍🧍🧍
1995 🧍🧍🧍🧍🧍🧍🧍🧍🧍
1996 🧍🧍🧍🧍🧍

Advertising spend of the 'top five' chocolate manufacturers in the UK in 1996. £ = £10 000

Company A £ £ £ £ £ £ £ £ £ £ £ £ £ £ £ £ £

Company B £ £ £ £ £ £ £ £ £ £ £ £ £

Company C £ £ £ £ £ £ £ £ £

Company D £ £ £ £ £ £

Company E £ £ £

Figure 8.11 Some examples of pictograms.

Map charts

Map charts (cartograms) also use symbols to represent values, usually of geographical data, such as the difference in market share of products and brands (or the whole organization) in regional areas of the UK, EC and international markets. The maps can be produced in a number of different ways – shading using lines, dots and complete colouring are some of the techniques used.

Figure 8.12 illustrates a map chart.

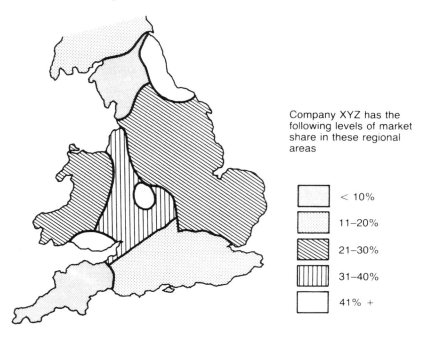

Company XYZ has the following levels of market share in these regional areas

	< 10%
	11–20%
	21–30%
	31–40%
	41% +

Figure 8.12   Map chart.

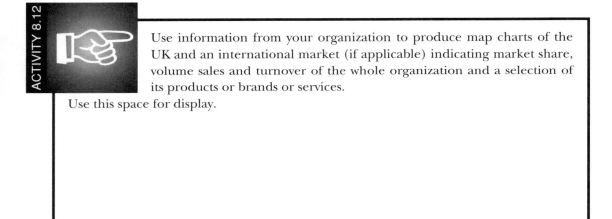

Use information from your organization to produce map charts of the UK and an international market (if applicable) indicating market share, volume sales and turnover of the whole organization and a selection of its products or brands or services.

Use this space for display.

Photographs

Photographs are often found in annual reports of organizations and other brochures and flyers as they are visually appealing and of interest to readers, especially if it is important for them to put a name to a face.

They are commonly used in surveys of large geographical areas and selective locations to show a number of important characteristics, such as suitable land sites and their proximity to towns, cities and natural resources, for the purposes of building processing and manufacturing plants, distribution centres and so on. They can also be used to highlight dangerous physical situations and in evidence to settle disputes.

Drawings and diagrams

Drawings and diagrams can be extremely useful in showing the dimensions and parts of products, equipment and machinery and how they operate; they are extensively used in instruction manuals for a large range of technical products.

Figure 8.13 is a diagram of a typewriter and its components.

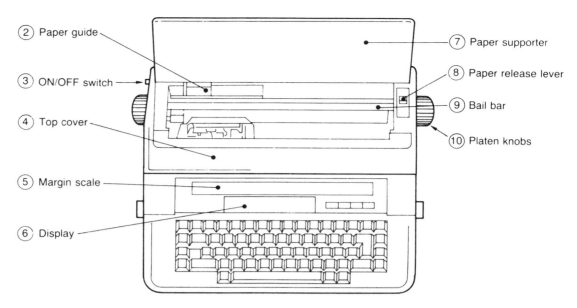

Figure 8.13 Diagram of a typewriter.

Flow charts

Flow charts are useful for demonstrating conceptual relationships, processes and procedures and business activities, where numerical values are not important. The relationships between various parts of the activity being demonstrated are shown in sequence from beginning to end and use geometric shapes to distinguish between various aspects.

Figure 8.14 demonstrates a flow chart.

Organization charts

Organization charts are frequently used in business organizations to show the hierarchical positions and relationships of employees, which also represent the main formal channels of communication.

An example of an organizational chart is shown in Unit 1.

Graphical presentation of statistical data through the use of tables, charts, maps, diagrams and pictograms demonstrates the significance of important variables and the relationships between them. They are used extensively in business to enhance and complement the information to be communicated and frequently by the sales and marketing functions.

Graphs must be kept as simple as possible and be attractive to the reader. They must also reflect the needs of the audience in terms of type, level and format for presentation of the information. Using colour, contrast and shading can make the visual easier to follow; greater appreciation of differences can take place and its appeal will be enhanced. An example is shown in Unit 1.

SUMMARY

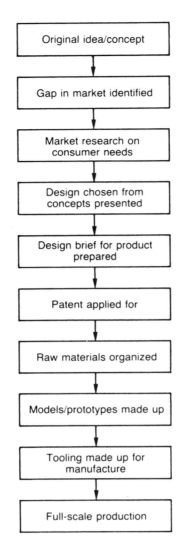

Figure 8.14   A flow chart for the stages involved in the introduction of a new product.

This unit has taken you through a selected range of statistical techniques that can act as important visuals in business communication, either as part of a verbal presentation such as a speech or meeting or a written document, for example a report.

It is vital for the purposes of the exam that you learn the rules that govern each of the statistical techniques described and use one or more that are *most suitable* in a given context where the raw data will be provided.

The compulsory question is the one most likely to ask you to present raw data in a statistical format, and other questions are likely to ask for your *written* interpretation based on a chart or graph which is presented.

Specimen examination question 1

You have recently joined Robinsons's, a grocery chain with 96 outlets in the north of England. Following a survey which was carried out by the magazine, '*Food Retailer*', you are required to analyse the information given below and to deliver a presentation to senior management. For use with an overhead projector, draft out the visual information you would include on 3 acetates/slides. Draw out *any graphs or charts in a way which gives a clear indication of how* you consider the material should appear.

Survey Details

A total of 1750 shoppers were interviewed in the north of England. Most of those interviewed were women. The area was divided into convenient sections and electoral registers were used to make random selections of houses. The refusal rate was under 0.7 per cent. The average age of women interviewed was 40, and 78 per cent of those interviewed had children.

Table 1 How often do you shop for groceries not including the times when you have forgotten something?

	%
More than twice a week	7
Twice a week	17
Once a week	60
Every two weeks	11
Every three weeks	1
Less often	2
Miscellaneous	1
No response	1

Table 2 On what day or days of the week do you usually do most of your grocery shopping?*

	%
Monday	12
Tuesday	4
Wednesday	8
Thursday	24
Friday	40
Saturday	31
Sunday	6

* results add up to more than 100% because respondents could choose more than one day.

Table 3 What is the main reason you do most of your grocery shopping on that day?

	%
Most convenient time	45
Fits in with pay-day	30
Good day for special offers	26
Habit	19
Not crowded	8
Stock up for the weekend	7
Leaves weekend free	6
Run out of food on that day	6
Better selection of groceries	3
Miscellaneous	13

Table 4 At which one store do you shop for groceries most often?

Top UK Retailers	%
Sainsbury	11.2
Tesco	10.4
Co-Op	6.9
Asda	5.7
Safeway	4.7
Robinsons	4.5
Fine Fare	4.5
Gateway	4.4
Spar	4.2
Kwiksave	3.2
Others	40.3

Table 5 What are your reasons for shopping at (name of shop) most often?

	%
Convenient location	42
Special offers/low prices	38
Good meat	25
Carry all brands	22
Friendly assistants	20
Quality of fresh produce	17
Good display	14
Adequate parking	12
From habit/miscellaneous	47

Table 6 What are your reasons for not shopping at the other stores?

	%
Prices too high	45
Too far to travel	27
Slow check-out	22
Prefer the shop I go to	17
Very few special offers	17
Poor selection	15
Unattractive store	7
Too small	7
Too overcrowded	5
No particular reason	3
Miscellaneous	28

Table 7 On your major grocery shopping trips, how often do you buy advertised special offers?

	%
Frequently	35
Occasionally	15
Seldom	10
Never	38
No response	2

Table 8 Which of the following are your best source of special offers? Which second and which third?

	Source		
	First	Second	Third
Newspapers	40%	10%	21%
Store leaflets	25%	24%	15%
Leaflet drops	15%	31%	19%

Table 9 Please look at all these advertisements and tell me the reference number of the one you like best.

	%
Safeway	20
Fine Fare	16
Asda	14
Gateway	13
Kwiksave	10
Tesco	9
Sainsbury	8
Co-Op	6
Robinsons	2
Aldi	1
No response	1

Table 10 Why do you like the advertisement you picked?

	%
Special offers are easy to find	42
Eye catching	38
Easy to read/large print	27
Easy to find specific brands	19
More bargains	17
Good variety of items	15
Other replies none more than 8%	45
No response	3

The first point to note is that 15 marks are allocated to this part of the question, and therefore we can safely conclude that 5 marks per drawing of a chart or graph will be awarded. The tables are all reproduced below (by kind permission of the CIM) and it is a question of personal choice as to which are to be used in answer to the question. You must make sure that each graph or chart is clearly labelled, both on each axis and also given a title.

I have presented below a different graph for each set of data corresponding to the first five tables.

Table 1. I have chosen a column/bar chart to represent the data in this table.

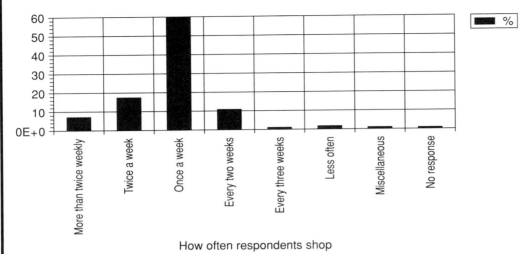

Figure 8.15 Shopping for groceries

Table 2. I have chosen a pie chart to represent this data.

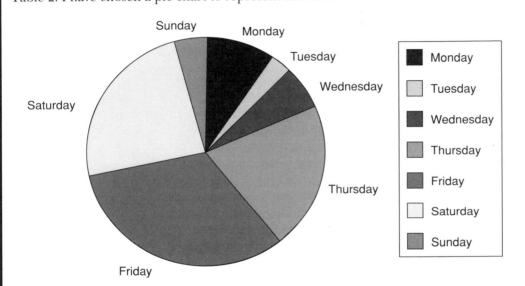

Figure 8.16 Shopping days

Table 3. I have chosen an area graph to represent this data.

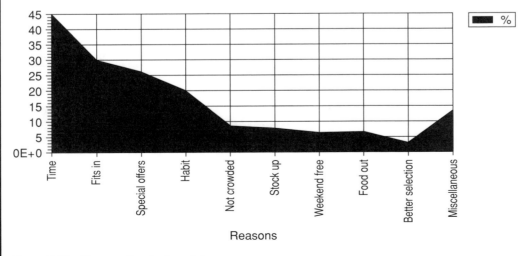

Figure 8.17 Reasons for choice of day

Table 4. I have chosen a standard line graph for the data in this table.

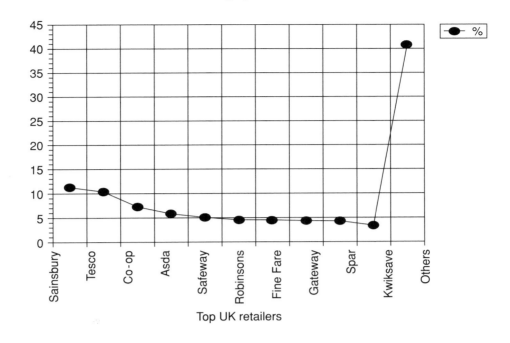

Table 5. I have chosen a 3-dimensional column/bar chart for this data.

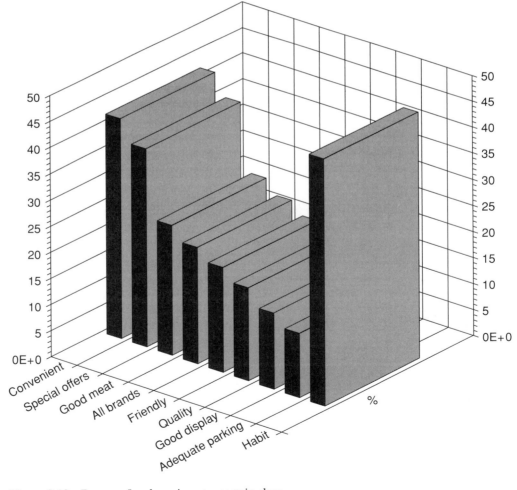

Figure 8.19 Reasons for shopping at a certain shop

Specimen examination question 2

(a) The sales manager has asked you to write a brief note on the value of column/bar charts and pie charts in the presentation of sales data. (10 marks)

(b) Study the undernoted information on the American cigarette market and choose a suitable method for graphical presentation of the data. (10 marks)

The American Cigarette Market, 1993
Courtesy: Merrill Lynch. Source: *The Sunday Times*, March 1994

Brand name sales	(billions of cigarettes)	Percentage share of the market
Marlboro	108.5	24%
Basic	24.4	5%
Benson and Hedges	11.5	2%
Merit	10.6	2%
Virginia Slims	10.4	2%
Winston	31	7%
Salem	18.1	4%
Camel	17.9	4%
Carlton	6.9	1%
Pall Mall	5.8	1%
Kool	12	3%
Newport	23	5%
Other	181.3	39%

(a) Pie charts are represented by a circle, divided by radial lines into sections, so that each one is proportional to the size of the figure represented. It therefore shows the sizes of component figures in proportion to each other and to the overall total. There are many uses for pie charts in presenting sales data, as whole numbers or percentages can be depicted, but the main value is that by using shading or contrast the segments can be easily distinguished and, if this is compared to past data, it serves a useful basis for planning.

Column/bar charts represent data by a series of columns/bars and are a valuable visual as the differences between the data are easy to distinguish, enhanced by the use of contrast or shading.

Column/bar charts can be used to show the relative values of data or brand performance in terms of turnover, percentages, perhaps relative to other brands, internal or external (if the data is available).

(b)

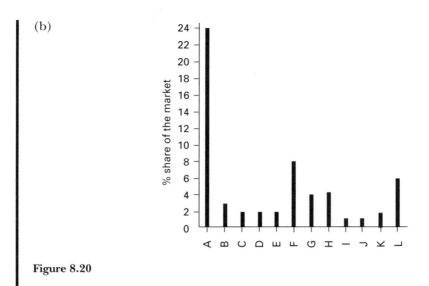

Figure 8.20

Clearly the number of statistical techniques or other visuals to present sales or marketing data are enormous and you need to learn how each can be used to best advantage in the presentation of information. In meetings and discussions or when written communication is received, analyse whether any visuals have been used and, if not, could they have contributed to a better appreciation of the information presented?

Experiment with the range of techniques developed in this unit and ask for feedback on their effectiveness and value to the recipients in your own business communications. Monitor and evaluate this activity over a period of time until you feel confident that the most suitable visual is used in a given situation.

Information systems and technology

In this unit you will:

- Define the terms associated with information systems, data processing and information technology.
- Understand and appreciate the significant developments that have taken place in the world of electronic equipment and how this has influenced the business communication process.
- Unravel the functions that can be performed by a computer and its applications in the marketing and general business environments.

By the end of this unit you will:

- Feel competent enough to explain the uses of electronic equipment in making business communications more effective and successful.
- Appreciate that there are significant cost advantages in the long run to be derived from using electronic systems of communication.
- Understand that this is a rapidly developing industry enabling business people to communicate faster and more effectively than ever before.

Information technology is a vast subject area and we can only present some of its most basic aspects in this unit. However, it has been included as part of the syllabus for Business Communications because it is through this very medium that not only does the majority of business communication take place, but in terms of an industry it has achieved phenomenal growth, particularly during the last decade, and therefore provided significant market opportunities for business organizations. Do you work in an IT organization or one that is related to this industrial sector?

The aim of this unit is therefore to give everyone a basic knowledge of IT and in particular how it has enhanced the business communication process, making it more efficient, cost-effective and fun!

Completion of this unit will take about 4 hours and you will require a further 4 to tackle the questions, tasks and to study the specimen examination question given at the end of the unit.

You should begin this unit by thinking about the situations in which you are required to use IT for the purposes of communication.

Your thoughts might turn to making an interview appointment on the telephone, sending a business letter or document through a facsimile machine, or even participation at a video conference.

Whatever the case, make some rough notes now and refer back to these as you progress through study of the unit.

The list of situations in which IT is now used is endless. However, there are only a limited number of methods for transmitting information (some mentioned above), though new products are still coming on to the market and their degree of sophistication continues to increase.

You should also refer back to the personal communications plan in Unit 1, as IT may have been identified as an area in which you need some, or further, training. Use the knowledge gained from this unit as a means of strengthening your practical experience of IT in the business environment.

Finally, keep up-to-date with this fast-changing dynamic sector, as you may be asked to draw upon current information in the examination.

Why is information important? Can you establish why information is generally important to business organizations and specifically to marketing?

Introduction

We shall begin our study of this unit by considering the notion of an *Information System.*

The definition of an Information System is that which describes an organization as a *whole* in terms of its information requirements and information utilization. The Information System of a business organization is therefore all the equipment and software required for data and information management.

The requirements for data and information management are met, in part, by the *Data Processing Systems* of the business organization.

Data processing is the collection, manipulation and interpretation of data which produces useful information for decision-makers.

Today, the main methods used to undertake this process are electronic and computer-based (electronic data processing (EDP) we shall return to this later in the unit.

Data therefore is a term used to describe basic *facts* about the activities of a business organization.

They are usually numerically based, for example, sales turnover figures, sales volume figures, percentage profitability or market share figures, etc. There is also a growing trend in marketing and selling to qualify qualitative data with numbers, numerically based rating scales such as Likert scales, semantic differential scales and so on.

Information is obtained from this data in a business organization by *organizing* it into a meaningful form. There are a number of techniques that can be used, and some of the statistically based ones are described in Unit 8. Clearly, in organizations where a large amount of data is available and frequently used, software packages on computer-based systems that allow the manipulation of this data (data processing) to make it meaningful to the decision-maker are extremely valuable in saving time and making the data an easily accessible unit of information.

The information can then be presented in written or visual format (see graphs, tables and charts in Unit 8) and communicated through the medium of a report, memo, brief or letter (see Units 2 and 3); transmission could even take place through the same computer-based system using, for example, E-mail, if the recipient is a networked user.

Figure 9.1 below describes the fundamental data processing to information stages, beginning with data collection and finishing with the production of a suitable communication that will provide information for a decision-maker in any large, medium or small business.

DATA COLLECTION Data collection can take place from either primary (original) or secondary (published) sources, depending on the nature of the information required and other factors such as time available for data collection, research budget and the needs of the recipient or data user. ↓
DATA PREPARATION The data must be prepared for input into the computer-based system. This may involve sorting, organizing or transcripting the data (especially if it was qualitative), to make it suitable for input. ↓
INPUT OF THE DATA Data may be put into the system by a number of different people (sales managers, customer credit personnel, etc.), but in most business organizations, if there are vast amounts of data, staff responsible for this function will be employed. ↓
DATA PROCESSING The data processing stage is usually when the computer software takes over the task of sorting, manipulating and providing statistical inferences or other calculation, where appropriate, of the data. ↓
OUTPUT The final stage is where the (manipulated) data is retrieved and used by a group or individual as information for decision-making.

Figure 9.1

In business organizations, each department or functional area, such as marketing or sales, is a *centre* of information.

These centres identify the need for information, analyse it and prepare a range of communications (written, verbal and visual) to disseminate this information to others, both internal and external.

When this information has been received it must flow through to individuals and groups so that they can make decisions and solve problems based on the facts that are presented.

In business organizations, managers make a range of decisions on strategic and tactical issues, ultimately to meet their functional and corporate objectives. Strategic decisions and tactical decisions are entirely different, as are those taken by managers in the various functional areas. Therefore the type of information that they need and the frequency with which they will need it vary considerably.

In marketing, managers need information on customers (level of sales, strength of demand, price sensitivity), competitors (for example, new, existing, the relative market shares of each and how this is likely to change under a set of new conditions such as increase in advertising), the STEP (social, technological, economic and political) factors, their own internal constraints (for example with physical, financial or human resources), suppliers (for example, their ability to respond to changes in an organization's production schedule) and so on.

Factual information usually arises from numerical data which is then *arranged* to make the variables meaningful and to show significant relationships between them (this is discussed more fully in Unit 8) or in the form of summaries, reports, plans and proposals from internal and external sources that prompt the flexible and responsive organization to react.

The type of information needed depends on the issue under investigation for solving an internal or external problem or because the organization wishes to take advantage of a perceived opportunity in the business environment. Whatever the situation, for information to be of value to an organization, it must be *relevant, accurate, clearly presented and timely.*

The business organization not only needs good communicators to collect, analyse and disseminate the information, but good systems of business communication to enable the collection, processing, storing and distributing to be fast, convenient and accurate. The systems of business communication are described under the heading of IT.

QUESTION 9.2

What is IT? In your studies to date and experience at work, can you explain what is meant by the term IT and the relationship it has to communication in business organizations?

DEFINITION 9.5

certain. defi
definition *n.*
precise mea
distinct, cle
definitive *a.* f
something;

IT is the equipment, tools and systems used to *create, produce, reproduce, distribute and store* business communications. IT systems enhance the channels of communication that are used in business by their ability to send and receive information quickly and conveniently and increasingly at lower cost than traditionally used channels such as the postal system (for letters, reports etc.) and the telephone.

In summary, all systems have the following functions for handling information:

Inputs

Information that is received into the business organization or department is placed on to computerized systems, for example through word-processing packages or scanners, so that it may be retrieved at a later date. Information is also input through electronic technology as a means of immediate communication with parties who have suitable systems for receiving it, for example, the increasing use of E-mail as a fast and efficient means of business communication (this is discussed more fully in the following unit).

Storage

This usually takes place on a range of computer files, for example magnetic tape or floppy disks, and has the obvious benefits of cutting down on storage space in the office environment. Information is much more conveniently retrieved, especially as messages stored originally in one part of the organization can be accessed in another part of the building or in a separate building altogether, which is locally, nationally or internationally placed.

Processing

This is the *means* by which the information is placed on to a computerized or electronic system, which first may involve transcribing the information manually and then inputting through a software package which is text-, numerically or graphically based.

Output

This is the stage involving distribution of the information that has been collected, processed and stored.

There are numerous ways in which business information can be accessed or distributed locally, nationally and internationally, not least because of the rapid growth and sophisticated means made available by the telecommunications industry, which enables any organization to maximize its IT potential.

Private data-transmission circuits via telephone lines and fibre-optic networks are just two examples that enable businesses to transmit information from one venue to another.

Feedback

We have discussed the significance and value of feedback in the process of communication in Unit 1. In the context of IT, it is important for the individuals involved in the design and implementation of IT systems to reflect on the way in which a mechanism for receiving feedback should be incorporated and which must be efficient and convenient to both sender and receiver.

One example of a successful feedback mechanism is the visual tag that travels with E-mail messages. When the communication has been received, a message on the sender's monitor indicates that this is the case and therefore is confirmation that the message was sent and received.

ACTIVITY 9.1

In your professional capacity, you must receive a variety of communications through a number of different channels. Some of these will be frequent and some relatively infrequent.

Frequent channels may be written communication through memos or verbal communication through the telephone, and the type of information received may be on sales forecasts and actual figures or forthcoming promotional campaigns.

Make a list of the channels that are used to communicate with *you* and the types of information that you receive under the headings of 'Frequent' and 'Infrequent', as follows:

Channel and type of information received	Frequent	Infrequent
Telephone		
Memo		

Letter

Report

Fax

Telex

Computer-based system
(be specific)

Other

Can you draw any conclusions from this in terms of whether you are receiving the type of information you need as frequently as you would like, and are the channels used the most effective in speed, convenience and accuracy?

Most individuals who use electronic systems for handling information would agree that the methods available today make the process of communication and the ability to take decisions or analyse and solve problems much faster than used to be the case when information was accessed through manual means.

The marketing and sales environments have benefited enormously from the developments in electronic equipment that have made business communication – verbal, written and visual – faster and more efficient, especially as these environments are dynamic and therefore consistently changing, requiring up-to-date information and the ability to access and transmit this quickly.

Electronic technology in the business organization

The *electronic office* is a term used to describe a section of an organization that only uses electronic systems for transmitting information and storing documents.

DEFINITION 9.6

An electronic office is capable of communicating faster, both internally and externally, than one which uses traditional manual systems, based on paper. The electronic office is therefore able to provide information for decision-making quicker and more frequently, saving both time and money to the organization. Managers are able to respond faster to the business environment in which they compete and provide a higher level of service to their customers and suppliers because of their availability, accessibility and the quality of the information at their disposal.

Observe your office environment and make notes as to what extent you operate in an electronic office.

	Send information	Receive information	Store information
Type of equipment or channel of communication			
1			
2			
3			
4			

Computers

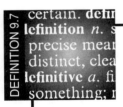

certain. defi
lefinition *n.* s
precise mear
distinct, clea
lefinitive *a.* fi
something; r

A computer is an electronic piece of equipment which allows the range of functions, input, storage, feedback, etc., described earlier in the unit.

There are basically two types of computer.

Digital computers are the type used in data processing, and therefore function by taking discrete numbers and performing calculations on them; this type of computer is commonly found in all business organizations.

Analog computers are capable of different functions, for example the measure of physical changes to variables, such as temperature or chemical reactions. They are commonly used for scientific data rather than commercial/business data.

Today, computers are capable of going far beyond the functions described above, and for the purposes of business communications they can incorporate use of the telephone, telex and television in order to produce information as text, pictures and voice messages.

Computers (mainframe, microcomputers and workstations) have undoubtedly revolutionized the business communication process through the range of functions they can perform and the extensive facilities that they can provide, depending on the hardware and software available in the organization. Some of the most important functions of computers are described below:

1   Word processing – documents can be created, prepared and arranged in a variety of written formats. This undoubtedly speeds up the process of preparing correspondence,

especially as frequently used messages/names and addresses can be stored and accessed quickly.

2 Data processing – (numerical) raw data, as mentioned earlier, is arranged into factual information for better analysis and interpretation. Graphs can be produced to make the variables and their relationships easier to appreciate; this is usually achieved through the use of database packages. Databases are extensively used in marketing to keep records on customer segment profiles, the value of their purchases, geographical location, etc. and a whole host of other factors in order to target promotional campaigns and as a basis for carrying out marketing research.

Data processing is achieved in a number of ways, depending on the distinct needs of the department or organization, as follows:

(a) Batch processing is used by organizations that require large print runs on a regular (daily, monthly, etc.) basis, for example the printing of customers' bills.

(b) On-line processing is the availability of the organization's database to all employees who wish to access this frequently, particularly if they are to provide customers with up-to-date information, for example on credit availability.

(c) Stand-alone data-processing is achieved by the individual user on his/her own personal computer (PC) and for distinct purposes, such as the manipulation of variables to analyse their effect.

(d) Time-shared processing is undertaken by smaller organizations who use a third party to provide them with their processing requirements and make a payment according to the service used and the speed with which it is required.

(e) The processing mix is a development achieved through open systems integration (OSI), whereby data links and network control allow access to both work- and home-based employees to the computer systems of the organization. Since the growth in employment away from the office base, including sales people who spend much time in the field, this medium serves as an important communication function, as all data can be accessed.

3 Forecasts can be made to project changes in data if variables are changed. This is usually achieved through the use of spreadsheet packages and is frequently used by managers in the sales and marketing functions, for example to plan for product changes, in order to analyse the effect of price changes on demand and so on.

4 Designs and models can be produced to visualize a product, component or parts of it, in order to assess feasibility and practicality before any production activity takes place and which can be tested as a concept on the potential consumer or business market.

5 Desktop publishing is the production of documents and publications which are more like professional printed matter, and which can be changed quickly and easily, saving on time and cost. The use of a laser printer in conjunction with a desktop publishing package increases the quality of the printed material. Many organizations use this function to produce/print a range of internal correspondence, pro formas and material which is used to communicate with external audiences, such as brochures, price lists and catalogues.

Electronic networks

When computers are linked electronically between parts of the organization (which may be in different geographical locations) and individual employees, it is usually through local-area networks (LANs) or wide-area networks (WANs), which facilitates the business communication process and speed of information access and exchange.

Value-added networks (VANs) are systems which can be accessed by a number of organizations through a third-party provider. The provider sets up an electronic mailbox for the user, who can then send and receive messages.

DEFINITION 9.8

certain. defir
lefinition *n.* s
precise mear
distinct, clea
lefinitive *a.* fi
something; r

> LANs use parallel communications between computers based on a minimum of eight electronic wires to send the information. WANs use serial connections, which are a single or twisted wire that carry the communication down the line.

Telephone networks carry sound-based messages and use a modem (modulator–demodulator) to transmit the communication.

certain. defir
lefinition *n.* s
precise mear
distinct, clea
lefinitive *a.* fi
something; r

> Electronic data interchange (EDI) is a network used to make an electronic link between an organization and its suppliers in order to establish a system for ordering supplies, making enquiries and settling accounts faster and more conveniently than would be the case otherwise.

Specifically, electronic technology has the following roles to play:

Creating and producing documents

The tasks of creating and producing written documents such as letters, memos and reports are all made significantly faster and easier through the use of electronic typewriters and word-processors, usually by an individual using a PC or network (discussed later). Word-processors have the advantage that the text can be arranged and edited as suitable; the information can also be stored on a computer disk, which cuts down storage space and makes reference to documentation easier to access at a later stage.

Some electronic typewriters have large memories for storing complete letters or key names, addresses and phrases and a facility where the text can be viewed before it is printed on to the notepaper.

Verbal communications, such as key statements to personnel or complete speeches, presentations and demonstrations, can be created and produced using audiotapes (where the presenter can be heard), videotapes (where the presenter can be seen and heard) and videodiscs, which use laser equipment to access the information.

Reproducing documents

Reproduction of written documents through ever-increasingly sophisticated photocopiers and offset printing machines (for larger numbers) have substantially cut down printing time, as most reproduction activities can take place in each department. This is much faster than having to send the communication to a separate print section and wait for its return. A number of accessories are also available for use with photocopiers that sort and staple documents together.

Processing and distributing information

Documents and information can be distributed and transmitted both physically and electronically. The method chosen will depend on factors such as convenience, delivery time, confidentiality, cost, availability and accessibility to systems of distribution.

Physical systems include delivering documents personally, through internal mail, meetings and speeches and using the postal system. The latter has grown in the range of services it provides and the private sector has also entered the market to offer its services through providing messengers/couriers and local, national and international mail and parcel delivery.

Electronic systems for the delivery and transmission of documents and information are numerous. The most commonly used are described below:

1 The telephone is possibly the most widely used electronic system in business for verbal communication. It is convenient, fast, efficient and immediate feedback is

available. A number of organizations have telephone systems with multiple lines, where individuals in various parts of the building or in different locations can communicate internally; calls can be transferred from one person to another and also put on hold. These functions can also be achieved by a private branch exchange (PBX) system or private automatic branch exchange system (PABX), where a computer routes most of the calls.

2 Written communication, by electronic coding and using telephone lines, can be transmitted to other locations. There are many methods available; some of the most commonly used are described below.

Electronic mail

There is no doubt that electronic mail has revolutionized business communications.

The main advantages of this computer-based system, which requires both sender and receiver to have a VDU (visual display unit) for reading the message (and storing, etc.) and be linked up to the 'network', are as follows:

- Employees can communicate short or long messages from their office or keyboard (with modem) to anywhere in the world.
- Messages are transmitted *immediately*; therefore there is no reliance on the relatively slow postal systems or other methods of communication.
- The cost is absolutely minimal, relative to using other systems of communication; it also saves a considerable amount of time which is required when preparing letters and other documentation to make them suitable for posting.
- A signal is sent to the recipient on his/her screen to indicate that a message has arrived. Messages can also be stored easily and efficiently for future reference.

Facsimile machines

The fax machine, as it is often called, has also made a major contribution to business communications. In particular:

- It is capable of sending letters and other documents via a telephone line to be received anywhere in the world (assuming that the recipient has a fax too).
- It is a relatively cheap and efficient method of sending information – the prices of fax machines have come down greatly over the past few years and look likely to continue falling, though less dramatically. The cost of sending the fax through telephone lines is determined by the usual rates charged by the telephone company, though for large businesses these are negotiable.
- One of the further benefits is that security can be maintained in sending the document, though this cannot be controlled at the other end. However, it is generally agreed that sending information by fax is safer than by other methods.

Video technology

Video technology has become a vital part of business communication. Sales people travelling nationwide and internationally now frequently carry portable self-contained playback units to show clients video presentations of new products, services and other relevant information, perhaps depicted by statistical charts and graphs or diagrams and drawings.

Business organizations are beginning to replace the company newsletter with video bulleting, such as news reports and other information which is distributed throughout the organization.

Conferences make increasing use of video technology alongside more familiar techniques such as film and slides.

Every video system consists of a 'source' and a 'display'. Sometimes they can be connected directly together, but often in a business video there is a need for additional switching or 'interfacing' equipment between them.

Examples of 'sources' are equipment such as video-cassette players, video-disk players and computers.

'Displays' include items such as tiny flat screen displays, television sets, video projectors and video walls.

In order to present successful business communications using video technology, the user must ask him/herself a number of important questions as follows:

First, what is the *environment* in which the video presentation is to take place; second, what size of display must I have and finally, what sources do I need now and may need to add in the future.

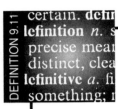

certain. defi
lefinition *n.* s
precise mea
distinct, clea
lefinitive *a.* fi
something; 1

'Video' is based on television and is mostly concerned with moving images. All the standards for video have been derived from the needs of broadcasting, and the capabilities of TV cameras. Computer graphics however, are created within a computer's memory, their resolution or image quality is a function of the size of that memory.

Since computer graphics can be shown to a higher resolution than standard video, the *screens* on which they are seen are usually different, it is now possible to feed video pictures through a computer, but only by changing the nature of the image signal from analogue to digital.

Increasingly the broadcasting industry is moving towards 'digitalization'. For the business communicator, the main points in terms of this trend are that digital video is the basis of computer sourced video and that digital video equipment is now use in professional video production, it is gradually replacing analogue equipment as there is almost no 'generation loss' when copies are made from digitally originated material.

Video conferencing

Video conferencing is an exciting development in the business communication process. Compared with all the other methods described above, it is the only one in which a face-to-face interaction of business people can take place without anyone having to leave their location of work, or even their desk.

However, it has taken time to become established. One of the reasons is the different time zones in which employees operate around the world and therefore the availability of all the participants.

The main advantages of video conferencing are as follows:

- Face-to-face interactions such as meetings can take place without participants having to travel to be in the same place as each other.
- This makes it a cost-effective means of communication.
- In face-to-face interactions, participants can not only talk to each other, but also observe behaviour (such as body language) which can be important in assessing the nature of the message.
- A record of the meeting can take place which can be used for future reference.

The mobile telephone

Another more recent revolution that has taken place is that of the mobile telephone. People are no longer having to 'tie' themselves to one location in order to speak to another individual.

The main advantage has been to people who are continuously 'on the move' but need to keep in touch with the office or contact other people. In the marketing environment, sales people in particular have benefited from this technology as they are largely an 'absent workforce'.

Mobile telephones operate through analog or digital systems which record the time used in making calls and therefore the charges due. The user tariffs in this relatively new industry are extremely variable, but in general it is safe to conclude that the cost of making a call from a mobile telephone is *higher* than through the traditional telephone system.

Storing documents

The traditional method of storing documents is to place them in different types of files and then put them in a filing cabinet. However the main disadvantage is that this requires storage space, which must be paid for. Since electronic equipment has become extensively used in the production of documentation, many electronic storing devices through the use of magnetic and laser technology which scan, digest and store are now available. Information can of course be stored in the hardware itself.

Feedback

Information exchange is only complete when feedback on the communication has been provided, if only to acknowledge that the message has been received. Electronic feedback devices such as the visual tag are used to display on the sender's computer monitor that the message has been received.

The Data Protection Act 1984

Organizations usually carry a substantial amount of information on databases, not least on customer profiles, which are used as a basis for planning a range of marketing initiatives.

However, in 1984 the Data Protection Act was passed to safeguard the interests of individuals and prevent their names, addresses and personal details being passed around from organization to organization; data must therefore be obtained lawfully, only used for registered purposes, be accurate and up-to-date and not be kept longer than necessary.

The electronic business communication industry today

The electronics industry providing new equipment to facilitate the process of business communication is booming.

A recent article in the *Financial Times* (March 1994) quoted the chief executive of Casio, the electronics giant, suggesting:

> communication is the key to our business success and that of the customers that buy our products . . . the challenge of the communication age will be met by the development of products using technical skills and will enable effective, innovative communication expertise to all that wish to acquire it.

Some of the new products that are in the pipeline include communication diaries and a visual radio that can broadcast text information as well as sound on an FM frequency.

The world of presentation has also changed enormously in recent years.

Once the emphasis in business communications/presentations was on printed material and graphics, perhaps supported with audio-visuals, today every presentation usually comprises of a mix of media, otherwise known as multi media.

Multi-media communications and presentations will include audio elements, perhaps with originally composed music and songs, interactive computer software programmes specially designed for the task, as well as the necessary hardware to operate it. Computers will also be used to produce graphics and animation to enhance the presentation of information and product visualization, perhaps before a prototype is made.

Video is another aspect of multi media which has been discussed under 'video technology' earlier in this chapter. Also briefly mentioned in that section was 'image processing', in other words the production of everything from 35 mm slides and OHP's to 'frame grab' from video, all of which may be required by the business communicator.

Finally, it is not a requirement of the Business Communications syllabus that you are to know how to produce pages (Web's) for the Internet, but many of the rules discussed under written and visual communications will of course apply.

The use of the Internet by organizations wishing to communicate information and those wanting to receive it has undoubtedly presented itself as an interesting and growing opportunity which looks set to expand well into the future.

In this unit I have introduced you to the following aspects of IT.

It grew rapidly in the 1980s and continues to do so today, providing an extensive range of devices suitable for every business need, most of which are capable of being integrated to perform an even greater number of business functions. The telephone and cellular/portable phone, facsimile and cellular fax machines, electronic typewriter, computer/microcomputer and laptop, word-processor and computer printer, photocopier, audio and video tapes, videodiscs and calculator are some of the most commonly used business machines and tools.

Information systems in business are capable of inputting all types of data, for example, sales figures in terms of volumes and values, orders, advertising costs, budgets, production costs and outputs. This data is then stored and processed to provide an output of the type of information that will be of significance to the user.

IT has substantially increased the speed of business communication, both internally and externally, and often provides better-quality information to aid in decision-making, planning and control of all business activities with its electronic technology, relative to the manual systems used in the past. However, the costs of processing and accessing the information should not outweigh the benefits derived from electronic systems.

IT systems have the following functions:

1 Inputs – information that is received into the business organization or department is placed on to computerized systems so that it may be retrieved at a later date.

2 Storage – this usually takes place on a range of computer files, for example magnetic tape or hard disks, and has the benefits of cutting down on storage space in the office and is more conveniently retrieved.

3 Processing – this is the means by which information is placed on to a computerized or electronic system, which first may involve transcribing the information manually and then inputting through a software package which is text; numerically or graphically based.

4 Output – this is the stage involving distribution of the information that has been collected, processed and stored.

5 Feedback – information exchange is only complete when feedback on the communication has been provided, if only to acknowledge that the message has been received. Electronic feedback devices such as the visual tag are used to display on the sender's computer monitor that the message has been received.

Organizations cannot function without information. It is one of the most important resources that they have, critical for decision-making, planning, monitoring and controlling all business activities.

The value of information depends on its relevance, completeness, accuracy and timeliness to the decision-making process and the ability of the organization to respond to the dynamic environment in which it operates.

Information can be communicated through technology in a number of different ways, depending on the need of the sender and recipient, convenience, time, availability and accessibility of equipment. The most commonly used channels are:

- Telephone – this is one of the fastest and most commonly used methods, with the advantage that immediate feedback can be solicited. The telephone is also used for tele-conferencing.
- Fax – which sends copied documents through telephone lines.
- Typewriters send messages through electronic coding and telephone lines to recipient teletypewriter printers.
- Word/information processors – send messages using computer memory from terminal to terminal.

- Computer networks – two or more computers are linked together for sending E-mail and other messages.
- Video technology – for video-conferencing and training/demonstrating through the use of videos.
- Audio tapes – for training and preparing notes/documents which may be used to produce hard copies at a later stage.

REVISION TIPS

You must be able to do the following:

1   Explain the term IT and its value in business communication, especially in the sales and marketing environments.
2   Briefly describe the main electronic channels used by business organizations for the transmission of information and documents.
3   Explain why an IT system should be designed to reflect the culture and structures of a business organization.

EXAM HINTS

The examiner may ask you to do any of the following:

(a)   Write an essay or report to a (designated) person on one or more of the topics covered in this unit – you would therefore be expected to have a good depth of knowledge, enough to enable you to cover the points to achieve the mark allocation.
(b)   The subject of IT and its use in business communications may be used as part of a verbal or written presentation – you must therefore be in a position to identify the appropriate format (memo, report, speech, etc.) and take into consideration the usual factors of audience/individual recipient (and his/her/their level of understanding, need, etc.), time allocation (in the case of a meeting or speech) or length in terms of a written piece, etc.
(c)   Write a piece (with or without some of the other units to consider, as stated in (b)) on the future role of IT and its use in business communications.

EXAM QUESTION

Specimen examination question 1 (4 December 1995)
You are a buyer for a large multinational organization which has recently taken over a small mail order company marketing specialist gardening equipment and materials. You have been instructed to discuss with their office manager the purchase of a new computer system which will be compatible with head office. The firm is old-fashioned and does not use information technology.

(a)   Write some preparatory notes for the meeting and set out your ideas on the problems with the current system, the requirements of the firm, the benefits of the up-to-date technology which is available and costs involved.   (10 marks)
(b)   Write a letter to arrange an initial meeting and use this communication to allay any fears you suspect the office manager may have about discussing this issue.
(10 marks)

(a) If the firm does not currently use IT, it is missing out on some important opportunities, as follows:

IT can make its employees more efficient because the speed with which data and information can be saved/stored, retrieved and used is much greater than with any traditional manual system, no matter how well it may be organized. Efficiency in the organization brings with it a number of other advantages.

Firstly, the business can respond faster to customers' enquiries and requirements (through establishing a database and monitoring this information).

Secondly, the company can 'build up' profiles on the market, customers and other variables that have an impact on other activities, such as promotion, pricing, etc.

In the long run the company will save money (less storage space needed, etc.), and this will make it a 'healthier' business.

The system which is bought must be compatible with head office for two main reasons.

Firstly, head office managers will use the data and information available on the system to make decisions.

Secondly, information and data which is put in at head office should also be retrievable by the mail order firm, benefiting it with, for example, market research data which is expensive to buy.

(b)

MNE PLC
Raffles City
Singapore

Tel: 241 555

December 4th 1996

Krishna Dogra
Office Manager
Green Gardening Equipment Suppliers Ltd
44–45 The Park
Preston
Lancashire LH6 87Y

Dear Ms Dogra,
I would like to arrange a meeting to discuss the purchase of a new computer system for your company which would be compatible with the one we operate at Head Office in Singapore.

Please rest assured that the aim of this exercise is to enable your office to benefit from all the national and international market research information held on our databases and also to help you in your general office management.

I will shortly be arriving in the UK and would like to meet you on 23 December 1995 at 2 p.m. Please confirm that both the date and time are suitable.

I look forward to meeting you.
Yours sincerely,

Candidate name
Computer Systems Buyer

'Communication technology is changing the way we do business'. Discuss this statement, indicating what these changes are and outlining their impact on business communications. (20 marks)

ANSWER GUIDELINE

Information is needed by business organizations for a variety of different reasons, but whatever the situation, for information to be of value to an organization, it must be relevant, accurate, clear and timely. IT can help business organizations to achieve efficiency and accuracy for decision-making faster than manual systems and this is particularly important for the dynamic business environments of sales and marketing.

IT is the equipment, tools and systems used to create, produce, reproduce, distribute and store business communications that are fast, efficient and convenient. IT systems enhance the channels of communication that are used in business by their ability to send and receive information quickly and conveniently, usually saving both time and money to the organization.

All systems have the following functions for handling information:

1   Input and processing – this is the process of putting data and other written or verbal communication into a system that can be accessed at a later date.
2   Storage – there are a large number of ways in which electronic information can be stored. The hard disk of a computer is capable of storing information, but is constrained by the size of its memory. Therefore, a range of suitable disks have been designed to take the storage load and to keep it on file.
3   Output – this is the stage where the information that has been processed and stored is accessed.
4   Although electronic information greatly speeds up the process of communication, it is not complete without a mechanism that allows feedback. One example is the visual tag used by those on E-mail systems. This enables the sender to check that the communication has been received.

The electronic office is a term used to describe a section of an organization that only uses electronic systems for transmitting information and storing documents.

An electronic office is capable of communicating faster, both internally and externally, than one which used traditional manual systems, based on paper. The electronic office is therefore able to provide information for decision-making quicker and more frequently, saving both time and money to the organization.

Computers are the most common electronic tool for handling information and have a range of functions that offer a large number of benefits to any organization. The main functions are described below:

1   Word processing – documents can be created, prepared and arranged in a variety of written formats to meet the needs of the recipient.
2   Data processing – (numerical) raw data is arranged into factual information and enables a number of cross-correlations, calculations and graphical presentations to take place.
3   Forecasts can be made to project changes in data if variables are changed. The most commonly used packages for this purpose are spreadsheets, which also have the advantage that they are capable of absorbing large amounts of data.
4   Models can be produced, sometimes in 3-D, to visualize a product, component or parts of it, in order to assess its feasibility.
5   Desktop publishing is a package that enables the production of documents and publications that are of a quality which cannot be achieved through manual sys-

tems in our business; it may also save time and money on some of our printing needs.

In summary, IT provides an extensive range of devices suitable for every business need, most of which are capable of being integrated to perform an even greater number of business functions.

The facsimile and cellular fax machines, electronic typewriter, computer/microcomputer and laptop, word-processor and computer printer, photocopier, audio and video tapes, videodiscs and calculator are some of the most commonly used business machines and tools.

IT has substantially increased the speed of business communication, both internally and externally, and often provides better-quality information to aid decision-making, planning and control of all business activities with its electronic technology, relative to the manual systems used in the past.

EXTENDING KNOWLEDGE

My recommendation would be for you to use the many different pieces of electronic equipment available in the various functional departments of your organization. The aim should be to carry out an evaluation of the advantages and disadvantages of using the range of electronic equipment for sending business communications in terms of their efficiency, convenience and savings made to your department or organization in time and money, relative to other channels of communication.

You should also keep up-to-date with the developments taking place in the IT industry generally and specifically in the electronic equipment designed to make business communication easier, faster and cheaper.

Guidance on syllabus and examination

Syllabus overview
Aims and objectives
- To enable students to maximize their personal effectiveness by improving personal communication skills – necessary for communication inside and outside the organization.
- To provide students with the knowledge and techniques which will assist them when working with colleagues and customers in face-to-face and telephone situations.
- To provide them with the framework for preparing reports and other written forms of communication.
- To provide students with an understanding of the elements of visual communication and with electronic channels of communication.
- To provide a range of communication opportunities to enable students to practise and develop their confidence in a safe environment.

Learning outcomes
Students will be able to:

- Communicate effectively with a range of internal and external audiences in both verbal and written format.
- Recognize alternative methods of business communication including the telephone.
- Write a persuasive business report and plan and prepare a business presentation.
- Recognize the elements of effective visual communications and use graphics, colour and design to improve a range of communication tasks.
- Organize and effectively present statistical information and data collected from a research project.
- Appreciate the importance of language and body language in interpersonal communication and use it more effectively when communicating with others.
- Plan and lead a meeting, discussion, or interview.
- Understand the role of internal marketing as an influencer and be aware of how to market themselves, their ideas and their services effectively within their own organization.
- Appreciate the role of information technology in communication, with internal and external audiences.

Indicative content and weighting
The process of communication (15%)
- How and why people communicate and the major barriers to successful communication.
- Communication routes through organizations.
- The importance of reading and listening skills.
- Non-verbal communication and role of perception, attitude, congeniality and credibility and expectation.
- The process of planning business messages, developing an audience profile, establishing the main idea and selecting the channel of communication.

Written communication (20%)

- Advantages and disadvantages of written communication – types of written communication.
- Formats for memos, letters, briefs, direct mail, reports, press releases, adverts and job descriptions.

Statistical information (10%)

- Presentation of facts, figures and findings – the use of tables, charts and diagrams.

Verbal communication (15%)

- The importance of verbal skills, questioning styles and persuasive language.
- The formal presentation – preparation and techniques.
- Effective use of the telephone.

Visual communication (10%)

- Planning, designing and producing visual aids.
- The value, impact and perception of colour, shapes and styles.
- The role of logos, letterheads and images in marketing.

Meetings, discussions and interviews (15%)

- The role of meetings and interviews.
- Different types of meeting and interviews – structure and procedures.
- Participants, terminology and necessary documentation.

Information technology for business communication (15%)

- IT and electronic office equipment systems.
- Desk-top computing, electronic networks and fax, telex and view data systems.
- IT and telephone communication.
- Documents and data processing.

Tutor's guidance notes
Notional taught hours: 45

Weighting of Learning Experience	%
(a) The process of communication	15
(b) Written communication	20
(c) Statistical information	10
(d) Verbal communication	15
(e) Visual communication	10
(f) Meetings, discussions and interviews	15
(g) Information technology for business communication	15

Method of assessment: 3 hour written examination
Number of questions: 8 (Compulsory question 1 in Part A, 40% and three from Part B
Pass mark: 50%

Preferred sequence of studies

It is strongly advised that this paper is studied at the earliest opportunity in the course by students as it endorses all the presentation styles and formats that may be specified for the presentation of responses in the other subjects.

Aims and objectives

- to enable students to maximize their personal effectiveness by improving personal communication skills necessary for communication both inside and outside the organization.
- to provide students with the knowledge and techniques which will assist them when working with colleagues and customers in face-to-face and telephone situations.
- to provide them with the framework for preparing reports and other forms of written communication and understanding the importance of both visual communication and electronic channels of communication. By the end of their studies students should be able to:

(a) Communicate effectively with a range of internal and external audiences in both verbal and written format.

(b) Recognize and use appropriately a range of written communications.

(c) Effectively use the telephone and prepare formal, personal business presentations.

(d) Recognize the elements of effective visual communications.

(e) Appreciate the importance of language and body language in interpersonal communication and use it effectively when communicating with others.

(f) Organize and effectively present statistical information and data using tables, charts and diagrams in any given situation.

(g) Plan and lead/chair a meeting, discussion or interview.

(h) Appreciate the use of information technology in organizations.

Syllabus

(a) The process of communication

    (i) Definition of business communication and the stages of the communication process: the need to communicate a message, encoding, transmission, selecting the communication channel, decoding, interpreting and feedback.

    (ii) The major barriers in successful communication, emotional reactions, making assumptions, hostile, competitive or aggressive attitudes, inappropriate group size, lack of interest, information overload, prejudice or bias, lack of credibility, lack of feedback, poor use of language and listening skills and physical distractions or 'noise' in the environment.

    (iii) The four levels of communication: intrapersonal, interpersonal, individual to group, group to individual and communication routes through organizations: vertical, horizontal and diagonal.

    (iv) Formal and informal routes and organization charts: lines of authority and chains of command.

    (v) Key factors in effective communication, precision, credibility and congeniality.

    (vi) The three types of listening, content, critical and empathetic (active) and effective listening skills: concentration, remembering, being open-minded, working hard to listen and use of non-verbal cues.

    (vii) The functions and varieties of non-verbal communication: facial expressions and eye movements, gestures and postures, voice characteristics, personal appearance, physical contact, use of time and space.

    (viii) Verbal communication: essential speech characteristics.

    (ix) Effective reading skills: minimizing distractions and evaluating and interpreting the information.

(b) Written communication

    (i) The basic steps in the process of planning business messages.

    (ii) The general and specific purposes of business messages.

    (iii) Developing an audience profile.

    (iv) Establishing the main idea of the message.

    (v) Selecting the channel or medium of communication.

    (vi) Letters, memos and briefs.

    (vii) Essential elements of good business reports, factors affecting report format, style and organization and types of reports.

    (viii) Essential elements of good press releases and advertisements.

    (ix) Preparing a job description.

(c) Statistical information

    (i) Brief notes on collecting and calculating statistics.

    (ii) The essence of tables in business communication.

    (iii) The essence of line and surface charts.

    (iv) The essence of bar charts.

    (v) The essence of pie charts.

    (vi) The essence of flow charts and organization charts.

    (vii) The essence of maps, diagrams, drawings and photographs.

(d) Verbal communication

    (i) Categorize speeches and presentations according to their purpose.

    (ii) Planning a speech or presentation.

(iii)   Persuasive and rational language.

(iv)   Visual aids useful in presentations.

(v)   Effective telephoning technique and telephone tactics.

(e)   Visual communication

(i)   Planning, designing and producing visual aids. When to use visual aids, identifying points that require visual support and maintaining a balance between illustrations and words.

(ii)   The significance of colour in visual aids.

(iii)   The art of graphic design, continuity, contrast and emphasis.

(iv)   Logos, letterheads and corporate images.

(f)   Meetings, discussions and interviews

(i)   Categorizing interviews, job, information, persuasive, evaluation, counselling, conflict resolution and disciplinary.

(ii)   Planning the interview.

(iii)   Arranging meetings determining the purpose, selecting the participants, setting the agenda and preparing the location.

(g)   Information technology for business communication

(i)   Office technology origination equipment, production equipment, reproduction equipment, distribution/transmission equipment and storage equipment.

(ii)   The electronic office, desktop computing, electronic networks, fax, telex and view data systems.

(iii)   IT and telephone communications, mobile phones and organizational telephone systems.

(iv)   Documents and data processing, batch processing, real-time data processing, online data processing, timeshared data processing, standalone data processing and the processing mix.

Senior examiner's comments

The aim of this subject is to offer students the opportunity to develop and demonstrate their ability to appreciate and apply techniques of business communication.

One of the most critical dimensions of any work role or social relationship is communication, the process by which information, ideas, attitudes and emotions are transmitted from one person to another. The extent of understanding is determined by the skill of the transmitter and receiver, subject to appropriate conditions, i.e. lack of 'noise'. Ineffective communication costs money in time, lost business, delays and wrong decisions; it also has social costs, the atmosphere at work can suffer and this can mean unproductive activity and poor motivation.

The main focus of business communication is:

(a)   to give out information.

(b)   to make your ideas understood.

(c)   to initiate some action.

(d)   to share ideas, attitudes, beliefs.

(e)   to establish links with other people.

Students are expected to use the techniques of business communication both in Section A and B of the paper and the emphasis will be on demonstrating their ability to apply the techniques as well as keeping abreast of current technological developments in the office environment. The compulsory question will reflect the breadth of the syllabus and will normally require the student to draw material from different parts of it.

The topics in the syllabus are recommended to be studied in the sequence presented and much practice in writing memos, reports, letters, etc. is strongly advised. Credit in the examination will be given for clear and professionally presented work which demonstrates the student's practical communication skills.

In the near future it is anticipated that specimen papers will be made available at selected centres for continual assessment, although an option of assessment by examination will also be provided for the foreseeable future.

This module should be used creatively and flexibly by tutors to contribute to the integration and development of other Certificate studies.

The essential reading workbook will cover all the areas that may be examined and also acts as a reference tool.

Specific comments

In successful business communication the key planning process begins with recognizing the purpose of the communication and identifying the audience to whom the communication is directed, as well as recognizing the major barriers and essential skills required for effective communication, whether written or verbal. Therefore, students will be expected to know all the definitions and terms of business communication as stated in the syllabus and to use these appropriately in both short-answer questions, two-part questions where some of them will need to be applied and in fuller 'discussion' type questions.

Written communication

The paper will test the skill of the student in discerning the correct/appropriate information and presenting this in the designated or choice of format. All business communication, written or verbal, is based on facts, both primary and secondary, and requires skill in interpreting and presenting these facts. Students should therefore expect this paper to test their knowledge of sources of data and be able to analyse, interpret, conclude and recommend from it.

The level of sophistication in the response must reflect the person to whom the communication is directed; therefore it is imperative that students practise defining the limitations of the topic in order to avoid going too far and including irrelevant material. Therefore, recognizing the purpose for the communication, audience and appropriate channel are the key elements in successful presentation of the message.

Although the choice of words is critical in evoking a precise image in the reader's mind, the students should be primarily concerned with getting ideas and concepts on paper as quickly and completely as possible and then developing the piece as time allows, in terms of the main theme, style, tone and readability.

All writing, including business letters, memos and reports, should be clear, concise and complete and reflect all the principles discussed above. However, at times the different types of business letters, reports and memos require different organization and different features, any of which may be tested, along with the advantages and disadvantages of one medium against another.

Visual communication

Whether business communication and presentation is long or short, written or verbal, visual aids will usually enhance it. When business data seems complex, visuals can make interpretation of these facts much easier. Students must therefore be able to produce and choose from graphs, charts and tables to clarify the data presented to them and must reflect the audience, purpose of communication and type of data being presented.

Logos and letterheads are important vehicles for communicating an organization's identity and image, which is also an important area of marketing. Students will therefore be required to demonstrate an appreciation of the different messages that may be communicated through logos and letterheads and be able to incorporate these into business communications.

Verbal communication

Because speaking is such a natural activity, we tend to do it without much thought, but this casual approach could be a problem in business. Students must therefore learn that speech is a tool for accomplishing objectives and therefore how to plan what to say, how to say it and to manage the impression that they are trying to create by tailoring remarks and delivery style to suit the occasion or situation. Students must be prepared to demonstrate telephone techniques, listening techniques and an appreciation of non-verbal communication such as body language.

During a business career the student will be required to make a variety of verbal presentations. These may be short, such as for introducing a speaker, or as long as one hour, such as for making a technical presentation. The size of the audience will also vary, from one to hundreds, as well as the purpose, from informative to comparative to persuasive. The student will be asked to demonstrate his/her ability in planning presentations, which includes determining the major topics and minor areas and integrating them in a logical order, reflecting time allotted, audience size and level of understanding.

Meetings, discussions and interviews

Personal communication, whether one to group (as in a meeting or conference) or one-to-one (as in an interview), is a useful medium for information exchange at all organizational levels. The key to successful meetings, discussions and interviews is to have a system and students will be expected to know the general guidelines and rules that apply in the conduct of the above and also to identify which is the most appropriate in different situations which may be presented.

Information technology for business communication

The majority of students will be aware that computers are now being used for everyday tasks such as letter writing, report preparation and the development of visual aids; new methods of receiving mail and telephone calls too have become common. It is advised that students keep abreast of developments in the 'electronic and automated office' by reading quality newspapers and, where appropriate, gaining 'hands-on' experience at work. Tutors are advised to collect articles on changes in information technology and to bring these to the attention of students.

Recommended reading
Essential reading

Business Communication 1997–98, Shashi Misiura (CIM/Butterworth-Heinemann)

Additional reading

How to Improve Your Presentation Skills, Michael Stevens (Kogan Page)
Common Sense Time Management, B. Pearson (Mercury Business Books)
Make the Most of Your Mind, T. Buzan (Pan Books)
Business Communication Today, Sue Smithson (ICSA Publication)
Communication, Nicki Stanton (Macmillan Education)
The Essence of Effective Communication, Ron Ludlow and Fergus Panton (Prentice Hall)
Personal Effectiveness, A. Murdock and C. Scutt (Butterworth-Heinemann)

Note: It is intended that increasingly colleges will be invited to undertake assessment of this element of the course internally. Emphasis should be given to the development of practical skills and competences, and opportunities for developing these skill areas in the context of other parts of the certificate course should be identified and developed.

(NB   Instructions in Rubric, renumbering of questions and rough workings shown for illustration purposes only)

Certificate in Selling

Business Communications

3 Hours Duration

This examination is in two sections.

Part A is compulsory and worth 40% of total marks.

Part B has nine questions, select three. Each answer will be worth 20% of the total marks.

DO NOT repeat the question in your answer but show clearly the number of the question attempted on the appropriate pages of the answer book.

Rough workings should be included in the answer book and ruled through after use.

The copyright of all The Chartered Institute of Marketing examination material is held by the Institute. No Case Study or Questions may be reproduced without its prior permission which must be obtained in writing.

PART A

You are working as a Marketing Assistant at Sugarfield Limited which produces a range of sugar confectionery products.

Beatrix Dubois, brand manager of 'Chewy Minto' one of Sugarfield's best selling brands has recently appointed a new sales promotion consultancy, 'Incentive and Promotion Solutions'. She asks you to collect research data on the branded mints market and last year's 'Rollo the mint with the hollow' sales promotion campaign. You have collected the following data.

Rollo is brand leader in the market and therefore a major competitor of 'Chewy Minto'. Hestler-Crabtree, owners of the Rollo brand, have had a three-pronged marketing strategy; advertising, added value promotions (10% extra) and theme promotions, to support their brand in the last year. The last theme promotion, the Moneybags Bonanza, led to a sales increase of 25% during the promotion.

Value of sales in the branded mints sector grew by nearly 70% from 1988 to 1994. Sales increased from £106M in 1988 and in each subsequent year to £117M; £128.7M; £141.57M; £156M; £175M culminating in sales of £180M in 1994.

Rollo's advertising spend for 1993 amounted to £2.7M. Spend on sugar confectionery brands, in general, tends to be low, equal to 1.7% of sales compared with almost 3% for chocolate. Extra strong mints totalled 22% of total sales in 1994, minty boiled sweets account for 27% of the market, mild pressed mints, such as, Rollo, held 30% of the market whilst the remainder of branded mint sales were soft and chewy mints, with 21% of the market. This data was found in Nielsen.

The general trend in the sector has been towards stronger tasting mints. Sugar-free mint sales have grown steadily over the past three years due to greater awareness of the links between sugar consumption and tooth decay.

To support the Moneybags Bonanza the following awareness campaign was used:

- extensive advertising on breakfast TV and in the national press
- coverage in children's comics
- press releases featuring prize winners were sent to appropriate regional newspapers

Moneybags bonanza sales promotion campaign

- instant taste and win concept
- used product rather than packaging as the prize vehicle
- 1400 winning mint prizes were spaced so they would appear nationally in several million promotional packs
- winning mints were stamped in blue with prize money amount
- 20 possible prizes of £1,000
- 30 possible prizes of £100
- 250 possible prizes of £20
- 1,100 prizes of £5
- redemption rates not revealed
- many would-be winners rang the 0800 number to claim their cash prize and 1000 were crank calls or fraudulent claims
- other fraudulent practices included marking mints in blue pen with a prize amount or finding a £100 prize mint, breaking it and attempting to claim a £1,000 prize
- duration of promotion: 10 weeks
- promotion budget: £500,000 (according to industry reports)
- making consumers want the Rollo brand more i.e. increased sales of up to 20% was the objective of the promotion
- not all prizes were claimed obviously some consumers had eaten the mint before the blue lettering could be seen
- genuine winners were identified over the phone as hidden security codes had been incorporated into the winning Rollos – packs could also be identified with a serial number

Advertising research results

Target Group	% Respondents aware of Rollo Moneybags Bonanza Promotion
children 5–16	77
adults 17–30	55
adults 31–64	23
adults 65+	53

Source: this information has been adapted but based on an article from November/December 1993 issue of Promotions and Incentives.

Question 1

Using the information which you have collated (as given above) you are required to complete the following tasks:

(a) Produce three visual aids which could be used at a presentation on the branded mints sector. Use a variety of graphical/visual communications to present some of this material. (Marks will be awarded for presentation and layout). (**15 marks**)

(b) Write an informal report for Scott Collingwood, the Chewy Minto account manager at Incentive and Promotion Solutions, on the 1993 Rollo sales promotion campaign. (**15 marks**)

(c) Reply to a memo from Beatrix Dubois which asks you about potential problems associated with prize claims in instant taste and win promotions. (**10 marks**)

PART B – Answer THREE questions only

Question 2

As manager of current accounts at a branch of the Midshire Bank Plc., you have to write a circular letter to customers informing them that a market research survey is to take place over the next few weeks. The Bank has asked an independent market research company, TMI Limited, to conduct telephone interviews with a random sample of customers. You need to persuade customers to co-operate with the market research company in giving their views but also mention that they may not be chosen to be part of the sample. You should reassure customers that their responses will be completely confidential. (**20 marks**)

Question 3

In the role of Jay Kingston, senior administrator for the oral surgery department at the Westfield District Hospital, you are responsible for customer care training for other administrative staff.

You are aware that a letter has been sent out from your department to patients confirming a date for their operation. Unfortunately there has been a mistake and there will be no surgeons available on this date.

(a) For a training session on effective use of the telephone, write down five reminders which you could put on the first slide of the presentation. **(5 marks)**

(b) Using the scenario described above, illustrate how you would deal with the problem of contacting patients by telephone to inform them of the last-minute postponement of their operation. Draft an example of the telephone conversation which might occur if both parties were efficient in the use of the telephone. Indicate how you might deal with an angry individual who feels inconvenienced by this situation. **(15 marks)**

Question 4

The recent fortnightly sales meeting you have just attended has ended in disarray. Most people appeared to have either misunderstood or lost interest in what the newly appointed, regional sales manager was trying to say. This was partly caused by his tendency to mumble whilst looking down at his copious notes. He seemed to move from one topic to another in a disjointed manner. Furthermore he presented his sales figures by reading out a long list in a monotonous voice.

The situation was exacerbated by the fact that the marketing manager who was leading the meeting, allowed it to disintegrate as people argued and chatted amongst themselves. There appeared to be no running order and several topics seemed to be discussed at length whilst other people did not have an opportunity to have their say.

(a) As the UK sales manager, advise your regional sales manager how he should deliver future presentations to his colleagues. Put your ideas in a memo so it can be used for future reference, even though you intend to talk the matter through with him in further detail. **(10 marks)**

(b) Plan the conversation you intend to have with the Marketing Manager with regard to improvements you would like to see at future meetings. Write your ideas in note form and provide him with appropriate examples of documentation you would expect to see used during and after meetings. **(10 marks)**

Question 5

(a) Using examples, where appropriate, explain the benefits of three of the following:
- computerised accounts
- computerised databases
- electronic mail
- facsimile machines
- video conferencing **(12 marks)**

(b) Discuss the implications for the security and storage of sensitive information held on computers and floppy discs. Suggest ways in which access to an organisation's computer network and software could be made more secure. **(8 marks)**

Question 6

Along with an ex-college friend, you have started up a small successful business called Labelling and Signage Designs. The firm designs logos, company letterheads and graphical symbols for the workplace, such as, 'no smoking' and 'wear helmets in restricted access area' signs which are displayed in prominent areas.

You have the opportunity to gain some favourable publicity as you have been invited to write a brief article (maximum 600 words) for a local newspaper explaining why logo, letterhead design and graphical symbols are important for companies' internal and external communications. **(20 marks)**

Question 7

Identify four ways management can communicate with

    (a)   its staff   **(4 marks)**

    (b)   its customers   **(4 marks)**

    (c)   Choose one method of interpersonal communication and explain how incorrect use of language and body language can cause distortion of the message. **(12 marks)**

Question 8

As marketing assistant at the local leisure centre you are always keen to find ways of extending the membership and increasing the number of users. Following several improvements to the facilities: new showers; extra steam rooms; and the refurbishment of the bar by the Boddway Brewery, you decide to write a press release to be sent to several local magazines and newspapers.   **(20 marks)**

Question 9

You are the sales manager of a well-known electrical retailer in the town centre. Due to maternity leave and holiday absence you need to employ additional sales assistants on a temporary basis to help with the summer sales in August.

    (a)   Design the job advertisement to be placed in the evening newspaper. Use your illustration to indicate the space the advert would take up and the size of the lettering. Include all necessary details to assist a prospective applicant's response.

                    (10 marks)

    (b)   Draft an appropriate job description which would indicate the duties involved in such a job.   **(10 marks)**

Question 10

    (a)   Using the information presented in Figure 1, explain how Castleford X is perceived by consumers in contrast to the consumers' ideal beer and discuss the characteristics of the competing brands in relation to Castleford X.   **(10 marks)**

    (b)   Use appropriate graphical/visual communication to illustrate Castleford X's sales data and market share information.   **(10 marks)**

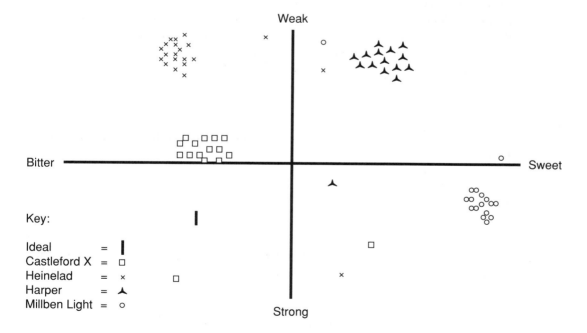

Figure 1 Scatter diagram showing research conducted into consumer preception of a range of competing lager beers.

Sales date and market share information

1993/4 market share figures were as follows: Harper 16%; Millben Light 10%; Castleford X 34%; Heinelad 27% with several other smaller brands standing at 13%.

UK sales of Castleford X have increased in recent years. Sales of cans in the take-out market reached £98M in 93/94 and the previous year stood at £91.4M. Although there was a serious low point in 1990–91 with only £65.7M cans sold, this was preceded by high sales of £80M. The problems with distribution to off licences and supermarkets reached crisis point in 1990. Although delisting by Bettabuys came as a crucial blow to the owners of the Castleford X brand, major changes in the senior management team and distribution strategy meant that sales were once more on target at £84.7M by 91/92. Since then the brewers of Castleford X have had to face stiff competition from Heinelad whose owners spent £2.5M on a particularly creative campaign last year. Castleford X's Marketing Director said: 'Despite the slow recovery in general economic terms we remain the brand leader in the carry-out lager market and trends indicate can sales of over £100M in the year ahead.'

Specimen answers   12 June 1995

Question 1(a)

The first point to note is that you are likely to receive approximately *5 marks* (the total available is 15 marks) for *each* visual (three required); therefore you should apportion the same amount of time to each one. You must also make sure that they are all clearly *labelled* and distinguishable, both from each other and in terms of the *data* that is used to produce them.

The first visual will be a column graph (figure 1), which is easy to draw (only pencil and ruler required) and effective in demonstrating the data available (see fourth paragraph in the question paper).

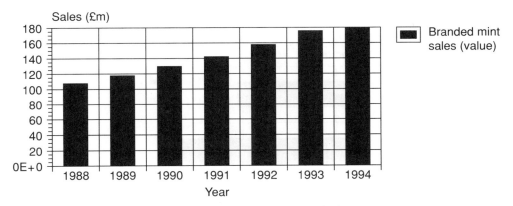

Figure 1 Sales (Value) in the branded mints sector 1988–1994.

An alternative visual (pie chart) using the same data is presented in figure 2. Notes on how to draw pie charts are given in the book (Unit 8) and will not be reproduced here.

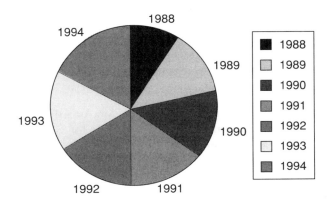

Figure 2 Sales (Value) in the branded mints sector 1988–1994.

The next set of data which can be used to draw a graphical visual aid is given in the fifth paragraph of the question paper.

The data initially relates to the market for confectionery as a whole, but from the third sentence there is information on the *total sales* (in percentage terms) of mints in the market.

The data can be translated into a number of effective visuals such as column charts, bar charts, pie charts, etc. I have firstly chosen a line chart (figure 3) and then a bar chart (figure 4) to represent this data.

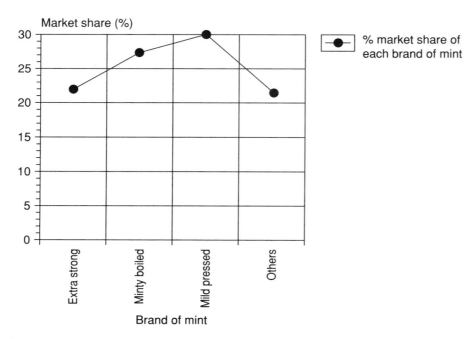

Figure 3   The branded mints sector (percentage market share) 1994.

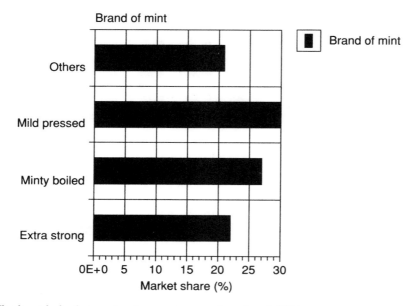

Figure 4   The branded mints sector (percentage market share) 1994.

No. 3 The third visual should use some of the other data or information presented, or a combination of both. Do remember that the question asks for visuals on the *branded mints sector*, and not on a specific brand or campaign.

The following would be an effective introductory (synopsis) visual to highlight the main aspects of this sector; it could be used both in verbal and written (report) presentations, as could the others demonstrated above.

THE BRANDED MINTS SECTOR: AN INTRODUCTION

1 SALES OF SUGAR-FREE MINTS HAVE GROWN STEADILY OVER THE PAST THREE YEARS. **WHY?** BECAUSE OF THE GREATER AWARENESS OF THE LINKS BETWEEN SUGAR CONSUMPTION AND TOOTH DECAY

2   THE GENERAL TREND IS TOWARDS STRONGER TASTING MINTS
3   ADVERTISING SPEND IN THIS SECTOR IS LOW (EQUAL ONLY TO 1.7% OF TOTAL SALES) COMPARED WITH CHOCOLATE CONFECTIONERY (3% OF TOTAL SALES)

(b)   REPORT

THE 1993 ROLLO SALES PROMOTION CAMPAIGN

by

Candidate name

12 June 1995

Introduction

The aim of this report (based on my research derived from secondary sources) is to demonstrate the significant aspects of the Rollo sales promotion campaign, 1993.

Findings

The research indicates that Rollo is clearly the *brand leader* in the market for confectionery mints, with a significant share of the mild pressed mints market that accounts for 30% of the total sales for branded mints.

Hestler-Crabtree are the owners of Rollo and firmly believe that advertising spend will generate an increase in sales. (*The total advertising spend for Rollo in 1993 was £2.7m.*)

Their commitment to the brand is demonstrated by their three-pronged marketing strategy (advertising, added-value promotions, theme promotions), which last year with the theme promotion alone generated an increase in sales of *25%* during the campaign. Indeed, the themed campaign described below in detail was backed by an extensive advertising campaign on breakfast television, the national press and coverage in children's comics, together with a PR campaign whereby press releases featuring prize winners were sent to appropriate regional newspapers.

Research was carried out on the advertising campaign and the results appear in the Appendix to this report. The most notable feature is that the target group of 5–16-year-olds achieved a *77% awareness* of the Rollo promotion.

The themed campaign

The duration of the promotional campaign entitled 'Moneybags Bonanza' was ten weeks. The objective was to increase sales of Rollo by 20%.

The firm used an advertising campaign to create and raise consumer awareness in support of the promotional campaign.

The main concept was an instant taste and win promotion whereby the 1400 winning mint prizes were stamped with the prize amount. Interestingly, the product rather than the packaging was used as the vehicle for promoting the winning prizes.

The number of possible prizes was as follows:

£1,000 available to 20 winners
£100   "   to 30   "
£20   "   to 250   "
£5   "   to 1100   "

Conclusion

In conclusion, the Rollo Moneybags Bonanza promotion by the agency to Hestler-Crabtree exceeded its target of a 20% increase in sales by 5%, a total increase of 25%.

The budget for this campaign was £500,000 and a total of £33,500 was available in cash prizes to the winning consumers.

The advertising and promotional campaign undoubtedly raised a great deal of awareness in all the target groups (by age), in particular those in the 5–16 year category (see Appendix).

Appendix

Advertising research results

Target group	% of respondents aware of the Rollo promotional campaign
15–16 years	77
17–30 years	55
31–64 years	23
65+	53

(c)   MEMO

To: Beatrix Dubois (Brand Manager)
From: Candidate name (Marketing Assistant)
Date: 12 June 1995
Re: Problems with prize claims

Although the Rollo campaign which featured a prize claim promotion was a marketing success in generating both an increase in awareness of the campaign and therefore the brand (up to 77%) and total sales (up by 25%), it nonetheless had a number of associated problems.

The main concept of the promotion was an 'instant taste and win'; however, results indicated that a number of the prizes were not claimed because some consumers had eaten the mint before a win could be identified; this is the problem of 'stamping' the mint directly, as opposed to presenting the winning prize on the packaging or through some other mechanism such as a loose leaflet inside the pack.

A number of people also called the telephone number and tried to fraudulently claim a prize. There were several ways in which this happened:

(a)   Some people marked the mint in blue themselves and attempted to claim a winning prize.
(b)   Others broke the winning mint of, for example £100, in order to claim £1,000.

In order to mitigate against fraudulent claimants, hidden security codes were incorporated onto winning packs which could then identify a winner with the appropriate serial number.

Part B, Question 2

The first point to note in relation to this question is that a *circular letter* is an ordinary (business, in this context) letter which should contain the essential elements (addresses, salutation, etc.) as shown below.

There are 20 marks available for this question which are relatively easy to achieve as long as the essential elements are in the correct place and the content of the letter contains all the information required. You should also present the information in a *logical* manner and keep the language straightforward but businesslike. The tone should be *pleasant and reassuring*, as you are asking the customers both to give up their valuable time and also for personal views.

Note: The bank is identified as 'Midshire'. Shires are unique to England, and 'mid' would mean somewhere in the middle of the country – I have chosen the West Midlands to be on the safe side. However, for other countries, if you follow these general principles the addresses should be given the appropriate credit, as you would not be expected to have an intimate knowledge of UK geography.

MIDSHIRE BANK PLC

THE MALL

MERRY HILL

W. MIDLANDS WM15 6TT

Tel: 0121 5556666

June 12th 1995

Mrs K. Dogra
56 Station Road
Dudley WM14 6ST

Dear Mrs Dogra,

Midshire Bank PLC has recently appointed an independent market research company, TMI Ltd, to conduct telephone interviews with a random sample of our customers.

The aim of this exercise is so that we can learn how to respond better and faster to our customers' needs in the future.

The research will be taking place over the next few weeks. Although you may not be called by the survey team, in the event that they do telephone you I would be very grateful for your co-operation in expressing thoughts on our banking services. Please rest assured that your views and opinions will be treated with the strictest confidence.

Yours sincerely,

Candidate name
Branch Manager

Question 3(a)

There are 5 marks available for this question, and 'five reminders' on the effective use of the telephone are asked of the candidate; it would seem that there will be 1 mark available for each point made. Therefore, keep the point *short*, leaving the bulk of the time for part (b).

1   Before using the telephone, think about the purpose of the call and (roughly) plan what you want to say. If appropriate, also think about what information is required from the recipient of the call.
2   If you need to consult other information whilst speaking on the telephone, make sure that it is close to hand and 'highlight' the essential elements so that they are quick and easy to discern.
3   If you need to take down information from the conversation, make sure that pen and paper (or forms, if appropriate) are close at hand. You need to check, by repeating back, the accuracy of the information taken from the call.
4   Use suitable language, style and tone in relation to the context of the call and the needs of the recipient.
5   Before ending the call, make sure that all business has been completed and thank the recipient for his/her time, information given, etc.

At all times keep business calls as brief and succinct as possible.

(b) The aim of this part of the question is for you to put into practice (in writing) the points made in part a) above. Therefore, use them as a checklist whilst planning the telephone call to patients.

   You must use a confident and firm tone of voice, but at the same time be responsive to disappointment and possibly anger at the news these patients are about to receive. Don't forget that the mistake was made by your department and there are wider sensitive issues such as government 'cuts' which will be present in the minds of some recipients of the call. You will therefore have to *reassure*, but maintain a professional stance.

Recipient: Hello. This is Westfield 555777.

JK: Good morning/afternoon/evening. My name is Jay Kingston and I am the senior administrator of the oral surgery department at Westfield District Hospital. Could I please speak to Mr Christakos?

Recipient: This is he. How can I be of help?

JK: I am very sorry to inform you that your operation due on 12 June at 9 a.m. has had to be postponed.

Recipient: But I received a letter confirming this date.

JK: Unfortunately the letter was sent out by mistake, as there are no surgeons available on this date.

Recipient: But this is going to greatly inconvenience me as I have had to make arrangements in order to come into hospital on that date.

JK: I sincerely apologize for all the inconvenience you have been caused, but unfortunately there is nothing that I can do until another date is identified. However, if you could give me an indication of dates that would be suitable to you then I will do my utmost to arrange the operation for that period.

Recipient: I will think about it and call you back.

JK: As soon as you call I will act on the matter and confirm the new date in writing. Thank you for being so understanding, and once again please accept my sincerest apologies.

Recipient: Goodbye.

JK: Goodbye.

Question 4(a)

There are two items required of candidates in this question, for which 10 marks are available.

Firstly, you need to present the information in *memo* format, and secondly, you need to have at least eight (ten to be on the safe side) guidelines for effective presentations; these are standard and described in the book. Once again, the tone of your memo to the Regional Sales Manager should be pleasant but firm, making sure that he/she does not feel 'singled out' in this matter.

MEMO

To: Peter Steinberg (Regional Sales Manager)
From: Suzannah Taylor (UK Sales Manager)
Date: June 12th 1995
Subject: Guidelines for making verbal presentations

Peter, from time to time it is necessary for an individual to speak to a number of colleagues in a group situation, such as a meeting.

I have therefore produced a set of guidelines which I hope that all members of the team will find helpful and which will serve as a useful checklist in the preparation for future presentations.

I would very much like us to sit down together and talk these through, and the meeting which has just taken place, at a mutually convenient time in the near future.

In the meantime, I hope that you will actively use these points, and of course do not hesitate to call me if I can be of any further help.

GUIDELINES FOR PRESENTATIONS

A.   What is the purpose of giving the presentation?

Since you are presenting a paper on a topic in your functional area of business, you should have the subject matter in hand, but you also need to address the likely reaction of the audience to the issue raised or points made during the presentation.

B. The audience. Who will they be and what will be their level of knowledge and understanding?

This is a key question, and your content, theme and style of presentation must reflect and satisfy the needs of those attending the conference and listening to your paper.

Keep the presentation informative but 'to the point', and try to make sure that the issues presented are both relevant and interesting, which will help to keep attention focused on you.

C. What is the most logical sequence for presenting this information to my audience?

A brief introduction, followed by points building a logical argument, possibly presented on a visual aid such as an overhead projector (OHP) would be a useful medium for delivering the message. A full report can then be distributed to the delegates after the presentation, if appropriate.

Avoid reading directly from notes as far as possible.

D. Prepare the visual aids (OHP transparencies) in advance, practise your voice, expression and grammar and check your clothing (appearance) for the day.

E. Finally, ensure that your presentation finishes on time and that you have managed to complete all the necessary business.

(b) Notes for running successful meetings
Meetings are face-to-face interactions which have the following advantages:

- Group discussion can take place.
- Immediate feedback can be received and further information exchanged.
- They are an opportunity for fast and efficient dissemination of information.

Meetings do not generally work well if the following factors prevail:

- The purpose of the meeting is unclear or no background information to the meeting has been provided for the participants.
- The leader/chairperson does not control the meeting effectively or is biased in some respect.
- The participants do not wish to contribute, or communicate ineffectively at the meeting.

Preparation for successful meetings involves the following:

- A clearly defined objective, i.e. there should be a clear purpose for holding the meeting.
- Identifying the main subject(s) or topic(s) and sub-topics for discussion, by having analysed the situation leading to the call for a meeting and any (superficial) observations you have made.
- Selecting the participants and a chairperson who is objective, tactful and patient. Each participant should be given the opportunity to make a contribution if he/she so wishes and if it is relevant to the proceedings.
- Setting and distributing the agenda, i.e. the prepared logical list of matters to be discussed at the meeting, which should be agreed in advance with the chairperson and secretary to the meeting. A list of the participants, time, location of meeting and order of business should be included, and the agenda should be distributed several days in advance.
- Ensuring an outcome, i.e. some action should have arisen as the result of the meeting which can be effected in time.

Finally, standard documentation used in conjunction with meetings comprises of the following:

- A notice prior to the meeting taking place.
- An agenda, with a note of 'apologies for absence' and 'matters arising' from the previous meeting that should be discussed before the formal business of the meeting begins.
- Minutes of previous meetings which have to be agreed.
- Notes recorded, which will be translated into minutes to be agreed at the next meeting.

Example of an agenda

A meeting of the sales team will take place in the Executive Suite of the Royal Selangor Hotel, Kuala Lumpur at 10.00 a.m. on 12 June 1995.

Agenda

1. Apologies for absence
2. Minutes of the last meeting
3. Matters arising
4. Report from the North-West Regional Sales Manager (Carey Bamford)
5. UK sales promotions 1996–97
6. Any other business
7. Date of next meeting

minutes of the Sales Meeting held on 15 April 1995

Present: L. Atkinson, L. Cooper, H. May, S. Marie, A. Smith, K. Butt, M. Lewis, N. Archdale

1. Apologies for absence were received from A. Bullock.
2. Minutes of the last meeting were signed as a true record.
3. The report from the South-West Regional Sales Manager indicated that the product line X had exceeded its sales target, but other product lines, in particular line Z (65% down), were below target.
4. There were a number of issues that could have caused the decline, but the main one was lack of retail promotion which would have helped to push the products. Product line Z exceeded targets because of the recent retailer incentive which was helping sales.
5. No other business was discussed.
6. Date of next meeting agreed as 12 June 1995 in the Executive Suite of the Royal Selangor Hotel, Kuala Lumpur.

Question 5(a)

There are 12 marks available for the first part of this question, and as you are asked to address three of the five parts it is safe to assume that approximately 4 marks will be given to each. You should therefore attempt to write the same amount for each one. I have written responses to all of them.

Computerized accounts

The main benefits of computerized accounts are as follows:

- They enable speedy calculation and preparation of financial statements through spreadsheet packages.
- Data is accessible quickly and easily by those who need it for information and decision-making.
- Data input does not have to take place in one location or by a particular member of staff, other than a person with basic keyboarding skills.
- Storage of large amounts of data on computer disk makes it an efficient and cost-effective process, relative to manual systems.

Computerized databases

Some of the earlier points could be used together with the following:

- A large number of people can both input and access data through their terminals, and use it immediately.
- Data can be manipulated in a number of different ways and for a variety of purposes through the computer system and associated software packages.
- Computerized databases allow decision-makers to note at a glance whether sufficient information can be derived from the data available.

Electronic mail

There is no doubt that electronic mail has revolutionized business communications.

The main advantages are as follows:

- Personnel can communicate short or long messages from their office or keyboard (with modem) to anywhere in the world.
- Messages are transmitted immediately, therefore no reliance on the relatively slow postal systems.
- The cost is absolutely minimal, again relative to using the postal system, not to mention the preparation involved with letters and other documentation to make them suitable for posting.
- A signal is sent to the recipient on his/her screen to indicate that a message has arrived. Messages can also be stored easily and efficiently for future reference.

Facsimile machines

The fax machine, as it is often called, has also made a major contribution to business communications. In particular:

- It is capable of sending letters and other documents via a telephone line to be received anywhere in the world (assuming that the recipient has a fax too).
- It is a relatively cheap and efficient method of sending information.
- One of the further benefits is that security can be maintained in sending the document, though this cannot be controlled at the other end. However, it is generally agreed that sending information by fax is safer than by post, etc.
- The fax machine itself has come down in price substantially since it was launched, making it a good-value piece of equipment for the office or home business user.

Video conferencing

Video conferencing as a means of business communication has taken time to become established. One of the reasons is the different time zones in which employees operate around the world, as this means of communication really comes into its own when people do not have to be in the same room in order to have a face-to-face interaction.

The main advantages are as follows:

- Face-to-face interactions such as meetings can take place without participants having to travel to be in the same place as each other.
- This makes it a cost-effective means of communication.
- In face-to-face interactions, participants can not only talk to each other but also observe behaviour (such as body language) which can be important in assessing the nature of the message.
- A record of the meeting can take place which can be used for future reference.

(b) Only 8 marks for this question, so expect to write approximately two-thirds of the amount, compared with part a) above. There is also only a limited amount you can say on this topic.

Security and storage of sensitive information on computers and floppy disks need not be problematic for business organizations if some basic rules are observed.

Firstly, only the person who is required to use the sensitive information should be given access. The access can be controlled through the use of passwords, codes, etc., on the computer which will allow only the authorized user to retrieve the data.

Secondly, floppy disks should be stored in a safe place, preferably under lock and key or equivalent, with only the authorized user(s) having access to the mechanism which releases them.

Thirdly, all sensitive data should be copied in case it is sabotaged or removed, and the disks kept in a secure place.

Fourthly, staff using the area in which sensitive data is kept could be given a uniform, specific item of clothing (such as a laboratory coat) or badge which identifies them as authorized personnel where sensitive data is kept, and in particular if its frequent storage is problematic.

Question 6

All the rules for writing press releases and preparing messages should be observed in this question.

The first issue is that of a suitable *title* for the article. If you do not present one, then it will be created by the editor or his/her staff.

Identify your company and a suitable slogan which follows the AIDA principle.

Secondly, make the statements that you think will be of most interest to the readers. (You could potentially write a thesis on this topic!) The newspaper is a local one, which means that it will have a mixed audience, both passive but interested readers and also local businesses – try to appeal to both groups.

Finally, make sure that you give your company a 'plug' at the end, and it would also be useful to include a contact name and telephone number.

Keep to the word limit, otherwise the article is very likely to be 'chopped down' by the editor and you will lose control over the content and context in which it is written.

Labelling and Signage Designs Producing Designs for the Times

All companies have to engage in both internal and external communications for a variety of reasons.

Labelling and Signage Designs have built up a reputation as specialists in the design of logos, letterheads and other graphical symbols for local companies.

All of these help business organizations in a number of ways:

- Identifying staff through nameplates on office doors, badges and even T-shirts and other merchandise which are particularly useful on special occasions.
- Signs can pinpoint exit areas (crucial safety), which departments or personnel are located in which areas of the building (for example, on different floors).
- A large sign on the outside of a building signals to customers and others where the building is located. The sign should be in suitable lettering style, colour, be of an appropriate size and incorporate the logo if possible and suitable.
- Logos are usually made up of symbols that conjure up an image of the organization or the nature of an issue. For example, the Coca-Cola sign is recognized throughout the world even if it is in a foreign language – the style of lettering and combination of red and white colours is unique and consistent.

Many organizations use symbols without any letters or words attached; for example in the UK (and internationally where the company is known) most people would associate the 'spread eagle' with Barclays Bank PLC or the 'black horse' with Lloyds Bank PLC.

The use of symbols and logos and slogans in general is aimed at creating a corporate identity for the business organization which is unique; this process of differentiation is designed to distinguish the firm from its competitors and for the other reasons described above.

Logos should therefore be easy to associate with the organization, interesting and eye-catching.

Logos can be used on letterheads too, and definitely 'add value' to the letterhead style, as well as on all other forms of communication, both internal and external.

If Labelling and Signage Designs can help your business to reflect its value to all with whom it associates and the public at large, please call 0171–445 2233 and ask for Harry Brown or Jane Slipazchek.

Question 7

There are 4 marks available for parts a) and b), and with four methods requested we can safely conclude that 1 mark will be given for each correct response.

Four ways in which management can communicate with:

(a) Its staff:

1   Internal newsletter, either frequent or periodical.
2   Staff noticeboard, on which a number of items of information can appear, both professional and personal/leisure.
3   Video – this method has proved particularly useful in organizations where the staff are largely 'absent' from desk duty, such as airline staff (cabin crew).
4   Meetings and briefings, either in large or small groups, for general or specific issue.

(b) Its customers:

1   Advertising has to be one of the most commonly used methods, particularly in fmcg (fast moving consumer goods) markets.
2   Demonstrations, either personal or at exhibitions, etc.
3   Business letter, to inform about promotions, new products or other developments, etc.
4   Telephone, fax, E-mail, Internet, etc.

(c) I would suggest that you begin with a general 'essay' on interpersonal communication and then introduce an example/context in which this takes place. The example should be a business one and, as far as possible, related to marketing or selling, as this is the Certificate which you are pursuing. However, the communication process has to take place for a variety of reasons (interviews, selection, meetings, etc.) and these are common to *all* business organizations.

Interpersonal communication takes place between two or more individuals for a variety of reasons. The key to successful interpersonal communication is good use of language and body language, together with voice skills, organization and planning.

Messages are designed to give information, but it may also be necessary to receive information in an interpersonal conversation or meeting. Therefore, it is critical that the sender has a clear objective for his/her communication, uses the most suitable language for his/her needs and that of the receiver, and conducts him/herself through use of body language in such a way that this will enhance the communication process and effective delivery of the message.

In interpersonal communication it is all too easy to use gestures, postures and other body signals that can confuse the reciever of the message. The potential for this is greatest when the parties are unfamiliar with each other, there are different cultures at play (for example, people are not using their 'mother tongue' or are in an unfamiliar environment) or when the nature of the message is sensitive.

One method of interpersonal communication is a meeting between an account manager of an advertising agency and his/her client. The culture of an advertising agency is vastly different from that which prevails in most other organizations, even though all are 'professional' and businesslike in their own way.

Advertising through the media is a very expensive business, and it is therefore critically important that the brief is expressed by the client in a clear manner, both verbally and through the use of appropriate body language.

The account manager should explain all media terminology that is used unless he/she is certain that the client is familiar with this type of language.

Finally in this context, the use of storyboards, video or radio sketches will all enhance the interpersonal communication process.

Question 8

You msut follow the general principles for writing press releases and then use your own creativity in presenting the information given.

The tone used in presenting the press release should be firm and factual (avoid 'puffery' at all times). The correct format should also be used, i.e. double line spacing and wide margins.

Do not forget to give a contact name and number, either at the end or the beginning of the release.

Press Release

12 June 1995

THE BODDWAY LEISURE CENTRE
IS NOW OPEN FOR YOU

The Boddway Leisure Centre, which has served Boddway for 25 years, has recently undertaken a massive refurbishment to make our facilities better for you.

The new improvements are:

- New showers for ladies and gentlemen
- Extra steam rooms for ladies and gentlemen
- The bar has been completely refurbished by Boddway Brewery and is now open throughout the day for drinks, snacks, bar meals and coffee.

As a special opening offer, we are giving a free three-week trial pass to all new members taking a one-year subscription. If you do not like what you see, we will refund the subscription.

Call into the Boddway Leisure Centre or telephone the marketing assistant (Candidate name) on 0121 342 7896

Question 9(a)

The first part of the question (equal marks of 10 given to both parts) requires you to design and present a job *advertisement*.

The space of the advert can be stated in writing or *indicated* through your illustration; it might, however, be helpful to the examiner if you did both.

The size of lettering is important, not just to show an effective and suitable communication through the press for the retailer, but it also has implications for cost.

SDB Ltd
High Street
Chiswick

Temporary Sales Assistants

Sales assistants are required for August only to help in our busy high street shop with SDB's summer sale.

Sales experience in any retail outlet would be an advantage, particularly with electrical goods. However, training can be given.

For further details, please call into SDB, telephone 0171 749 2788 or write to The Sales Manager, SDB Ltd, 44–46 High Street, Chiswick, London

(b) SDB Ltd

Job title: Temporary Sales Assistant

Location: SDB Ltd, High Street, Chiswick

Responsible to: Sales Manager

Duties: Serving customers in the shop and taking telephone enquiries.
Demonstrating the electrical products and accessories.
Cleaning the stock in the morning and at times throughout the day.
Stocking the shelves with items as required from the storeroom.
Assistance with displays in the shop window.
Any other duties as may be deemed necessary from time to time.

Qualifications and experience: No formal qualifications are required, but good command of English (or that of your own mother tongue), accuracy and good general ability in Maths and a willingness to be of help to our customers, both in the shop and on the telephone, are important.

Remuneration: The hourly rate will be £4.50 and approximately 5 hours per day will be available on weekdays, 7 on Saturdays. The number of hours and days is negotiable.

You will get a paid hour for lunch and have use of the tea/coffee-making facilities in the shop.

Other requirements: Staff are expected to dress smartly and will be given a name badge.

Question 10(a)
There is no model format that can be applied to the presentation of the answer to part (a). Candidates should therefore use a good essay style, making sure that all relevant points are covered.

The consumer perception of Castleford X compared with consumers' ideal beer and competing brands

Customer perception
Castleford X is perceived by consumers of beer to have a bitter but neither particularly weak nor strong flavour, relative to the other brands. However, in terms of the ideal taste, it is slightly weaker but with the right amount of bitter taste.

Competition for Castleford X
The 1993/4 market share figures reveal that Castleford X has a leading (34%) share of the market, it is followed in second place by Heinelad (27%), Harper (16%), collective smaller brands (13%) and Millben Light (10%).

In the period 1991–2 sales of Castleford X reached £84.7m and the trend continues upwards, despite the temporary setback caused by Bettabuys decision to delist the brand, major changes in the senior management team and distribution strategy.

Castleford X is the brand leader in the carry-out lager maket, and 'trends indicate can sales of over £100m in the year ahead' (Castleford X Marketing Director).

(b) In part (b) there are a number of visuals that can be used to depict the sales data (second paragraph) and market share information (first paragraph). Visuals which make the data easy to discern and are interesting should be used in preference to those that are quick to draw.

The first visual graph (figure 1) is a line chart which represents the market share figures for Castleford X and its competitors.

The second visual (figure 2) is a bar chart which demonstrates the UK sales of Castleford X from 1989 to 1995 inclusive.

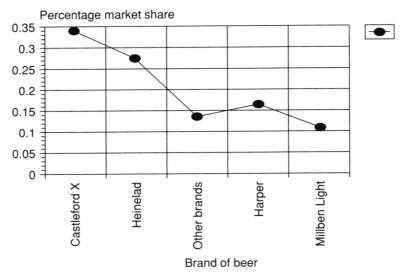

Figure 1 Market share figures for Castleford X and competitive brands of beer.

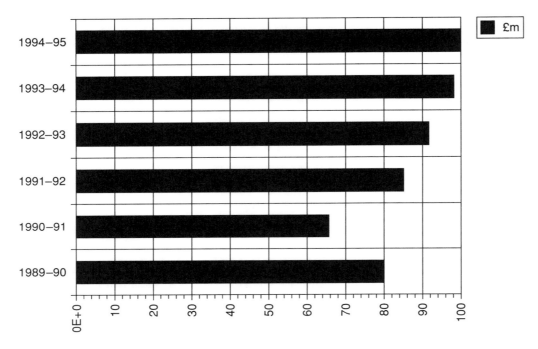

Figure 2 UK sales of Castleford X 1989–95.

(NB   Instructions in Rubric, renumbering of questions and rough workings shown for illustration purposes only)

Certificate in Selling

Business Communications

3 Hours Duration

This examination is in two sections.

Part A is compulsory and worth 40% of total marks.

Part B has nine questions, select three. Each answer will be worth 20% of the total marks.

DO NOT repeat the question in your answer but show clearly the number of the question attempted on the appropriate pages of the answer book.

Rough workings should be included in the answer book and ruled through after use.

PART A

You work at the Target Data Market Research Consultancy. Your line manager, Jessica Freil, is keen that you get involved in all aspects of the work that is carried out at the firm. The local college, located on the edge of town, is one of the firm's new clients. Jessica asks you to analyse some of the research data about the college.

The research has been commissioned to investigate the attitudes and perceptions held by three distinct stakeholder groups. These comprise: the general public; school pupils and local employers. The research is being carried out over a two month period and the following information only forms part of the data.

Consider the research data below.

College Research Data

Survey Of Local Residents

Figure 1 – Attitudes to attending college.

Respondents were asked to indicate their strength of agreement or disagreement with a range of statements about attending the college.

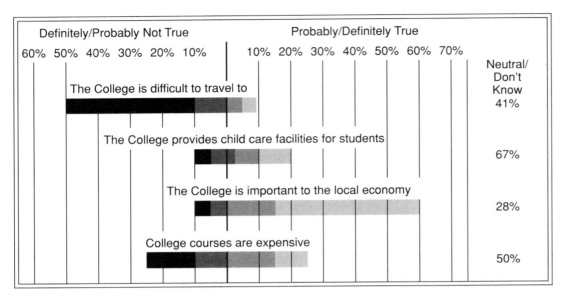

Def. not true
Prob. not true
Prob. true
Def. true

Figure 2 – Strengths and weaknesses of the college.

Respondents were asked to indicate their strength of agreement or disagreement with other aspects of the college.

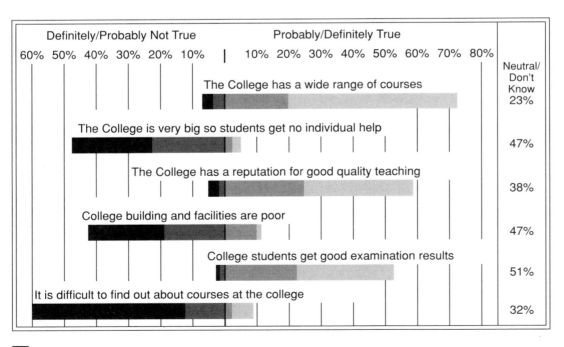

Def. not true
Prob. not true
Prob. true
Def. true

Survey Of Pupils At School

Figure 3 – Attractions of attending college. Pupils were asked to identify which aspects of attending college they considered to be important. Figure 3 ranks the attractions in terms of the proportion of pupils selecting each attraction.

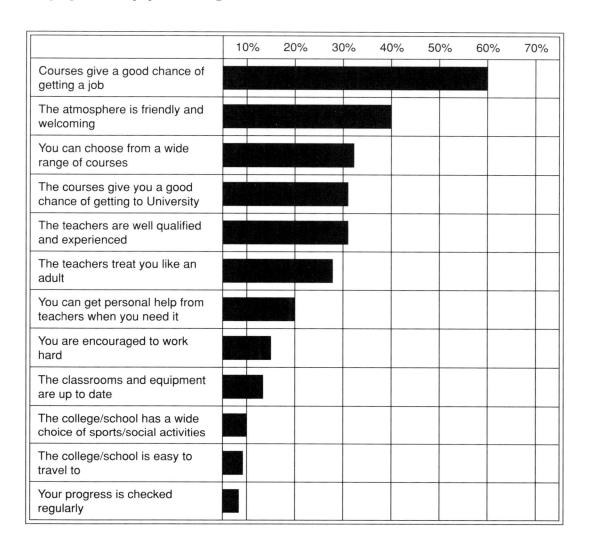

Survey Of Local Employers

Figure 4 – Quality of college communications with local firms/employers.

Local employers were asked to comment on the statement 'It is easy to obtain information and guidance about standard courses and customised packages of training.'

= Not true

= True

Question 1

(a) Produce a report in a suitable format which will provide an overview of the attitudes and perceptions held by the three target audiences of the college's market.

(20 marks)

(b) Provide a notice and agenda for the forthcoming meeting with the college's marketing manager which has been organised to discuss these initial findings and to provide a focus for the next stage of the research. **(10 marks)**

(c) A postal questionnaire with the offer of free entry to a prize draw is to be sent to residents living inside a five mile radius of the college. The questionnaire has already been designed. Write the explanatory letter and design a response mechanism which will enable residents to put their names and addresses into the prize draw. A freepost envelope will be provided. **(10 marks)**

(40 marks total)

PART B – Answer THREE questions only

Question 2

(a) Draw a diagram to represent the communications process and illustrate where 'noise' can occur. **(4 marks)**

(b) Explain how each of the following can create a barrier to communication and use an example for each to indicate how the impact of noise could be reduced.
   i)   lack of credibility
   ii) perceptual bias
   iii) information overload
   iv) contradictory non-verbal signals **(4 marks each)**

(20 marks total)

Question 3

As the Sales & Marketing Manager at Greenland Foods, you have decided to use the next staff meeting to discuss a number of issues which will involve and affect staff.

These include the following matters: the stages in the product development process connected with the planned launch of a new vegetarian product; the sales figures of three different recipes of frozen pizza; the current holiday requests, which if granted, would mean a lack of staff cover during August; and the performance of individual sales staff over the last six months.

Choose one of each of the following presentation formats to communicate each of the issues mentioned above. Make relevant assumptions to enable you to draw the relevant visual communication in each case.

   i)   gantt chart
   ii) line graph
   iii) multiple bar chart
   iv) flow chart **(5 marks each)**

(20 marks total)

Question 4

Write a brief informal report for your line manager about the development of office telecommunications facilities which could be introduced to improve the efficiency and effectiveness of internal and/or external communication within your organisation.

(20 marks)

Question 5

You work in the Marketing Communications Department of Visibility, a specialist signage and point of sale company. You are covering for your line manager and he has asked you to write an advertorial to be used in the local newspaper. The copy should publicise and explain how logos, letterhead design, point of sale and graphical symbols can help organisations communicate with both their internal and external markets. You have been given a maximum of 500 words. **(20 marks)**

Question 6

(a) You are self employed and run your own marketing consultancy. You have recently completed some consultancy work for a large firm. You were hopeful that this was the beginning of a fruitful business relationship from which you would get repeat business. However, it has been 6 months since you completed the job and you have not yet been paid, in spite of a number of telephone calls which you have made to the accounts department.

Write an appropriate letter to the accounts department of your client.

(10 marks)

(b) With the introduction of individual work stations in your office you have become concerned about the inconsistency in the appearance and tone of business letters. In particular, the work of a number of junior staff features poor layout and presentation. Write a memo to staff which will highlight good practice. **(10 marks)**

(20 marks total)

Question 7

You have received a letter inviting you for interview as a press and public relations/communications officer for a pressure group concerned with conservation issues. With the letter inviting you for interview, you are asked to prepare a presentation highlighting what activities are necessary to fulfil the role successfully. The presentation is to last no more than 10 minutes.

i)   Prepare three slides for the presentation, in draft form, which show the main points of your presentation. A colleague has offered to help produce the slides. Provide clear instructions for their production. **(12 marks)**

ii) How will you ensure that your presentation delivery is effective? **(8 marks)**

(20 marks total)

Specimen answers   2 December 1996

Answer – Question 1

a.

College Survey Report

Prepared for:	**Jessica Freil, Research Manager**
Prepared by:	**Any Candidate, Research Assistant**
Date:	**2nd December 1996**

1.0 Terms Of Reference

This report provides an overview of the attitudes and perceptions held by Anytown College's target audiences. This interim report is based on the initial data which has been collated.

2.0 Procedure

The data was gathered over a two month period. Three distinct stakeholder groups: local residents; school pupils and local employers, were questioned as part of the survey.

3.0 Findings

3.1 Local residents' attitudes to attending college

This group were asked whether they agreed or disagreed with a range of statements about the college.

A majority of those questioned (62%) thought the college was important to the local economy.

There were different views on the question of whether the college is difficult to travel to. 50% disagreed with the statement, 9% agreed but 41% did not know.

Views were mixed regarding the cost of courses, 25% agreed they are expensive, 25% disagreed and 50% were not sure.

20% agreed with the statement that the college provides child care facilities, whilst a minority of 10% did not and a further 67% did not know.

3.2 Local residents' strength of agreement or disagreement with statements about other aspects of the college

71% of those asked agreed, with the statement 'the college has a wide range of courses', with over 50% of those strongly agreeing with that statement.

48% strongly disagreed with the statement that the college is very big so students get no individual help, although 47% did not know whether this was a true statement or not.

58% thought the statement 'the college has a reputation for good quality teaching' to be true, with over half of those strongly agreeing with that statement. 38% of respondents did not know how true or not this statement was.

Over 40% considered the statement 'the college buildings and facilities are poor' was untrue, just over 10% thought it was true and 47% were not sure.

47% agreed with the statement 'college students get good exam results, 2% did not agree and 51% were not sure.

60% thought the statement 'it is difficult to find out about courses at the college' was untrue, 81% thought it was true and 32% did not know.

3.3 Pupils perceptions of the attractions of attending college

Pupils considered that the most important aspect of attending college was that courses gave a good chance of getting a job. Of secondary importance was the friendly atmosphere. 32% cited the wide range of courses, teachers' experience/qualifications and the chances of getting to University as important reasons for going to a college.

Less important but still chosen by 27% of pupils, was the fact that teachers treat students like adults and 20% thought it important that personal help is available when necessary. The following reasons were considered least important: that students are encouraged to work hard; that classrooms are up to date; that there is a wide choice of sports/social activities; that progress is checked regularly and that college is easy to travel to.

3.4 Local Employers

Employers were split in their view about the ease with which information and guidance about courses and training is obtained, with half considering it easy to obtain information and the other half considering it difficult.

Conclusions And Recommendations

Local residents generally have a favourable impression of the college in terms of its importance to the local economy and ease of travel to the college but views were mixed on the cost of college courses.

Importantly, many people were unaware of the following: the costs of college courses; how easy it is to travel to the college and whether child care facilities are provided.

A large majority had a positive view of the college in terms of the range of courses, the help given, the exam results, the teaching reputation and the quality of buildings and facilities. However, significant numbers (51%) were not aware if students obtained good exam results, 47% were unaware of the quality of buildings/facilities or if the size of college affected the amount of individual help students received.

It seems that the college's marketing and promotion needs to address these issues and raise awareness among the local residents.

School pupils thought the college attractive in terms of job success, the atmosphere and the wide range of courses. These aspects can be emphasised when marketing the college to school pupils.

However, communications need to be improved so that employers can easily obtain information about standard courses and customised training.

b.

NOTICE
Anytown College Marketing Research Project Meeting

Meeting to be held on 2nd December 1996 at 2.30 pm in the Target Data conference room.

Agenda

1. Apologies for absence.
2. Minutes of the last meeting.
3. Matters arising from the minutes.
4. Local residents survey.
5. School pupils survey.
6. Local employers' survey.
7. Promotion research and effectiveness of advertising.
8. Any other business.
9. Date of next meeting.

c.

Anytown College
Anytown Road
Anytown
Any Country

2nd December 1996

Dear Local Resident

I am interested in your opinion about our college and would like to hear your views about a number of issues. In this way I can find out how we can improve our service to the local community and firms in the area.

At the same time I would like to offer you the opportunity to take part in a prize draw. The first prize is a Sony Laptop computer.

I would be very grateful if you would take just a few minutes to complete the attached questionnaire.

To enter our prize draw please complete your details on the tear-off slip below and send it along with your completed questionnaire in the freepost envelope provided.

Yours faithfully

Richard Hopeless
College Principal

- -

Name: _____

Address: _____

_____

_____

I would like you to send me further details of college courses: Yes ❏   No ❏

I am interested in the following subjects _____

_____

Answer – Question 2

a.

The Communications Process

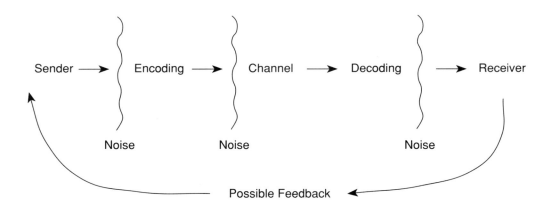

b.

(i)   Lack of credibility can be a barrier to communication if, for example, a young inex-
perienced salesperson, lacking in product/market knowledge tries to sell a high value,
specialist, technical product. This barrier to communication could only be overcome
if the salesperson had thorough training in both sales technique and the product/
market.

     The noise could be reduced somewhat if the salesperson had a professional appear-
ance in terms of dress and used a professional demonstration kit to illustrate the
product to potential customers. It would also be useful if the salesperson worked for
a well known company and had testimonials from previous satisfied clients to show
potential customers. In this way customers would concentrate less on the weakness
of the salesperson and focus more on the credibility of the manufacturer and the
product.

(ii)   Perceptual bias can mean people hearing what they want to hear. By filling in the
gaps and making assumptions a significant barrier to the real message can be created.
If a manager addressed a departmental meeting about job losses, then it could be that
some staff would 'tune out' to information relating to investment in new equipment
and they may only hear the negative aspects of what was being said or assume that the
manager was not being open with them.

     The noise could only be effectively reduced if he spoke openly about the rumours
and denied them. He would need to allay their fears and invite his audience to ask
questions at the end, to clarify any points or issues.

(iii) Information overload is a barrier to communication as too much information means
people do not absorb the message that is being conveyed. An example of this could

be a talk given to the local CIM branch on the effectiveness of a new advertising campaign. If the speaker gave the audience too many facts and figures, the overall message might be lost in the detailed information and the audience might become bored and stop listening.

To reduce the impact of the noise, the speaker could reduce the amount of material and emphasise the main points by using visual aids, illustration and interesting examples. The in-depth detail could be provided in the form of background notes for those who wanted to read this information in their own time.

(iv)   Contradictory non-verbal signals might be conveyed by a person whose words say one thing but their body language says something else. An example of this could be when a customer is complaining about the service in a bank. The cashier could be enquiring about the problem but avoiding eye contact with the customer, looking at other papers and perhaps sounding uninterested in the customer's problem by speaking with a monotone voice.

To reduce the noise, the cashier would need to support the words being used by using a sympathetic tone, eye contact, and positive body language such as nodding, to show that the customer's problem was understood.

Answer – Question 3
(i)   Gantt Chart indicating lack of staff cover

Holiday Requests For Sales & Marketing Dept

August

	1	2	3	4	5	6	7	8	9	10	11	12	13	14
Paul	X		X	X	X			X		X				
Grace				X	X				X	X	X			
Natasha									X		X			
Suresh	X	X	X	X	X			X	X	X	X	X		
Phil	X	X	X	X	X			X	X	X	X	X		
Pilar	X	X			X									

X = annual leave booked

(ii)   Line Graph showing frozen pizza sales

Frozen Pizza Sales (93–96)

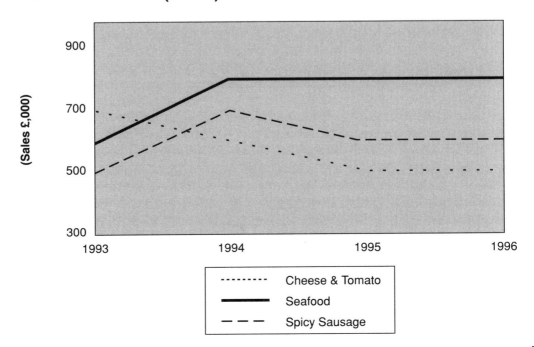

(iii)   Multiple Bar Chart showing staff performance

Monthly Sales (£,000) Performance Of Staff (2nd Half 1996)

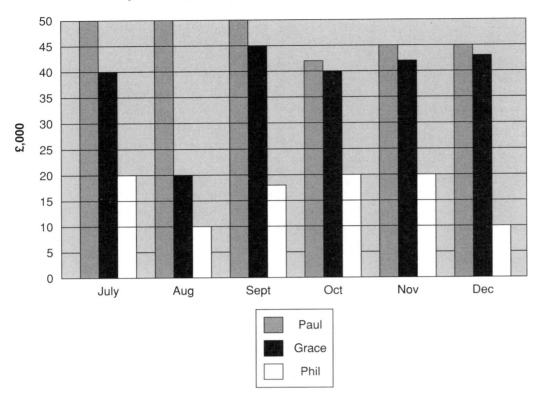

(iv)   Flow Chart to show product development process of new vegetarian food

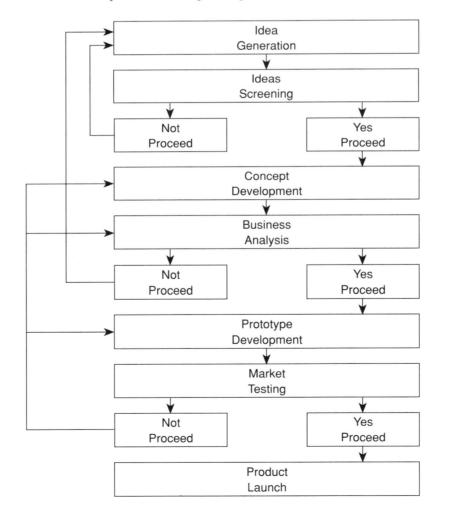

Answer – Question 4

Report On Office Telecommunications Facilities

To: Mark Scrivens
From   Jo Goodwin
Date: 2nd December 1996

Introduction
Various office equipment that is available now could be used by our company to improve the efficiency and effectiveness of our internal and external communication.

Findings
Fax Machine
This would mean we could receive written orders, designs and other text and visual messages very quickly without having to rely on the postal system. We could also receive information out of office hours which would help our overseas clients where there is a time difference. Equally we could send this information very quickly for the price of a telephone call and at the same time have a record of information that has been sent. This is not possible with a telephone call.

Voice Mail
During busy periods customers often have problems getting through to the switchboard with our current telephone system. With a voice mail system connected to a computer, customers could use an interactive menu system which would mean they could ring up and choose to be connected to any one of a number of departments without having to go through the switchboard. Customers could also leave messages when a person is not at their desk which saves colleagues spending time taking messages.

Networked Laptop Computers
Laptop computers could be used by managers out on business to input data after they have visited a customer. Laptop computers can also be used via the telephone network which enables staff to be connected to our various district offices, which would enable managers to have up to date sales and stock data at their fingertips.

Conclusion
I recommend that all three telecommunication facilities be introduced into the company to improve both our internal and external communications.

Answer – Question 5

The Importance Of *Visibility*

What impression do you have of an organisation when you see scruffy, hand-written signs which say 'wet paint' or 'toilets'? It indicates that someone has done something in a rush or that it is a temporary situation.

If you want to communicate with your staff or customers about anything other than a very temporary situation, then it is necessary to communicate in a professional and consistent manner. It is also important that the information stands out in an environment already crowded with signs, symbols and other 'noise'.

A local firm, Visibility, specialises in creating signs and point of sale material for inside shops, office premises and other public areas.

Many companies find that they have to promote themselves on a number of different levels, through advertising, leaflets, brochures, exhibitions, and can even take the opportunity to do this through their letters, company vans and the exterior of their buildings.

They need to use a distinctive corporate identity incorporated in their logo and letter heading to communicate their line of work and to differentiate them from other competitors.

The designers at Visibility use a combination of graphical symbols, visual communication, typefaces and colour to give an appropriate image to a company and/or its products or services.

When a corporate image is established it can give customers the reassurance of dealing with something known and familiar. It provides credibility and means an organisation has at least one less communication barrier to deal with.

Visibility also manufacture point of sale material which is used by shops and their suppliers. These items, such as, hanging signs, perspex dispensers, posters and shelf signs are essential promotion tools for companies that need to make their goods stand out in retail outlets.

Even companies that do not deal directly with customers in their office premises may need signs which communicate information to staff, such as, arrows, door signs or instructions, for example: No Smoking.

An organisation which wants to create a positive image in its dealings with employees and customers, will need to use professional signs which use colour and illustration to communicate a message effectively.

If your business could benefit from effective graphic design services for corporate literature, signs or point of sale material, then call Vivien Sobers on 01625 356789.

Answer – Question 6

a.

Fix-it Marketing Consultancy
63 The Park
Parklands
Parkville
PO5 6FG

Mr Smith
Accounts Dept
Moat House Forte Hotels
Mottershead
Basingstoke
BS7 2ER

2nd December 1996

Dear Mr Smith

Purchase order no: FI/57890

As you are aware I successfully completed a customer research project for Moat House Forte Hotels in July of this year.

Since then I have invoiced your company in August and again in September. The invoice amounted to £3,500. Since the invoice was still not paid I have telephoned your department on five separate occasions. Each time I was advised that the invoice had been received and the matter was being dealt with.

I must now insist that this matter be dealt with immediately and therefore attach another copy of the invoice.

If this matter is not settled within 28 days of receipt of this letter I will have to put the matter in the hands of a solicitor.

Yours sincerely

Andy Mann
Marketing Consultant

b.

MEMORANDUM

To: **Admin & Sales Staff**
From: **Any Candidate, Office Manager**
Subject: **Office Correspondence**
Date: **2nd December 1996**

Since the introduction of work stations in the office, staff are able to produce and send routine letters and documents to clients without secretarial help.

This saves time and is an efficient way of working. However, I am concerned about the inconsistency in the tone and the layout being adopted.

In particular, I would like to remind staff that they should use a professional tone which is not too informal.

Please use our company headed paper for letters and include the recipient's name and address on the top left hand side, with the date below this and the appropriate reference below that, before starting the salutation and the main body of the letter.

Please start letters with the standard salutation, 'Dear' and the name, if known, and at the end use the complimentary close, 'Yours sincerely'. If you do not know the name of the recipient then please start the letter, 'Dear Sir or Madam' and end the letter with 'Yours faithfully'.

Please include your designation (underlined) below your name at the end of the letter.

Our company house style is to send letters typed in 12 pt typesize using the Times New Roman font. Standard payment reminder letters, appointment letters and others are available for you to see in the file marked 'standard letters' on my bookshelf.

Thank you for your co-operation in this matter.

Answer – Question 7

a.

Slide 1

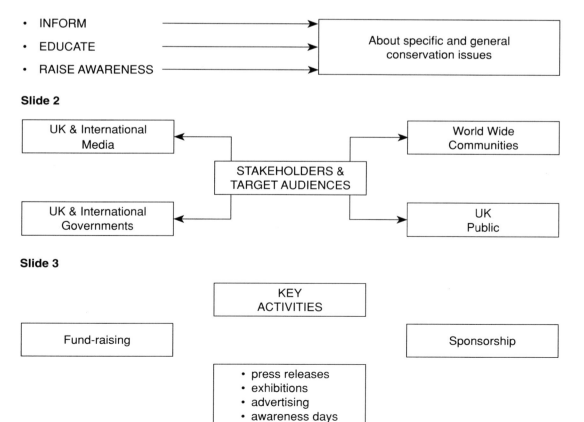

181

Guidelines For Production Of Slides 1–3

Use the colour printer and use green for drawing lines and boxes but use black text.

The background of boxes should have yellow shading. Text should be 22 pt and please use Times New Roman typeface. As indicated on my draft, please use capitals where they are shown, otherwise use upper and lower case text.

b.

To ensure effective presentation delivery it would be necessary to do the following:

- Research the content so it is relevant to the purpose of the presentation and the audience.
- Prepare visual aids.
- Have a clear structure – beginning, middle, and sum up at the end.
- Use a clear voice.
- Be concise.
- Maintain eye contact with the audience.
- Be enthusiastic about the presentation and use tone and voice pitch and body language to show this.
- Use appropriate pace so the delivery is not too rushed.
- Be prepared to be asked questions at the end.

Glossary of terms

AIDA a useful principle for use in planning written communication: acronym for Attention, Interest, Desire, Action.

Attentive listening used when receiving instruction or (new) information e.g. sales conferences, demonstrations.

Averages measures of *central tendency*, used to find the number which is representative of a group of numbers: the *mean*, *median* or *mode*.

Block-based images simple images on VDU using graphic, alphabetic and numerical characters.

Body language medium for non-verbal communication: facial expression, gestures, postures, physical contact, providing clues as to our own and other people's behaviour and real feelings.

Briefs documents 'carried' or given to a barrister which are the necessary details required to help them prepare a case for trial.

Business communication the process of which information is transferred and received from one individual or group to another both within and outside the organization.

Claimor adjustment letters in marketing, letters dealing with faculty, mishandled or lost merchandise and other customer complaints.

Communication Process
- *Decoding* the message is received and meaning assigned by the recipient.
- *Encoding* putting thought into symbolic or word form, ready for transmission.
- *Feedback* the message is communicated back to the sender.
- *Transmission* the process of sending the message, via a selected channel or medium, for example, telephone call or advertisement.

Computer an electronic piece of equipment which allows the range of functions, input, storage, feedback etc.

Critical listening used where the aim is to evaluate the strength and implications of the message e.g. management–employee negotiations.

Data term used to describe basic *facts*, usually numerically based.

Data processing the collection, manipulation and interpretation of data which produces useful information for decision makers.

Diagonal communication communication between departments in relation to specific tasks for which there is no obvious line of authority.

Downwards, vertical information information passed from superiors to subordinates.

EDI Electronic Data Interchange: a network used to make an electronic link between an organization and its suppliers.

Electronic office a term used to describe a section of an organization that only uses electronic systems for transmitting information and storing documents.

Empathetic listening used in situations where feedback is required e.g. appraisal/joint review interviews.

External market the total of the individuals and groups who have an indirect relationship with a business organization e.g. customers, suppliers.

Graphs visual representations which show the relationships between two variables by means of a straight line or curve.

Histograms column/bar charts which show a continuous distribution of data and can demonstrate the basic shape of the distribution with the display of columns/bars.

Horizontal information   information passed between departments and individuals at the same level in an organization.

Informal reports   reports used where the information to be presented deals with relatively simple issues.

Information   obtained from data by organizing it into a meaningful form.

Information reports   reports designed primarily to provide information to others; mainly summaries of longer/complex material.

Information system   that which describes an organization as a *whole* in terms of its information requirements and information utilization, e.g. the information system of a business organization is all the equipment and software required for data and information management.

Internal market   those who are involved with the internal processes of a business organization e.g. employees, shareholders, the board.

Investigation reports   records of the investigation of a problem/situation or a proposal for change; usually offers recommendations and proposals for future action or consideration in the final sections.

IT   the equipment, tools and systems used to *create, produce, reproduce, distribute* and *store* business communications.

LANs   Local Area Networks: use parallel communications between computers based on a minimum of eight electronic wires to send the information.

Letters of recommendation   usually confidential, letters that convey information about people, their characteristics and suitability for a particular position.

Long formal reports   long reports designed to provide information and arguments based on an investigational problem or opportunity.

Mean   an average figure, found by totalling the sum of all the numbers in the group and then dividing by the number of numbers in that group.

Median   the value of the *middle* number in a group; particularly useful when analysing extreme values in a distribution of numbers.

Memorandum   internal correspondence conveying short specific information.

Mode   the most frequently occurring item in a list of numbers; useful when a frequency from a list can be commonly and easily identified.

Motions   definition proposals put to a meeting and which require a decision, usually through a vote.

Non-verbal communications
- *Body language*   gestures, postures, eye movements, type of physical contact and voice characteristics.
- *Personal appearance*   clothes, hair, make-up.
- *Use of time and personal space*   manners, hospitality, respect, physical space.

Pixel-based images   images on VDU built up from a large number of dots ('pixels').

Press releases   documents which convey topical and newsworthy information for the purposes of publicity and generating feelings of goodwill amongst the public.

Primary data   data collected specifically for the investigation or survey being carried out by using observation, experimental techniques, interviews and panel surveys or questionnaires.

Reports   factual documents prepared to fulfil the needs of decision makers in organizations.

Secondary data   information that has already been collected and published elsewhere.

Short formal reports   clear, concise statements pertaining to some organizational problem which can be solved, or a decision made relatively quickly, based on the facts which are presented.

Statistics   a group of figures which relate to some important attribute or variable, presented in a manner which allows easy interpretation.

Table   a matrix structure where data is placed in titled rows and columns.

Upwards, vertical information   grassroots information passed from lower-level employees to superiors such as executives and managers.

VANs   Value-Added Networks: systems which can be accessed by a number of organizations through a third-party provider.

WANs   Wide Area Networks: use serial connections, which are a single or twisted wire that carry the communication down the line.

Index

your chance to bite back

Business Communications 1997–98

Dear Student

Both Butterworth-Heinemann and the CIM would like to hear your comments on this workbook.

If you have some suggestions please fill out the form below and send it to us at:

>College and Open Learning Division
>Butterworth-Heinemann
>FREEPOST
>Oxford OX2 8BR

Name: _____

College/course attended: _____

If you are not attending a college, please state how you are undertaking your study:

_____

_____

_____

How did you hear about the CIM/Butterworth-Heinemann workbook series?
Word of mouth	❏
Through my tutor	❏
CIM mailshot	❏

Advert in _____

Other _____

What do you like about this workbook (e.g. layout, subjects covered, depth of analysis):

_____

_____

What do you dislike about this workbook (e.g. layout, subjects covered, depth of analysis):

_____

_____

Are there any errors that we have missed (please state page number):

_____

_____